THE POLITICS OF SCARCITY

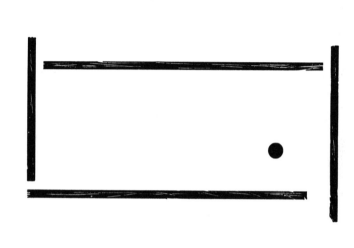

THE POLITICS OF SCARCITY

Public Pressure and Political Response in India

BY MYRON WEINER

THE  UNIVERSITY OF CHICAGO PRESS
Chicago & London

Library of Congress Catalog Card Number: 62-15047
THE UNIVERSITY OF CHICAGO PRESS, CHICAGO 60637
The University of Chicago Press, Ltd., London W.C. 1
© *1962 by The University of Chicago. All rights reserved*
Published 1962. Third Impression 1968
Printed in the United States of America

To Sheila and Beth

OF WHAT USE IS THE BARREN COW, WHICH GIVES NO MILK?
OF WHAT USE IS THE KING'S GRACE,
IF HE DOES NOT FULFILL THE HOPES OF SUPPLIANTS?

> *From "Nitivākyamrta: Nectar of Aphorisms
> on Polity," by Somadeva, a Digambara Jain
> teacher of the tenth century*

FOREWORD

Myron Weiner's book is at once an important contribution to political theory and a suggestive and prudent contribution to public policy. As political theory, *The Politics of Scarcity* provides us with some significant propositions about the process of political change. As public-policy guidance, it draws attention to opportunities for specific investments in the Indian political system which are likely to increase the chances that Indian modernization will realize its democratic potentialities and the democratic aims of its elites.

From the point of view of political theory, this study is the first full-length analysis of interest groups in a non-Western transitional political system. Weiner's classification scheme and his empirical research into the characteristics and activities of "community" associations, trade unions, business associations, agrarian movements, student organizations, and anomic movements in India are such as to make his work comparable to and cumulative with the best work of Western scholarship in the interest-group field. The general theorists of interest groups will have to take his work into account. It will suggest some revisions in their schemes of classification and draw their attention to aspects of interest-group phenomena in the West which are taken for granted and not theoretically explicated.

The central theme of his book is that the development of a legitimate and stable democratic infrastructure in India is contingent on the development of a bargaining culture in the key roles of the political system—in the political parties, in the bureaucracy, and among the interest groups themselves. Such a culture does not develop spontaneously. Indeed, Weiner draws our attention to a critical stage in the process of political modernization—the point at which the demands of industrial development and political development begin to conflict and diverge, and when, for lack of an appreciation of the specifically political aspects of development, the democratic side of the enterprise may be endangered. The Indian governmental and bureaucratic elites, overwhelmed by the problems of economic development and the scarcity of resources available to them, inevitably acquire a technocratic and antipolitical frame of mind. Particularistic demands of whatever kind are denied legitimacy. As a consequence, interest groups either become captives of the government and bureaucracy and lose much of their followings or are alienated from the political system. The situation he depicts in India gives us the beginnings of a model which can be used diagnostically in the study of this critical problem in other transitional systems.

Weiner has caught the process of political development in India at a stage in which the options are still open. This gives a special policy relevance and urgency to his study. He is describing a process of interest-group alienation which is still reversible, and his recommendations should be listened to with care by responsible Indian statesmen. Nothing can be more destructive of democratic culture than a conception of national interest which deprives special interests of the opportunity to bargain, to be heard, to enter creatively into the flow of demands and policies of the political process. The failure of effective linkage, thus far, is not simply a consequence of the undisciplined and centrifugal pressures of new and inexperienced interest groups and their elites. At least as important are the anxieties of inexperienced politicians and bureaucrats who react to the demands for autonomy on the part of linguistic groups, the demands for accommodation on the part of caste associations, the demands of trade unions and business and agrarian associations for benefits and exemptions, as though the India polity would fall apart if concessions were made and bargains reached. Weiner draws attention to the safe margin of bargaining power available to the governmental and bureaucratic elites, the concessions which might be made which would not undermine the integrity of governmental and economic planning processes. And at the same time, he points out that the choice available to these elites is not between the preservation of the integrity of governmental programs, on the one hand, and giving in to particularistic pressures, on the other. The choice quite frequently is between accommodating special interests in a peaceful and legitimate bargaining process and yielding in the end to demonstrations, strikes, and violence. His theme is that democratic development is an investment and capital-accumulation process, too. A political and governmental elite which treated the demands of special interests as legitimate —and bargained, accommodated, and within limits made concessions— might begin to develop similar attitudes and skills among the interest-group elites. These are investments in democratization well worth their price in economic irrationality or ethnic-political heterogeneity. The capital toward which such investments build is a democratic culture and infrastructure.

It brings one up short to realize that what Weiner tells us about contemporary Indian politics was being said not much more than two decades ago by Herring, Schattschneider, and others about American politics. The argument that the essence of democratic politics is bargaining, and the profession of politics, wheeling and dealing—coalition-making and compromising—caused a stir among the academic brethren in the United States only a little while ago. Our European colleagues still tend to look upon pressure group phenomena as somewhat sinful. The Indian situation is by no means an archaic one or an exotic one. We can take encouragement from the fact that what the Indian elites are striving to learn has only recently been learned in the West.

Weiner's work is important evidence of the great advantages of the comparative method. He began his study not only with the historical and cultural depth of the area specialist, but with the fund of knowledge and theory about interest groups and the political process which has developed out of recent Western political science scholarship. It is this combination of methods and approaches which enables him to locate with such accuracy the points at which the fateful decisions affecting the future of Indian democracy are being made.

GABRIEL A. ALMOND

ACKNOWLEDGMENTS

The history of this study constitutes a continuous stream of acknowledgments. The study began with assistance from the Social Science Research Committee of the University of Chicago, which permitted me to do some preliminary research before I embarked on a field study. The field work was conducted in 1957 and 1958 under a grant from the Committee on Comparative Politics of the Social Science Research Council. Apart from material support, the members of that Committee and the seminars in which I participated under the auspices of the Committee were an important stimulation to me, both before I left for India and upon my return.

In India there were countless individuals whom I interviewed in government, business, labor, universities, political parties, and other political organizations. Where possible, I have indicated the interview source of my information in the text, but for obvious reasons it has not always been possible to do so. In addition to those mentioned in the text, I wish to extend particular thanks to a number of individuals who kindly read and commented on portions of the manuscript: the late N. K. Siddhanta, former chancellor of the universities of Calcutta and Delhi; Humayun Kabir, Minister of Scientific Research and Cultural Affairs; Milton Singer and Bert Hoselitz, University of Chicago; Morris David Morris, Washington University; Bernard Cohn, University of Rochester; Howard Wriggins, U. S. Department of State; and Seyom Brown, University of Chicago.

Grants from the Social Science Research Committee and the Committee on Southern Asian Studies of the University of Chicago made it possible for me to employ graduate assistants, who all proved most helpful: Baldev Raj Nayar, Marcus Franda, Andrew Westwood, and Mrs. Margaret H. Case, who, along with my wife, edited the manuscript.

Though the field work for this study was conducted in 1957 and 1958, when I lived primarily in Calcutta, it is hard to separate what I learned during that period from what I learned on an earlier trip in 1953 and 1954, when most of my time was spent in New Delhi. On the more recent trip I had an opportunity to watch political groups operating in the state of West Bengal. Invariably much of what is described here is based heavily upon my research experience in West Bengal, and there are bound to be many who will accuse me of overgeneralizing. My only answer is that I have also discussed many of the problems raised in this study with businessmen in Bombay and Madras, trade union leaders in Kerala and Bombay, linguistic leaders in Poona, tribal leaders in Bihar, caste leaders in Madras, student leaders in Delhi, Uttar Pradesh, and Bihar, and party leaders, government officials, and administrators in almost every state. Any book on a country as large and diversified as India is bound to generalize on the basis of what inevitably must be limited experience.

I cannot close without some special word of affection for the Bengalis whom I interviewed and at whose tables I shared food. Despised as *babu's* by the British, and hated by all tourists who have the misfortune to pass briefly through Calcutta, Bengalis and Bengal remain for the garrulous scholar a sheer delight.

New Delhi

CONTENTS

INTRODUCTION

The efforts of people in the underdeveloped nations to raise their living standards through science and technology have quite appropriately and dramatically been called the great unfinished revolution of the twentieth century. It is plainly the objective of the people of the underdeveloped nations to raise their living standards; but the kind of political institutions through which they will work toward their goal remains uncertain. The relative advantages of democratic, authoritarian, and totalitarian political systems have been the subject of a running debate, both in the underdeveloped areas and in the West, as to which is the best means of rapidly building a modern society. This debate seems to be pointless, however, since there is abundant evidence that no correlation has existed historically between rates of growth and types of political systems. Some authoritarian systems have remained stagnant, while others have prospered. Some democratic systems have developed more quickly than some authoritarian and totalitarian systems; others have not. Democratic regimes have historically proven no less capable of pursuing wise economic policies than authoritarian and totalitarian regimes.

Each political system is, nonetheless, accompanied by its own special problems when its leaders attempt to hasten economic growth. In this study we shall explore some of the political difficulties confronting India, the largest country of the underdeveloped world that is trying to modernize and at the same time create and maintain free institutions. The chief political problem of economic development in a free society arises from the very freedom of men to try to influence government policies and administration. Vast numbers of Indians, availing themselves of opportunities provided in a society of free political institutions, have organized to press a host of demands upon government. Given the limited resources possessed by government, a vast gap remains between what organized groups demand and what government is capable of providing. Indeed, the government's concern for long-term economic planning means that it must place limits on the extent to which it will satisfy the demands of specific groups. The requirements of political responsiveness and the requirements of economic planning are thus often at odds with one another.

The present study has been guided by a set of questions rather than by an attempt to explore the utility of some conceptual framework. How does government behave toward organized groups when it views the demands of such groups as threatening to its development program? Why do violence and other forms of coercion play such a large role in the behavior of organized groups toward government? How have tribes, castes, and religious and linguistic communities adapted themselves to the new political framework? How have business organizations operated in a political framework in which government's stated objective is the creation of a "socialistic pattern of society"? How, if at all, are the productive requirements of the state reconciled with the consumption requirements of organized groups? To what extent has government been responsive or unresponsive to organized demands, and what has been the consequence? Finally, what strategy is available to a government that seeks to maximize the use of its resources through government planning, but is also committed to the development of free institutions and the participation of organized groups in public life— essential components of a free society?

At the heart of this study is a simple problem. In a free society, there is an increase in the freedom of choice and in the capacity to affect one's environment—a freedom and a capacity exercised by people who voluntarily associate to influence the course of public policy. Freedom of association, freedom of assembly, a free press, and free speech are the freedoms maintained in a democratic society so that citizens may affect their government. On the other hand, voluntary associations would defeat their own purposes if they were to effectively paralyze government, destroy orderly rule, or threaten to Balkanize the political system. The difficulty is obviously not unique to India, and has been of concern to many who have written on the theory and practice of democratic government. If the problem is particularly pressing in India, it is because the gap between government plans and decisions and the many demands of organized groups is so great that the danger is ever present that neither democratic institutions nor effective government policy will survive.

In one sense this study is in the tradition of that body of literature labeled the group approach to politics or group theory. How people organize, what they organize for, how they attempt to influence policy, and what factors affect their attempts to influence policy have been major questions raised by those who have studied the role of groups in a political system. This study breaks with that tradition in its emphasis on the attitude of the participants in government and political life toward government and politics. What do leaders of interest groups expect of government, and what are their notions about the correct ways of achieving their objectives; what behavior do government officials expect from politicians and what do they think about the nature and function of government itself? To understand, for example, the political role played by caste, tribal, religious, linguistic, and ethnic associations (which will be referred to here as "community" associations), one must analyze the hostility they have evoked among bureaucrats, national politicians, and a large part of India's intellectual community. Likewise, the political role of Indian business has to be seen in the context of popular attitudes—shared by many government officials and often even by businessmen—toward private gain. Throughout this study we shall explore those attitudes which affect the behavior of men and their expectations of the behavior of others. Above all, we shall explore some of the consequences which flow from divergent political orientations.

I. GOVERNMENT AND POLITICAL DEMANDS

New social classes emerged throughout India in the nineteenth century as a consequence of changes in land-tenure systems, the development of a new educational system, and the establishment of the modern occupations of medicine, journalism, law, and administration. By the latter half of the nineteenth century, these classes had begun to establish political associations. At the same time, spurred by the new political forms which the British government had introduced, those social classes that had existed earlier also formed and joined political associations.

By the beginning of the twentieth century, these associations multiplied, and many of them began to oppose British rule. Others, such as trade unions and peasant organizations, were organized or harnessed by the nationalists to press simultaneously for immediate rewards and for independence. Still others, especially many of the caste, religious, and other "community" associations, often worked within the governmental framework to press for their own interests. There were many differences among these associations, but all of them—nationalist, nationalist-front, and collaborationist—shared a belief that the role of government had to be enlarged.

In 1947, a nationalist leadership organized by the Indian National Congress took power in New Delhi and the state capitals. The government of free India undertook to expand its own functions, not because of real or imagined threats of external intervention such as motivated Turkey and Japan in an earlier era, but as a response to the ideals and goals of its own leadership and to the growing aspirations within Indian society. Indian leaders saw their task as that of reducing scarcity, which was more acutely felt at the time of Independence than it had been fifty years before, not necessarily because there was greater poverty in India, but because popular aspirations had expanded much more rapidly than had the society's ability to fulfill public demands. The new leadership believed, moreover, that the initiative for modernization must come from the government, because government, in their judgment, is best able to assess the society's total resources, material and human, and most efficiently to allocate those resources for economic development. All this, they believed, must be done within the framework of a unified national state, a stable political order, and institutions of representative government. To assess resources adequately, of course, a government must have information; and once sufficient information was available, the new leadership believed they could plan rationally for the country's economic development. After Independence, therefore, a host of commissions were appointed—a taxation-inquiry commission and a planning commission; commissions to investigate the textile industry, the coal industry, cottage industries, and handicrafts; permanent commissions and *ad hoc* commissions; commissions made up exclusively of governmental personnel and public-private commissions; commissions to deal with immediate issues and commissions to do long-range planning.

Out of the pillared halls of Parliament in New Delhi and from the nearby secretariat buildings has since come a torrent of reforms and development programs. Reform measures have been passed with the object of freeing the individual from the bonds of custom: untouchability has been constitutionally abolished, women have been given inheritance rights, divorce is permitted, dowries have been legally abolished, the arbitrary powers of the princes have been eliminated, and peasants have been freed from the grip of landlord control. The state has also increased its control over various economic activities in order to promote development. Since 1951 there have been three five-year plans; and the Industrial (Development and Regulation) Act, the Industrial Disputes Act, the industrial-policy resolutions, and acts nationalizing life insurance, the Imperial Bank, and the airlines are all expressions of the state's concern for economic development.

The new leadership did not believe—as the nineteenth-century utilitarians had believed—that it was enough for the state merely to release the energies within society; society by itself, they argued, could not generate its own economic dynamism, partly because much of the society was so poor that without external assistance it would remain stagnant, partly because educating the present generation to the new values of science and modern thought was a slow process, and partly because those individuals who did have capital did not seem willing to forego immediate returns in the expectation of long-range profits. Therefore, as the new leadership launched the government in 1947, it held the firm conviction that the state not only must plan and develop from above, accumulate capital, and invest it; but also that it must stimulate enthusiasm from below, encourage belief in the new values of science, social equality, political democracy, and national unity, and above all, encourage participation in development programs. The new leadership began with a sense of confidence. As leaders of the nationalist movement, they had aroused the population to work for independence; and surely, they reasoned, they were also capable of arousing the population to work for national development. And, in the main, the new leaders believed themselves to be capable of the tasks of planning, for they saw themselves as practical men, free from the prejudices, narrow-mindedness, and superstitious values of many of India's citizens. Their loyalties to family, caste, and even region had largely been displaced by a new rationalism and dedication to modern national development.

The first years of independence were years of high hopes, great challenges, and miraculous accomplishments. The country and the government survived a bloody partition, the assassination of Gandhi, a struggle over Kashmir, and a Communist insurrection in the south, and moved on to formulate a new constitution, hold national elections, and undertake the first five-year plan. But disappointment soon came. Economic development, especially agricultural development, did not accelerate as rapidly as the leadership had hoped. Perhaps even more disappointing were the political developments that emerged. In place of a growing sense of national unity, caste, tribal, religious, and linguistic bodies multiplied. Instead of being dedicated to increase production, trade unions, under leftist control, were launching strikes. Harmony was not growing in the countryside—the Communists and Socialists were busily fomenting class struggle. Young people did not seem determined to increase their technical skills, but instead student "indiscipline" increased. And instead of uniting to work as a single force to rally the country, the Congress party became increasingly split by factionalism. From the point of view of the national leadership, it was "politics"—in the sense of narrow ambitions for power and the parochial loyalties of small men—which threatened national unity, economic development, and political order. Ambitious politicians, according to their view, catered to and nurtured parochial loyalties and selfish economic demands to satisfy their urges for political power, and were willing to resort to civil disobedience, and even violence, to achieve their objectives. In a society where respect for democratic institutions and orderly processes had not yet been inculcated, where men lived close to the economic margins, and where loyalties to caste, religion, tribe, and language were powerful, these politicians were working in fertile fields. The post-Independence developments, seen in this light, alarmed the new leadership.

The Management of Protest

Slowly and hesitantly a strategy for dealing with these developments emerged—although to refer to the political policy of the Congress party and the government as a "strategy" is perhaps to impute more deliberation than actually existed. Without forethought, the Congress party developed a policy of seeking to control political protest.

Almost immediately after Independence, the Congress party encouraged its trade union section to create a new national federation, the Indian National Trade Union Congress, as an answer to Communist, Socialist, and Marxist-left attempts to gain control of the working force. Many Congressmen were reluctant to see their party engage in trade union organizing on the grounds that Congress represented the interests of the working class; but this was countered by the more convincing argument that so long as free enterprise existed, unions were necessary to bargain with capitalists, and by the practical consideration that the Communists and Socialists were extremely active in the trade union field. Once formed, the new federation was dedicated to the principle of avoiding strikes; indeed, it staunchly supported the government policy of compulsory arbitration in industrial disputes, which was enunciated by the Industrial Disputes Act of 1947.

The Congress party hesitated, however, to organize separate student and peasant organizations, in spite of Socialist and Communist activities among students and peasants. Congressmen were convinced that students had no role to play in post-Independence politics. Even though the Communists had gained control of the All-India Student Federation during the war, and continued their organization efforts among students after Independence, Congress refrained from large-scale student organization until 1955, when it created the Youth Congress to counter leftist activities, to encourage participation in development programs, and to train youthful Congress party workers. On the peasant front, Congress initially took the position that no separate peasant organization was needed, since the Congress party was the spokesman and representative of India's peasant masses. The Congress party is, in fact, largely a rural organization. Its urban organization is strong; but in the cities it competes with other political parties, while in many rural areas it has little or no competition. Although the Congress urban vote has been decreasing, the Congress rural vote has continued to rise. However, in some parts of the country, particularly in Uttar Pradesh, Bihar, Bombay, and Andhra, peasant movements under Communist or Socialist control have been active. This activity has rarely—with the exception of Andhra—been of such a magnitude as to endanger the Congress party's control of the rural vote.

There are two aspects of these opposition movements that have concerned the government. They disrupt law and order by their demonstrations and civil-disobedience movements against high irrigation taxes, high prices, food shortages, and so on; and until recently they have been unwilling to encourage peasant participation in government programs to increase food production and improve village conditions. In 1952, therefore, the Planning Commission provided financial support for the creation of the Bharat Sevak Sangh (Indian Service Society) to promote rural participation in the Community Development Program and the National Extension Service. And in 1955, under the guidance of the Ministry of Agriculture, the Farmers' Forum was created to bring together government officials, Congress leaders, and the better-educated and prosperous local rural leaders. They were to exchange information on rural development programs, establish greater co-operation among those active in rural areas, and secure government support for such items as improved rural education, fair freight rates, adequate credit, low interest rates, improved marketing and distribution systems, and improved rural mail delivery.

Unlike the Bharat Sevak Sangh, the Farmers' Forum has made little effort to build any extensive local organization. Since the Congress leadership looks upon its own party as a peasant organization, it has been reluctant to see local party leaders and members dissipate their energies in creating what would, in their mind, be parallel organizations. Moreover, much of the local Congress leadership comes from non-cultivating classes—that is, petty landlords, local merchants, school teachers, lawyers, and doctors—and only secondarily from the tillers, and any attempt to build a peasant organization by the local Congress party might in effect split the organization. There are few local Congress officials who believe that any advantage could be gained for the party by organizationally separating tillers and non-tillers.

But recognizing the limits of these government-sponsored organizations, a commission appointed by the central government recommended that responsibilities for developmental and welfare activities be given to units of local government so as to encourage a greater measure of participation. Under this program a three-tiered system of local rural government would be established: the *panchayat* would be the unit of village government; the *panchayat samiti* would cover the area of the community development program; and the *zilla parishad* would serve as a co-ordinating and in some respects governing council for the district. In 1959 the program was launched in Rajasthan and Andhra, and it has since been extended to several other states. Apart from the beneficial effects this program might have on rural developmental activities, many Congressmen hoped that it would extend and strengthen the party's control in rural areas.

If the efforts of the Congress party to win control of various organized forms of protest are measured by the number of participants, or by success at the polls, then Congress has done quite well. The Indian National Trade Union Congress is the largest of the four trade union federations. The Youth Congress, which in 1957 claimed two hundred thousand members, has been growing rapidly; and its youth camps have received much attention and participation. Although the records of the Farmers' Forum and the Bharat Sevak Sangh are not as impressive, Congress has successfully maintained its political hold upon the rural areas. In the 1957 elections, the Congress party vote increased over that of 1952. And finally, the newly created *panchayat samiti*'s and *zilla parishad*'s are in the main under Congress control.

The Congress leadership, however, measures the success of these organizations by other standards as well. The Farmers' Forum and the Bharat Sevak Sangh are propagating new values, and their mission is to persuade the entire community in which they are active to accept these new values and to participate in the work of national development. So long as some trade unions encourage strikes and restrict production, so long as some peasants refuse to pay taxes and violate the law, so long as some students at schools and colleges riot against the authorities, the task of these organizations is not complete.

Techniques of Restraint and Coercion

Confronted with groups whose activities threaten public order, and unable either to control them or to persuade them of the new values, the Indian government has turned to various legal measures of restraint and coercion.[1] These measures include emergency provisions in the constitution, the Preventive Detention Act, Section 144 of the Criminal Code, the Press (Objectionable Matter) Act, restraining features of the Industrial Disputes Act, and the Maintenance of Essential Services Act. Each of these measures gives the government extraordinary powers which substantially modify the fundamental-rights provisions of the constitution.

Section 144 of the Criminal Code, which antedates Independence, enables government, including local authorities, to place an area under martial law and to forbid, within that area, any public meetings or demonstrations. Another measure which antedates Independence, but which is periodically renewed by Parliament at the request of the government, is the Preventive Detention Act. Even more rigorous than the Smith Act in the United States (which makes certain public statements illegal), the Preventive Detention Act permits the government to arrest individuals in *anticipation* of a public statement or an act that may endanger public safety and security, and to detain such individuals without trial and without habeas corpus. The Preventive Detention Act was originally intended to suppress Communist activities during a period of Communist violence, but the act is now more broadly used against many groups in a wide variety of situations.[2] When, for example, violent agitation occurred in the city of Bombay for the creation of a unilingual Maharashtrian state, the government arrested political leaders of the movement as they stepped off the plane at Bombay airport en route from the Parliament in New Delhi.

From time to time other coercive acts have been enacted. The Press (Objectionable Matter) Act is aimed in particular at inflammatory materials published by the Hindu communal press. The Maintenance of Es-

---

[1] These measures, it might be noted, are relatively mild compared with Sukarno's attempts at "guided democracy" in Indonesia, Ayub Khan's "controlled democracy" in Pakistan, or the deportation laws in Ghana. Devices to restrict the activities of organized groups when they appear to threaten the "modernizing" values of the new elite seem to be characteristic of virtually all newly independent countries of Asia and Africa.

[2] For a careful study of the political and legal aspects of the Preventive Detention Act, see David H. Bayley, "Violent Agitation and the Democratic Process in India" (unpublished Ph.D. thesis, Department of Politics, Princeton University, 1960).

sential Services Act was passed when the post and telegraph workers threatened a strike in 1958. And the Industrial Disputes Act has effectively enabled the government to ban strikes in any industry, essential or otherwise, merely by referring the dispute to a labor tribunal.

Of all the various measures of restraint and coercion, the emergency provisions of the constitution are the most comprehensive. Under these provisions the president of India, with the advice and consent of the prime minister and the cabinet, can abolish a state government and place it under direct "President's Rule." The president, operating directly through the administrative services and, if necessary, the military, thereupon directly governs the state. These emergency powers lapse within six months, unless renewed by Parliament.

Two mitigating features in the application of the many control measures have thus far prevented authoritarian rule by the Indian government. First, some of these measures, like the Preventive Detention Act, are temporary acts which must be renewed by Parliament, and which are viewed as unfortunate modifications of democratic institutions by India's policy-makers. Second, and more important, these measures have, on the whole, been moderately used, and have been limited to the purposes for which they were intended. During the violent tram strike in Calcutta in 1954 and the Bombay linguistic riots of 1956, the government used both the Preventive Detention Act and Section 144 of the Criminal Code. But there is no clear evidence that the government has ever used this legislation to improve its own political position, although there is an obvious danger that such legislation in the hands of government may be misused. While in theory it is difficult to draw the line between legislation which protects the state and legislation which protects the existing government, to cross that line is to enter the sphere of tyranny and authoritarian rule. Thus far the line has not been crossed.

Accommodation and Absorption

However, the strategies of control and coercion have not satisfactorily resolved the fundamental problem—how to modernize a state within a democratic framework, in spite of pressing political demands that appear to impede economic planning, national unity, and political order. Some groups within the Congress party, especially at the state level, have chosen to pursue a third strategy: accommodation and absorption. While the national government chastises "casteism, communalism, and provincialism," many state party organizations have made their peace with parochial groups. In Madras, the Congress party leadership has established ties with one of the anti-Brahman opposition parties. In Orissa, Congress formed a coalition government with a party of up-country ex-princes and tribals. In Rajasthan, Congress absorbed many ex-*jagidar*'s (feudal landlords), and in Kerala, Congress agreed to form an election coalition against the governing Communist party that included both the Praja Socialist party and Muslim League.

Most often, the sentiment for such a brokerage attitude has come from within state Congress party organizations where a sense of political reality—one might say political calculation—has developed. In several states a new, younger leadership has developed within the Congress party. Although it would be grossly unfair to say that these younger leaders are less concerned with development than are the national leaders, it is true that they are more sensitive to the political requirements of winning and maintaining power.[3]

Some of the leadership in New Delhi and the Westernized intelligentsia in general, however, view the strategy of accommodation and absorption as more likely to create than solve problems. Such a policy, it is argued, sacrifices the long for the short run. Some national leaders believe that concessions to special interests will impede national unity and economic development, and that concessions to some demands will encourage others, thereby setting in motion a destructive cycle. From this viewpoint, government must steadfastly pursue a "responsible" policy, which, in the economic sphere, involves allocating limited resources without regard to particularist demands so as best to achieve development goals. Another position grants that a policy of accommodation may result in a larger and temporarily more popular Congress party, but argues that the absorption of divergent viewpoints would prevent any kind of rigorous party ideology, which would serve in the long run to arouse popular (or at least intellectual) enthusiasm. This view is strongly argued by the Congress Socialist Forum, a "ginger" group within the Congress party made up of relatively younger Congressmen who strongly support socialist ideology and rural co-operatives. Still another view, supported chiefly outside the government and the Congress party, holds that parties and organized interests, as institutions, create further

[3] In 1960, the chief ministers of at least four states had served many years of their political apprenticeship in their district and state Congress committees: Kamraj Nadar in Madras, Sanjiva Reddy in Andhra, Y. B. Chavan in Bombay, and C. B. Gupta in Uttar Pradesh. When C. B. Gupta, as the leader of the Congress party organization in Uttar Pradesh, won the position of chief minister in 1960, *Link*, a New Delhi newsweekly, announced that "Tammany" had taken control of the state.

schisms at a time when the country needs to be united—that the very presence of parties and parliaments encourages the selfish struggle of individuals for power. This position, most forcefully taken by Jayaprakash Narayan, formerly a Socialist and now a committed Gandhian, culminates in the argument for party-less democracy, the abolition of Parliament, and the development of tiered structures of power built from the village up.

All these viewpoints—although often held by men who bitterly oppose one another—share a common distrust of politics and a desire to order the political process more rationally. They see the political process as an expression of the irrational and the traditional in Indian society, which they decry. They believe that peasants, workers, refugees, and linguistic, religious, caste, and tribal committees are organized by politicians, not in the interest of the organized, but rather to satisfy the power desires of the organizers. Those who argue from this position can cite one example after another of acts that, in their judgment, were politically motivated—of unrealistic and impractical demands made by spokesmen for refugee associations, of union and peasant demonstrations organized to press demands on which it was known the government already intended to act. The real interests of the masses, they assert, are not being represented by the organizations to which peasants, refugees, and workers belong, or by the political-party leaders who appear as their spokesmen. Therefore, it falls to the government to maintain the public interest, that is, to hold steadfastly to those policies that will achieve maximum economic development and social justice within the framework of representative institutions and national unity.

The Issue: Politics and Modernization

The fundamental issue, therefore, is whether organized interests in India do in fact impede the modernization process: do they make demands upon the government that are so violent and so beyond the government's capabilities that they have the effect of reducing both public order and economic development? This question is clearly heuristic, suggesting further questions and requiring a wealth of data beyond the scope of a single study. We can at present only wrestle with more specific questions, which may, at best, help throw light on the larger issues.

One of these questions concerns the multiplicity of caste, tribal, religious, and linguistic associations, which has been widely viewed as a threat to the sense of national unity in India, and which more recently has been described as a threat to the maintenance of orderly state governments. In chapter iii we shall examine briefly the reasons for the development of these associations and explore the extent to which they do in fact constitute threats to the Indian political system.

Workers' demands for higher wages and their proclivity to strike is pointed out as being detrimental to economic growth, especially in an underdeveloped economy. Is it possible to find ways of preventing strikes without destroying the goals of a free society—collective bargaining and trade unions? We shall explore this question in chapter iv.

Is it possible for the business community to operate in a system committed to socialism? Does business view government regulation and planning as so threatening that it will take steps to undermine democratic government? These are questions we shall discuss in chapter v.

To what extent are political organizations committed to the principle of class struggle in the countryside, thereby raising the possibility of rural warfare and endangering agricultural development? Or, on the other hand, is the Congress party so dependent on the support of certain classes in rural areas that it dares not pursue its policies, such as land reform or higher agricultural taxes, which are important from the viewpoints of social justice and economic planning? These questions will be taken up in chapter vi.

And finally, why and to what extent has "indiscipline" grown in India's colleges and universities? Does this indiscipline constitute a threat to India's political development? These questions will be examined in chapter vii.

Before turning to these issues, we shall explore in chapter ii the broad landscape of interest groups in India: To what extent are political demands organized? How were interest groups and the nationalist movement related? What effects has this relationship had on the character of post-Independence interest groups? What in general is known about levels of aspirations and expectations in India? And finally, what attitudes prevail in organized groups concerning appropriate demands and methods for dealing with the government?

II. THE DEVELOPMENT OF ORGANIZED DEMANDS

India has many power centers. In the villages and small towns, the sources of power lie in the petty landlords and the small tradesmen, and in the petty officials who deal with such men and who themselves wield power. The *patwari* (official keeper of land records) and the land-settlement officer are men of great power, for they determine how official documents will record the ownership of that most precious of rural commodities, land. The landlord, small as his holdings may be by American standards, has power over his tenants and hired laborers; and his power may shape their vote in village elections. The small tradesman, with his supply of credit, often determines who shall have money for seeds and whose land may be taken away in default of payment. Those who control land and credit are likely also to control the village *panchayat* (governing council) and other local organizations, such as credit societies and co-operatives, which make decisions important to the entire community. Those who have wealth have access to and may exert influence upon local government officials, including those in district administration. Such influence may be exerted through the ties of caste between official and landlord, moneylender, or businessman. Or the wealthy men of the village may be related by blood or marriage to the government official. Or the ties may be based upon mutual services: in return for protection or appropriate entries in land records, an official may receive acts of deference or, even more satisfying, financial remuneration. Ties of caste, marriage, or services provide the men who hold power in the village with the means of influencing those who administer and those who adjudicate the law.

But except in the case of large moneylenders, merchants, and land-lords, influence wielded in the village will not reach out to the higher levels of district administration; and only rarely will such influence reach into the state government. Local power cannot easily be extended for several reasons. For one, although the wealth involved may be great in the village, it is rarely significant as far as state and national governments are concerned. Only a few landlords have enough land to make their influence felt in the higher echelons of government. Second, local influ-ence is bound up in the local ties of caste, family, and services, which cannot be easily transferred to the more important levels of state and national government. Standards of administration are "higher" as one goes to the state capital or New Delhi; and the system of services con-sidered legitimate in the villages is less likely to be tolerated by the higher civil service, whose standards are closer to those of the British bureauc-racy than the village. Custom may tolerate small financial transactions in the village and district, for example, but such transactions in the state and national administrations would be viewed as corruption and subjected, when discovered, to the penalties of the law. And third, since their in-fluence in the village is so bound up with local ties and traditions, the landlords and other men of wealth rarely attempt to band together to exert influence. One landlord may, in fact, try to protect himself against, or inflict damage upon, another landlord through his influence on the administration. Conflicts between persons, families, factions, and castes virtually preclude joint enterprises by those who have wealth. They do not seek, as a group, to extend their influence to higher levels of gov-ernment, partly because they do not appreciate the ways in which the state and central governments may shape their lives by legislation, partly because they feel that whatever the "raj" may do at the top can be modi-fied by influencing the administration from the bottom, and partly be-cause they neither share a sense of group interests with other men of wealth nor see how, as individuals, they can influence state or national policy.

For the villager, government *is* administration. Until recent years the villager has had no contact with legislation, with legislators, or with elec-tions.[1] After the middle of the nineteenth century, the British tried not

[1]Ancient texts tell us that government's main function was to maintain the existing social order. "The primary duty of a king," according to the ninth-century *Sukra Niti*, "consists of the protection of his subjects and the constant keeping under con-trol of evil elements." Since the state was to preserve the existing order, much of the literature focused on the functions and organization of administration. More precisely, one might say that the king did not maintain the order, but that orderly society was

to interfere with rural life. Both landlords and peasants learned to obtain what they wanted through local administration; and issues of public policy were rarely felt in the villages. Even now that the government is passing and enacting legislation that substantially affects the position of moneylenders, local businessmen, and landlords, these persons have pursued ways of modifying government policy by influencing administration. Two illustrations may suggest how this is done.

In 1953 West Bengal passed the Estates Acquisition Act, a major land-reform bill that abolished the 150-year-old *zamindari,* or landlord, system. During the debates on the bill, the landlords with larger holdings, organized in the British India Association, soon realized that efforts to prevent the passage of the law would be of no avail. Accordingly, they focused their attention on obtaining provisions which would permit local landlords, often with the collaboration of local administrations, in practice to ignore limitations on the size of landholdings. The law provided that individual holdings were to be limited, but not the holdings of families. Many landlords thereupon transferred titles; and since a high limit was placed on *khas* lands (lands personally used by the landlord), many landlords evicted their tenants and enlarged such holdings. As a result, the initial effect of land-reform legislation in West Bengal, as in Bihar and Uttar Pradesh, was to increase the number of sharecroppers and landless laborers. Throughout much of India, in fact, local landlords,

---

regulated by Dharma, or cosmic law. The king himself was often considered Dharma incarnate, the protector of Dharma. The king maintained the Sacred Law through Danda, literally "a stick" to punish those who violated the Law. Neither king nor council were conceived of as legislative bodies. Rule-application and rule-adjudication rather than rule-making were their tasks. Thus the Indian state was limited in its activities, and was conceived of as an administrative structure. The state might expand externally—military expansion was in fact part of the dharma of the ruler, and is dealt with in great detail in the *Artha Sastra*—but internally it was to do only those tasks necessary to maintain the existing order. The reconciliation of conflicts was not conceived of as part of the function of the king, for Hindu political theory did not conceive of conflict as being part of the traditional order. To the contrary, "all the many groups of society are viewed as parts of a vast and complicated machine in which all parts are interdependent and must mesh for perfect operation" (W. Norman Brown, "Class and Cultural Traditions in India," in *Traditional India: Structure and Change,* ed. Milton Singer [Philadelphia: American Folklore Society, 1959], pp. 38–39). The Madisonian point of veiw is inconceivable in the classical texts. The state cannot be a broker reconciling conflicting interests, for so long as each individual and group conforms to the dharma that has been prescribed, there can be no conflict. The state must ensure the performance of dharma, not reconcile interests in a pluralistic and conflicting society. The views of contemporary Indian policy-makers are not far removed.

working with *patwari's*, have effectively neutralized much of the intended effect of land-reform legislation.[2]

The West Bengal government has also tried to regulate the procurement and distribution of some food commodities in the state in order to keep prices down and ensure a minimum supply to everyone. Modified rationing is administered by a director for the entire state, an official for each district, and an official for each subdistrict. These local officials recommend to the district officer, who in turn recommends to the state director of food, that certain local shops be licensed as fair-trade shops with fixed prices. About one hundred new licenses are issued each year to these fixed-price shops, which are then authorized to distribute government food. Although the local officer is expected to select the shops on the basis of shop size, convenience of location, local reputation, testimonials from local people as to the honesty of the shopkeeper, and so on, he obviously has considerable discretion; and opportunities for exercising "influence" are substantial. Hoarding by licensed shopkeepers and the resale of government commodities at higher prices than the fixed government prices often invalidate the government's intention of maintaining supplies at low prices.

The government's widespread permit system allows many opportunities for individual businessmen to obtain what they wish through local administration. It is widely reported, although no evidence is available, that the local Congress party organization works with local administration in making recommendations concerning who shall get a permit; and in this manner, the party organization improves its finances.[3] Since Congress is the ruling party, local administrators—subdivisional officers and even district magistrates—are now even more accessible to local influence than they were in the days before Independence.

The easy accessibility of administrative officers to individual businessmen has, in effect, minimized the need for local interest-group organizations. In fact, organization for concerted effort would defeat the merchant's

[2] For a discussion of *patwari*-landlord relations in the administration of land-reform legislation in Uttar Pradesh, see Daniel Thorner, *The Agrarian Prospect in India* (Delhi: University Press, 1956), pp. 14–15, 19–26, 47–50. For a discussion of land legislation in West Bengal, see *ibid.*, pp. 32–33. The capacity of local landlords to invalidate land reform is a recurrent theme of Thorner's book.

[3] The Congress party in Calcutta has a public-relations officer, whose responsibility is to be a "link between government and the people," which means that he helps businessmen obtain permits, Congress workers obtain jobs, Congress supporters secure admission of their sons to schools and colleges, and so on.

purpose, for each merchant competes with the others. Thus, many of those who wield power on the local level have little cause to organize themselves. They can obtain much of what they seek through local administration without concerted effort and organization.

The Unorganized and the Inarticulate

Those who do not share power on the local level—the sharecroppers, tenant farmers, poorer peasants, *harijan*'s (untouchables), tribals, the poor and depressed—have little access to administration and little access to policy-makers. Compared with some other sections of society, they are relatively unorganized and inarticulate—although not completely so, for as we shall see later, there are tribal, *harijan,* and peasant organizations. However, these groups are not always well organized, and thus far their membership is small. Both the peasants' traditional attitudes toward authority and their identification of government with administration have discouraged political organization among them. For neither alone nor in concert can the poor peasant or tenant compete with the dominant caste and the dominant economic group in the community in influencing local administration. Only when politics becomes increasingly legislative in character, and when elections and universal suffrage are introduced, do numbers, and consequently the organization of numbers, begin to count. Then such groups have the opportunity to leap over local administration and local status groups to influence legislation and the state government.[4]

One of the most important questions about India's political future concerns the way in which political parties and government will react to the entrance of these new groups into politics. In Britain, the working class was successfully absorbed into the party system and the parliamentary structure; in France, on the other hand, the working class turned toward totalitarian movements. In Ceylon, the two major coalitions successfully absorbed ever increasing numbers of rural, Buddhist- and Sinhalese-oriented middle classes and adopted the demands of this group for Sinhalese as the country's sole official language. But in the process, the

[4] It would be useful to explore systematically the relationship between the legislator—whether member of Parliament or member of the state legislative assembly—and his constituents. From the viewpoint of villagers, the role played by the M.L.A. as a liaison between the village and the district and state administration is even more important than his legislative functions. Even members of Parliament are approached by villagers for tubewells, roads, irrigation projects, and other local needs which can only be obtained through the state government.

Tamil people of Ceylon were alienated, Tamil-Sinhalese conflicts increased, and the country was plunged into disorder and violence.[5]

Since Independence, India too has witnessed a rise in "community-
minded" groups—linguistic-cultural groups (especially the Telugu and
the Maharashtrians), tribal groups (especially the Nagas in Assam and
many of the tribes of Orissa and Bihar), caste groups (such as the non-
Brahman castes of Madras), and to a lesser extent, religious groups (particularly the Punjabi Sikhs). Some of these groups have been absorbed
by the Congress party; but others have created parties of their own (such
as the Jharkhand party of tribals in Bihar and Orissa and the anti-Brahman Dravida Munnetra Kazhagam in Madras), or their cause has been
taken up by opposition parties (such as the Samyukta Maharashtra Samiti
in Bombay). M. N. Srinivas, a leading Indian anthopologist, reports that
in many areas of Mysore—and in other parts of the country as well—
caste restrictions have decreased, but caste identifications have grown
and have entered political life on a large scale. Whole castes demand
special privileges from government.

It may very well be that identification with one's community will become an increasingly important political force in India in the years ahead.
Improved communication and transportation, the creation of village
panchayat's, the presence of periodic elections, and increased competition for administrative jobs may all increase identifications with caste,
tribe, religion, or linguistic-regional community.

There are many tribes, castes, and other community groups that are
not yet politically organized or articulate, just as there are many agricultural laborers and factory workers who remain unorganized and inarticulate. The silence of many classes and communities thus far, and the
likelihood that many of these will organize in the future, raises questions
as to whether such groups will organize along community or occupational
lines, what kind of demands they will raise, how they will behave, and
how their demands will be dealt with by government.

Against this background of local power and a pervasive bureaucratic
structure, voluntary associations in India have developed—and have
had difficulties in developing. To a large extent, it took the external
stimulus of a nationalist movement to facilitate the emergence of voluntary political structures. The existence and character of the nationalist
movement greatly influenced the rise of voluntary political structures.

[5] See Howard Wriggins, *Ceylon: Dilemmas of a New Nation* (Princeton, N. J.:
Princeton University Press, 1960).

Mass Organizations and the Nationalist Movement

The earliest modern political groups in India were interest groups primarily concerned with influencing certain aspects of British policy. Among the earliest of these groups, and perhaps typical of them, was the India League in Calcutta, a group of young, educated, urban Indians— some of whom had studied in Great Britain—who were concerned with raising the age limit at which Indians could take qualifying examinations for the civil service and with increasing the number of government posts available to "natives." In 1885 a number of these groups joined together, with support and encouragement from British authorities, to create the Indian National Congress.

Like its predecessors, Congress declared its support for British rule and attempted to influence the government within the existing constitution. But with the rise of a new British-created, university-educated class, who were unable to find jobs in a society whose economy and government were not keeping pace with its education, discontent within the Congress grew. By the turn of the century, and especially in the decade preceding the First World War, the Congress movement began to split in two. On one side were those, known as the Extremists, who favored more militant measures against the British; on the other side were the Moderates, who, although unhappy with the slow pace of reform, continued to favor a moderate constitutional approach. Behind this conflict over tactics lay a more fundamental difference: the Moderates believed in the essential goodness of British rule, for the British had unified India, introduced the English language, helped destroy caste, suttee (cremation of a widow on her husband's funeral pyre), child marriage, and other "evils" of Hinduism, and opened up to Indian intellectuals the science and knowledge of the Western world; the Extremists, however, believed that the West had attacked and was destroying the "spiritual" tradition of India. The spirited defense of Hinduism by Ramakrishna and his world-famous disciple, Vivekananda, was behind the terrorist movement in the first decade of the century.

If the strength of the Extremist movement were measured by demonstrations and bomb-throwing, then it was indeed strong; but the struggle within Congress between the Extremists and Moderates remained largely unresolved until the advent of Gandhi shortly after the war. He came on the political scene at a time when there was increasing recognition within Congress that (a) their demands had far outstripped the concessions the British had thus far made or appeared likely to make in the near future, (b) neither terrorism nor the mere passage of resolutions served to push the British much faster, (c) some further sanctions were needed that would force the British to make concessions, and (d) terrorism, riots, and demonstrations were largely ineffectual, and the British far too well armed by modern military technology to make feasible a large-scale revolutionary war, as had been possible in the preceding century. A new military technology necessitated new political techniques. Gandhi offered an answer.

It is beyond the scope of this book to discuss the political and religious theories of Gandhi or even to discuss whether these new techniques might have been used by the nationalists if Gandhi himself had not proposed them.[6] The fact is that Gandhi pointed out, in a way that other nationalists had not, that the British could remain in India only because the population provided tacit support, that there must be mass organization against the British, and that only through the denial of support to the British in the form of civil disobedience could the nationalists force the British to accede to their demands. In the early 1920's a group of young politicians, including Nehru, Gandhi, Sardar Patel, and Rajendra Prasad, began to organize the peasantry and the working class; and Congress became the backbone of a nation-wide mass movement.

A few trade unions had existed before the First World War. The Bombay Millhands Association was founded in 1890, and the Amalgamated Society of Railroad Servants of India and Burma in 1897.[7] In India, as in England, philanthropists and social workers stood behind the trade union movement in its early development. In fact, much of the support and pressure for labor legislation in India prior to the First World War came not from Indian trade unions but from business groups in England. In 1888, for example, the Manchester Chamber of Commerce, wishing to minimize competition from Indian products, petitioned the secretary of state in support of legislation limiting the working hours of women and children in India.

But, as one writer has said, "the beginnings of the Indian labor movement can be placed in the year 1918. That year saw the birth of seven unions of a permanent character, followed the next year by ten more."[8]

[6] For an excellent, systematic exposition of Gandhi's political theories, see Joan V. Bondurant, *Conquest of Violence* (Princeton, N. J.: Princeton University Press, 1958).

[7] S. D. Punekar, *Trade Unionism in India* (Bombay: New Book Co., 1948), p. 59.

[8] Oscar A. Ornati, *Jobs and Workers in India* (Ithaca, N. Y.: Cornell International Industrial and Labor Relations Reports, 1955), p. 100.

Gandhi himself helped to organize the Ahmedabad Textile Labour Association, which is still known today as a Gandhian union, dedicated to non-violence and labor-management co-operation. Other Congress leaders were also deeply involved in organizing trade unions. In 1920 the All-India Trade Union Congress (AITUC) was born; Lala Lajpat Rai, the Congress president, was elected its first president. (Two other early presidents were simultaneously president of the Indian National Congress.) Through the 1920's other political groups became active in the labor movement. The Communists worked within the AITUC, soon dominated the Red Flag Textile Union (one of the cotton mill workers' unions in Bombay), and by 1929 controlled the AITUC. Thereupon, Congress-dominated unions split from the AITUC and created a new national organization, the Indian Trade Union Federation. This was the first of a series of splits, which have continued to plague the trade union movement. In 1931 the Communists broke away from the AITUC to form the Red Trade Union Congress. In the mid-thirties, the newly organized but growing socialist section of the Indian National Congress increased its activity in the trade union field. In 1935 the Communists dissolved their federation and returned to the AITUC; and a few years later, in 1940, the Congress-dominated federation returned to the AITUC, which was, for a brief period, the sole representative of organized labor in India. But not for long. With the start of the war, M. N. Roy, an ex-Communist, withdrew his supporters from the AITUC to form the Indian Federation of Labour, and supported the British war effort. During the war, while Congress leaders were under arrest for their antiwar activities, the Communists gained control of the AITUC. When the Congress leaders were released at the close of the war, they deserted the AITUC and formed a new national federation, the Indian National Trade Union Congress. The Socialists, fearful of being isolated in the Communist-dominated federation, also withdrew and created their own federation, the Hind Mazdoor Sabha. Similarly, the splinter Marxist-left parties pulled out of the AITUC and created their own United Trade Union Congress. There thus emerged, shortly after Independence, four national trade union federations, each controlled by one or more political parties.

That the trade union movement in India should be closely affiliated with political parties is not unusual. The trade union movement in England has been closely associated with the Labour party; and the Fabians played an active part in supporting and making trade unions respectable. Even in the United States, where the trade union movement has been less politically partisan, there have been close relations in recent years between the national federations and the Democratic party.

But in the United States as in Great Britain, trade unions—with the exception of the Communist-dominated unions—have played autonomous roles within the political parties. They have given or withheld support; they have not been dominated by parties. In India, on the contrary, trade unions have been instruments of political parties. In the early days, they were controlled by Congress nationalists, who regarded the organization of trade unions as necessary in strengthening the national struggle; and later they were dominated by the Communists, Socialists, and other political groups who have viewed the organization and control of the working class as a necessary phase in their own struggle for power.[9]

What has been said concerning the lack of autonomy in the trade union movement in India also applies to peasant organizations in India. As in the trade union field, there had been some peasant activity—and uprisings (especially in the Punjab)—prior to the First World War, but not until the postwar period, under Gandhi's leadership, did the nationalists concentrate on organizing the peasants.

The first peasant movement under nationalist leadership occurred in 1917 and 1918. This movement, which came to be known as the Champaran Struggle, involved a dispute between Gandhi and the British district government in Champaran district in Bihar. The controversy concerned certain privileges granted by the government to indigo planters, who were largely British; the privileges imposed many hardships upon the local peasantry. As a result of Gandhi's agitation and negotiations (during which he was arrested), an act was passed which relieved the peasants of a special indigo impost.

At about the same time that Gandhi was involved in Champaran, Sardar Patel was leading the Kaira *satyagraha* (civil-disobedience movement). This was a campaign against payment of land assessments to the government. The law provided that if the crop fell 25 per cent below the

[9] It should be noted that the dominant role played by political parties in India in controlling trade unions is duplicated in other former colonial countries of south and southeast Asia. The Trade Union Congress of Burma and the Anti-Fascist People's Freedom League (AFPFL) are closely related; so are the Central Trade Union Federation of Indonesia (SOBSI) and the Partai Kommunis Indonesia (SBII) and the Masjumi Party; the General Confederation of Labor of Viet Nam (Tong Lau Doan) and the Lien Viet movement and the Lau Dong (or Workers' Party); the All-Pakistan Confederation of Labor and the Muslim League, etc. See George E. Lichtblau, "The Politics of Trade Union Leadership in Southern Asia," *World Politics*, VII (October, 1954), 84–101.

normal yield, the land assessment was to be postponed. Patel's group maintained that the yield had dropped more than 25 per cent; the government refused to accept the Patel survey and began to collect the assessment. Patel urged the landowners not to pay the tax. At the end of a long struggle in which many landowners lost their property, the government claimed that it had collected all but 8 per cent of the assessments.

In 1928 Sardar Patel, later to be second only to Nehru in India's independent government, established himself as a national figure by his leadership in the famous Bardoli *satyagraha*. In this dispute, the government attempted to raise the land assessment. Once more a "non-payment of the land assessment" campaign was launched. However, this campaign was eminently more successful than any of the previous agitations; and in Indian political writings is called the "Bardoli Triumph."

It should be noted that the Bardoli *satyagraha*, like the previous ones, was directed against the colonial government, not against the landlords. In fact, some landlords joined in these struggles against colonial rule. Even through the 1920's, there was no widespread support in Congress for a program to abolish intermediaries between the state and the tiller. In the early 1930's, however, Nehru and the rising left wing, with which he was then associated, put pressure on Congress to support agrarian reform. In 1936 a number of scattered peasant organizations joined together to form the All-India Kisan Sabha, with official Congress blessings and under the presidency of Sardar Patel. The agrarian program issued at the first Kisan Sabha conference called for the abolition of the *zamindari* (landlord) system and the redistribution of land.

Soon after its formation, the Kisan Sabha broke with the Congress party. After the 1937 elections, Congress formed governments in seven states. Many Kisan Sabha leaders believed that these new governments were doing little for the peasantry, and organized mass meetings and huge marches in an attempt to pressure the Congress ministries. But the Kisan Sabha, once it broke from the Congress party, proved unable to build itself into a mass organization; having been a branch of Congress during its formative period, it had no substantial grass-roots organization of its own. During the Second World War, while the Congress leadership was in jail, the Communists gained control of the Kisan Sabha; and it was again the instrument of a political party.

Since Independence, other groups have entered the field of peasant organization. Congressmen and some Socialists have turned their attention to the Gandhian *bhoodan* movement, a "land gift" movement which encourages landlords and peasants alike to give up voluntarily part of their land to the landless. The Socialists have created the Hind Kisan Panchayat, and the non-Communist Marxist-left parties have created the United Kisan Sabha. These opposition parties have been active in fomenting peasant agitations. The recently formed Socialist party has declared that it looks upon such agitation as a means of bringing about the collapse of the Congress government; specific demands are made, therefore, with the intention of weakening the government rather than of passing legislation or improving the peasants' condition through administrative or legal action.

Most of India's major mass organizations—not only peasant groups and trade unions, but also women's organizations, youth and student groups, and many religious reform movements—grew out of, or were originally associated with, the nationalist movement. The nationalist movement helped create new movements, such as trade unions and peasant associations, and it absorbed nascent movements, such as religious reform associations. Even the demands to reorganize India's state boundaries along linguistic lines were adopted by the Indian National Congress in the 1920's as a part of its own program.

The nationalist movement very consciously assumed the character of a parallel government. Its annual convention was a national convention. The All-India Congress Committee, which represented all points of view within the movement, assumed the character of a national parliament. The Working Committee was its cabinet; and the Congress president was, symbolically at least, the country's prime minister. To the extent that all interest groups and mass movements turned toward the Congress party, rather than the government, for the fulfillment of their hopes, and to the extent that the national movement denied legtimacy to the British and refused to obey British laws, then Congress, in fact, became the nation's government.

Eager to win mass support for independence, nationalists of all shades —Gandhians, Communists, Socialists, Hindu Communalists—turned to all sections of society where discontent existed. While the Communists, and to a lesser extent the Socialists, stressed class struggle, the remaining—and dominant—nationalist leadership argued that one Indian class should not be turned against another, but that all should turn against their British rulers.

"Swaraj," in nationalist terms, came to mean more than independence. It meant the creation of a society in which the aspirations of the Indian people—of workers, peasants, students, women, untouchables, and linguistic groups—would be attained. It meant satisfaction of demands and freedom from deprivation as well as independence from alien rule. Students were told of the inadequacies of the British-created educational system, which prepared them only to be clerks for their British masters and trained too many of them for the few jobs available. Peasants were encouraged not to pay land taxes and to make their own salt to avoid salt taxes. They were told that their agricultural needs, such as expanded credit, irrigation facilities, and roads, were not being adequately satisfied by the British government. Land reform too would come with independence, they were told. Businessmen, who gave considerable financial support to the nationalist movement, were convinced by the nationalists that so long as the British ruled in the interests of their own commercial and industrial classes, import and export duties, freight rates, government credit facilities, and the like would never meet the requirements of Indian business and commerce. The middle classes were told that industrialization and modernization would never occur under colonial rule. Regional-linguistic groups were told that only with independence would the government reorganize the country's boundaries to fit regional-cultural feelings rather than to suit the administrative convenience of the rulers. The poor and underprivileged everywhere in India were promised that their only hope for improvement lay with a government of their own. The nationalists were creating a leviathan of aspirations.

Not all these aspirations, however, were directed toward the government. The religious revivalist movements that grew at the turn of the century as a defense against Christian attacks on the Hindu tradition were also reform movements that tried to purge Hinduism of untouchability, caste, bans against widow remarriage, and suttee. The Arya Samaj, the Hindu Mahasabha, and later, the Rashtriya Swayamsevak Sangh (RSS) emphasized both Hindu revivalism and revitalism. The RSS even argued that participation in the nationalist movement was of lesser importance than revitalizing Hindu youth. The Hindu Mahasabha, however, remained politically active; and with the rise of the Muslim League, politics soon overwhelmed its cultural and social-reform activities.

The Gandhians, on the other hand, successfully combined politics and social reform. While Gandhi's antistate sentiment was not shared by many of his Socialist and "modern" nationalist supporters, his close disciples actively built many constructive-work societies, which emphasized voluntary efforts at social and economic reform. Gandhi developed a fourteen-point constructive program, which stressed the role of voluntary effort in achieving his social aims: communal harmony, *harijan* betterment, prohibition, promotion of cottage industries, basic education, *adibasi* (tribal) welfare, promotion of *rashtra-bhasha* (Hindi as the official language), leprosy relief, women's welfare, promotion of *khadi* (hand-spun, hand-loomed cloth), *goseva* (cattle protection), labor welfare, and village sanitation and hygiene. To achieve these objectives the Gandhians created a host of social welfare associations, including the Nai Talimi Sangh to encourage basic education in the villages, the All-India Village Industries Association, the Harijan Sewak Sangh to improve the welfare of untouchables, and the Kasturba Gandhi National Memorial Trust for the advancement of village women. Since Independence, these organizations have continued their work and have been joined by the *bhoodan* movement, led by Vinoba Bhave, a leading Gandhian disciple, who walks from village to village securing gifts of land and money for redistribution to the landless.

Gandhian aspirations have not, one might add, been directed exclusively toward voluntary activities. Gandhians have actively sought government support for the development of cottage industries, for a tax on mill-made cloth to subsidize *khadi,* for Hindi as the official language, and for increased government allocations to the rural sector rather than for industrial development. So pervasive is politics, however, that even voluntary efforts aimed at satisfying aspirations through non-political, non-government channels have assumed a political character. Congress, the Praja Socialist party, and even the Communists have joined in supporting the *bhoodan* movement, and have urged their rank-and-file workers to take part. For any movement that assumes a mass character has a political potential that attracts all parties.

The most distinctive Gandhian contribution to the growth of aspirations and organized demands may have been the techniques that the Gandhians developed to influence government policy. Gandhi abjured violence, but he was a fervent advocate of civil disobedience and resistance to injustice. Behind this notion of civil disobedience lay elaborate theories concerning the nature of truth and justice, and precise principles that should guide a *satyagrahi*, i.e., one who commits civil disobedience.[10]

In actual practice, however, civil disobedience increasingly became a device by which discontented groups, acting in a non-violent fashion, attempted to coerce government into taking action on their behalf. So long as Gandhi was alive, his own civil-disobedience movements were guided by his principles. But with his death, civil disobedience became

[10] See Joan V. Bondurant, *op. cit.,* for a description of these assumptions and principles.

an instrument whereby groups opposed to the government increasingly encouraged violation of law. Gandhi was quite explicit in saying that the wanton use of civil disobedience was a misuse of his ideas. He called such movements *duragraha,* or "stubborn persistence." But Gandhi drew no distinction between the techniques that should be used against democratic and tyrannical governments. For him what was important was the presence, within any form of government, of injustice that had not been remedied through ordinary petition and persuasion. Nor could Gandhi define injustice so precisely that it excluded mere discontent. For many groups, the laws of an Indian government that had been democratically elected were no more legitimate than the laws of an authoritarian, alien ruler. The civil-disobedience campaigns now freely conducted by opposition parties, though criticized by many Gandhians as not being true *satyagraha*'s, claim to derive their sanction from Gandhi's precepts. And since many of those who now conduct civil-disobedience campaigns were once associated with Gandhi, their claim is lent some credence.

We have tried to suggest here that many of the problems faced by the Indian government, since it operates in a society of scarcity, have their origins in the circumstances surrounding colonial rule and a nationalist movement. Five features of current Indian politics can be traced to this earlier era: first, the high level of aspirations, which grew in part out of increasing Indian contact with Western material conditions and also out of efforts by nationalists to evoke aspirations among the Indian masses; second, the focusing of these aspirations toward government rather than toward voluntary or personal activities; third, the increasing organization of students and youth, peasants, workers, and other sections of society; fourth, the control and manipulation of these interest groups by political parties and political leaders; and last, the widespread readiness to violate law, which enables opposition party leaders to direct interest groups toward civil disobedience and sometimes toward the violation of public order.

How great are the present aspirations of the public, what is the substance of these aspirations, to what extent are they organized, and to what extent are they directed toward government for their fulfillment? These are questions which must be raised to understand the political process in India. There are four more-or-less useful indices for answering these questions: public opinion surveys, election data, the number (and membership) of political groups, and the number of petitions, civil-disobedience movements, and other kinds of public demonstrations organized to press demands.

Aspiration Levels

In recent years, fortunately, some information on public aspirations and attitudes toward government has been made available through the public opinion surveys of the Indian Institute of Public Opinion in New Delhi.[11] Since 1955 the Institute has asked a number of questions that have focused on levels of aspirations and the relationship of these aspirations to government.

In 1955 the IIPO asked a sample of fifteen hundred respondents in West Bengal the following question: "Thinking about the present social system, do you feel that a change is necessary?"[12] (See Table 1.)

TABLE 1

| ANSWER | WEST BENGAL | | | | CALCUTTA | |
| | Rural | | Urban | | Actual | Per Cent |
	Actual	Per Cent	Actual	Per Cent		
A change is necessary.....	125	62.5	305	50.8	548	78.0
You are quite satisfied.....	75	37.5	266	44.4	145	21.0
Don't know.............	...	...	29	4.8	7	1.0
Total................	200	100.0	600	100.0	700	100.0

When asked what kinds of changes were felt necessary the vast majority reported "social problems." The sample was then asked: "Could you suggest an agency or institution through which such change may be effected?" (See Table 2.)

In November, 1955, the Institute reported on a survey of public attitudes toward the dowry system. This survey was conducted in Travancore-Cochin and was based upon interviews with eleven hundred respondents. Of these, 65 per cent did not approve of the dowry system, while 35 per cent approved. But more significant was the finding that 65.2 per cent of those who disapproved of the system believed that it should be abolished by law.[13]

[11] Given the difficulties inherent in such an operation in India, in particular the lack of competent interviewers throughout the country, and the difficulty of sampling the usefulness of the Institute's data is limited. Then too, the sample employed in the surveys described here is largely urban, centers around Delhi, Calcutta, and the urban areas of Kerala (formerly called Travancore-Cochin), and draws heavily from educated and high-income groups. So long as we are aware of these features of the IIPO sample, however, and recognize that the data obtained cover only certain sections of the Indian public, it is possible to make some use of the surveys.

[12] *Public Opinion Surveys of the Indian Institute of Public Opinion,* I, No. 3 (October, 1955), 10.

[13] In May, 1961, the Parliament in New Delhi passed a law which banned the giving and accepting of dowries.

TABLE 2

AGENCY OR INSTITUTION	WEST BENGAL				CALCUTTA	
	Rural		Urban		Actual	Per Cent
	Actual	Per Cent	Actual	Per Cent		
Government and legislation.............	76	60.8	170	55.7	156	29.0
Press	5	...	...	...	...	1.0
Political organization......	5	4.0	48	15.7	50	9.0
Public institution.........	...	...	1	0.4	13	2.0
Religious institution.......	5	4.0	20	6.6	6	1.0
Co-operative movement....	4	3.2	8	2.6	32	6.0
Social reformer..........	5	4.0	15	4.9	6	1.0
Others*.................	30	24.0	65	21.3	273	50.0
Educational institution....	...	...	2	0.7	6	1.0
Total.................	125	100.0	329	107.9†	548	100.0

* No breakdowns given.
† Twenty-four double answers.

Two more surveys conducted in 1956, one in Calcutta, and the other in Calcutta, Travancore-Cochin, and Delhi, indicate the priorities given by the public to various problems, and the relative standing of government and private industry as agencies by which the problems should be handled. In assessing the significance of the question asked in Calcutta, one should note that the answers are structured, and that many issues, such as the slaughter of cows, the adoption of Hindi as the official language, and states reorganization, do not appear on the list. The responses do, however, give some approximation of public attitudes toward various economic issues (see Table 3).

The second question—which agency should handle the problems—also simplifies choices by posing government against private industry

TABLE 3

WHICH OF THESE PROBLEMS APPEAR TO YOU AS URGENT AND NEED THE IMMEDIATE
ATTENTION OF THE GOVERNMENT? (TOTAL RESPONDENTS: 796)*

PROBLEM	PREFERENCE (PER CENT)		
	1st	2d	3d
Ceiling on income......................	10.3	2.8	1.6
Rise in food prices....................	53.1	18.5	7.6
Low standard of living................	6.3	15.2	14.3
Unemployment........................	21.6	22.7	15.1
Rise in prices of cloth.................	2.4	24.2	19.0
Burdensome taxes.....................	0.9	2.8	3.3
Prohibition...........................	0.3	0.6	1.0
Housing problem......................	0.9	4.6	13.2
Lack of educational facilities...........	2.5	5.2	13.3
Refugee rehabilitation.................	1.8	2.6	8.8
Removal of untouchability.............	...	0.5	2.4

* *Public Opinion Surveys of the Indian Institute of Public Opinion*, II, No. 3 (December, 1956), 12.

rather than suggesting co-operatives, trade unions, or other voluntary agencies. The answers do, however, reveal the relative standing of the government vis-à-vis the private sector. A sample of 552 people in Calcutta were asked to suggest the agency or organization through which various objectives could be achieved. On almost every objective, a majority answered "government": more employment, 52 per cent (private industry, 3 per cent),[14] better wages, 51 per cent (6 per cent), better housing, 71 per cent (1 per cent), more and better food, 75 per cent (2 per cent), more clothing, 59 per cent (9.5 per cent), better educational facilities, 78 per cent (.3 per cent), and better medical facilities, 82 per cent (.2 per cent). On a few questions, government received only a plurality: better quality goods, 38 per cent (private industry, 16 per cent), workers' share in management, 31 per cent, (10 per cent), and profit sharing, 27 per cent (13 per cent). A sample of 300 taken in Travancore-Cochin gave similarly high majorities for government as against private industry. A sample of 234 in Delhi produced an unusually high number of "don't knows" (nearly 50 per cent for all questions); but those who did answer also reported that government rather than private industry should achieve these various objectives.[15]

The heavy demands placed upon the government are also evident in other surveys conducted by the IIPO. All these surveys indicate quite vividly the high level of scarcity that exists and the extent to which the public depends upon government to fill the gap between their aspirations and reality. How widespread these attitudes are in rural areas cannot be seen from these surveys (although the IIPO survey in West Bengal reported above included a small rural sample); but they do clearly indicate public attitudes in urban centers, from which opposition political parties, trade unions, and refugee and student associations draw their membership and leadership.

Election data show a high level of dissatisfaction with the existing government. Although Congress has won a majority of seats in all national and all but a handful of state elections, these victories have almost never been obtained by a majority vote. Slightly more than half of the Indian voters vote for opposition-party candidates or for independents. Those who argue that it is the Indian respect for authority that is keeping the present government in power would find little support from electoral data.

[14] The balance answered "both" or "don't know."
[15] *Public Opinion Surveys of the Indian Institute of Public Opinion*, I, Nos. 10, 11, 12 (May, June, and July, 1956), 14–19.

Since Independence, dissident political groups have been growing in number and size. Although no statistics are available on the numbers of caste, tribal, religious, and linguistic groups, clearly old associations have grown larger and new ones have emerged since 1947. There are at least two and one-half times as many trade unions in India today as there were at the time of Independence, and twice as many trade union members. Several hundred thousand students belong to Congress-, Communist-, or Socialist-dominated student or youth associations; and although it is difficult to say whether there are more or fewer than in the era before Independence, it is clear that students have remained politically active. The All-India Kisan Sabha, the largest single peasant association, claims a larger membership today than it did before the war. And community associations have mushroomed since Independence.

Membership statistics in India are notoriously unreliable. Nonetheless, the public activities of these groups do indicate that popular participation in movements making demands upon the government is considerable. The States Reorganization Commission reported that some 152,250 documents were submitted to it when it toured the country to investigate the demands for reorganizing India's states. In several states, community associations have demonstrated their capacity to bring hundreds of thousands of individuals into mass demonstrations or civil-disobedience movements—in the Naga hills, in the Telugu-speaking areas of Madras, in the Marathi-speaking districts of Bombay, in the city of Ahmedabad, and in the Sikh areas of the Punjab. In Kerala, the Communists and the anti-Communist groups have rallied hundreds of thousands of individuals into mass activities. In Calcutta, opposition groups have been able to bring out refugees and middle-class Bengalis to fill the main thoroughfares of the city, halt transportation, close shops, and in general paralyze the city. Student agitations have been large enough to force universities to close.

Large-scale organization and agitation in India's rural areas have not been as common as in the urban centers. The Communists successfully launched a movement against landlords in the Telengana area of Hyderabad immediately after Independence. Other sporadic peasant agitations, under Communist or Socialist leadership, have taken place in some districts of West Bengal, the Punjab, and Bombay. Linguistic agitation has filtered into some rural districts, especially some of the districts on state borders. A few of the agitations for separate states have originated in rural areas or small towns: the Naga agitation in Assam, much of the

Sikh unrest in the Punjab, and the activities of a number of hill tribes in northern India. But in the main, the bulk of the Indian countryside has remained relatively unaffected by the major agitation movements.

Electoral data substantiate the impression that disaffection from the Congress party is greater in the cities than in the rural areas. In Delhi, Calcutta, Madras, and Bombay, opposition groups have received far more support than they have in the rural areas. In the city of Madras, the Dravida Munnetra Kazhagam (DMK) opposition party has won municipal elections; and in Calcutta, the Communists and Marxist-left parties have elected most of the M.P.'s and M.L.A.'s (members of the legislative assembly). Reports of journalists and scholars in India suggest that there has been considerable disaffection among urban middle classes throughout the country. In contrast, Congress has done well in the rural districts. In many rural districts in the former princely states, there are now Congress party organizations where before Independence there were none. In many other states, Congress has established durable bureaucratic structures at the local level, where earlier there had been more diffuse patterns of organization. In most parts of India, Congress appears to win more votes in the rural constituencies than in the urban ones; and in many rural areas the Congress vote has been increasing.

The support given to Congress in the rural areas and the financial support provided it by many Indian businesses have been the major sources of post-Independence political strength for the Congress party and, one might even say, of India's comparative political stability. The existence of a complex social system and a system of overlapping tenure rights has mitigated against class struggle in the countryside. The close liaison between local administration, the local rural gentry, and the local Congress organization are also important factors in national Congress party strength. It is the relative stability of the countryside which makes it possible for the Congress party and the government to survive the turmoil and the high political demands more characteristic of the urban centers.

Demands upon the state are thus not uniform. As in almost everything else about India, diversity is the key. There are some rural districts where demands upon the state are virtually non-existent; other districts where demands for tubewells, credit, and seeds are growing; and large cities where refugees, the unemployed, and students make diffuse but violent demands upon the state.

Political Orientation

What attitudes do organized groups have toward government? There are considerable variations among the attitudes of trade unions, peasant organizations, student groups, and the like, and there are considerable differences between the attitudes of Socialists, Communists, and Hindu communalists. But behind these differences are certain common attitudes, widely shared by many political leaders of all groups not controlled by the Congress party and the government, and even by many Congressmen. Here we shall describe these attitudes in the broadest of terms, ignoring the variations and the many exceptions, just as we have generally put aside the variations and exceptions in considering the public philosophy of policy-makers.

We noted in the first chapter that many elected policy-makers have images of themselves as bearers of the national and general interest—an interest that is to be achieved through rational policy—and of the politicians out of government, especially those in opposition, as mere promoters of personal and group interests. Such policy-makers thus conceive of themselves as being influenced only by rational argument, by persuasion, and never by political threats or political and personal rewards.

The non-governmental politicians—and for purposes of simplification we are lumping together all those political leaders not in a position to make public policy—have a somewhat different image of the political process. The politician, Congressman and non-Congressman alike, conceives of himself as the bearer of the public will, that is, the spokesman for the downtrodden peasant, or worker, or middle class. The politician believes he is better informed on the needs of the masses than is the bureaucrat or the policy-maker. He often sees policy-makers and bureaucrats as conservative guardians of the existing order, more concerned with the maintenance of order than with social change. Or, if he is a local Congressman, and believes that the national leadership is concerned with social change, he often holds that it is too slow and too unresponsive to local needs. In any event, the politician often regards the policy-maker as particularly slow and inefficient, or even as a spokesman for selfish personal and group interests. Opposition leaders go further. To them the government is unresponsive because it *is* conservative; and only the pressures of politicians and the groups they lead will force the government to ameliorate the lot of the masses. Neither rational arguments nor petitions are likely to hasten government action, they believe; only mass activities, demonstrations, *hartal's* (strikes), civil disobedience, and other expressions of mass will can force the government to take action.

This is not to argue that the politician has no conception of a national interest. On the contrary, the major political groups have explicit conceptions of a public philosophy; and their conceptions are quite close to that of the present government. The goals of economic development and national unity are accepted by all, even though the major opposition parties deny that the government is acting in such a way as to best achieve these objectives. But perhaps because there is no debate on goals, Socialists, Communists, Jan Sangh, and other party leaders (with some exceptions in the Praja Socialist party) find it unnecessary to justify their demands in terms of some broader conception of the public interest. In 1958, for instance, students at the University of Calcutta struck against a decision of the authorities to raise tuition fees. In justifying or criticizing the strike, neither student leaders nor newspaper editors suggested that higher tuitions might be necessary for an improvement in faculty salaries or in university facilities, or that a failure to raise tuition fees might either lower standards or require the state government to allocate funds to the university that might better be used in development programs. No one criticized the students for the position they took, but only for the manner in which they acted.

Often the politician's identification with his group—union, party, peasant association, caste, or linguistic group—is so strong that he gives overriding precedence to the preservation and enhancement of that group and the community from which it derives. Few refugee leaders, for example, will attempt to persuade refugees of the possible advantages— to themselves as well as to the entire society—of accepting employment and land outside West Bengal.

Again, in Assam, both Congress and opposition-party politicians (in this case, with the support of the chief minister) demanded that the central government build an oil refinery in Assam. The oil was being extracted in that state, but a commission appointed by the central government had recommended Bihar or Calcutta as more satisfactory sites, given considerations of transport, costs, and so on. That the Assam politicians should demand preference for their state is not remarkable; but it is of special interest that Assam's case was presented not in terms of any national interest (such as Assam's special security problem because it is near the Burmese and Pakistan borders), but solely in terms of Assam's own requirements. One could cite case after case in which politicians neither considered the national interest in making demands nor argued for their group interests in terms of the national and public interest.

The policy-maker, with his public responsibility and image of the public interest, and the politician, with his responsiveness to group interests, often antagonize one another. Such antagonism is not only expressed in the inevitable conflicts between government and opposition, but often between the policy-maker and his own party; and it is most clearly and frequently evident between the state Congress party organizations and the state Congress governments. The central government tends to be the strongest defender of the responsible-rational national-interest outlook, and it is particularly anxious that control of state governments be in the hands of a like-minded leadership. In several states, including the important state of West Bengal, the central government has gone outside the party to select a chief minister, simply because it felt that the local party leadership had too narrow interests. And this was probably not an inaccurate appraisal, for many of the Congress party leaders are in fact largely concerned with pursuing policies that are politically popular or that are representative only of regional, class, or caste interests. Several state governments in India have, moreover, been paralyzed by government-Congress party conflicts when the party leadership has felt that the government was not being adequately responsive to popular wishes.

The politicians' criticism of the policy-maker is not altogether unfair. Since the policy-maker gives the public and national interest, as he conceives it, paramount if not sole priority, he is often indifferent to local demands, even when feelings are extremely intense. In the states-reorganization controversy between 1947 and 1953, when linguistic groups called for a reorganization of India's states to coincide with linguistic-cultural regions, the central government argued that economic-development plans deserved priority, and that considerations of administrative and other costs required that reorganization be postponed. Not until agitation reached the stage of violence in the Telugu-speaking areas of Madras did Nehru agree to create the Telugu state of Andhra. In 1955, other linguistic states were created. Bombay State, however, remained bilingual in spite of intense demands by the Maharashtrian-speaking peoples of Bombay. National policy-makers seemed unwilling to recognize that the Maharashtrians as a whole—not simply a few leaders—genuinely wanted a separate province, and that they would, if necessary, act forcefully if their demands were not met. From 1956 until 1959, Bombay State suffered frequent linguistic riots, until the central government finally conceded a separate Maharashtrian state.

One model thus feeds on the other. The politician makes demands to which the government fails to respond. He then turns toward force to which the government does respond, and is thereby convinced that only such mass pressures will move a static and conservative government. In turn, many a policy-maker is unwilling to listen, and often unwilling to respond when he does listen. He is accordingly unable to assess the consequences of his policies. When violence occurs, he is surprised. But then again, he is not, for violence vindicates his image of the political process as an irrational expression of narrow group interests.

III. COMMUNITY ASSOCIATIONS

"National integration" is a goal of India's national leadership. In the broadest sense, integration refers both to the absence of divisive movements that would Balkanize the nation or drastically jeopardize the power of the central government and to the presence of attitudes throughout the society that give preference to national and "public" interests as distinct from parochial interests. The persistence of primordial loyalties to one's own community—caste, religion, tribe, or language—is therefore viewed by the national leadership as the most serious threat to national integration. In 1961 a National Integration Conference was held in Delhi for representatives of all the national parties and many of the state parties to recommend steps that might be taken to diminish divisive tendencies. And prior to the elections in 1962, national leaders of the Congress party, and of other national parties as well, spoke of passing legislation which would outlaw "communal" appeals to the electorate.[1]

At the same time that national leaders decry the existence of community associations and community loyalties, all parties, including Congress, continue to take into consideration—as one of the criteria for selection—the community affiliations of prospective candidates for the state assemblies and the national Parliament. Community associations and community political parties have persisted; and in some areas, many such old

[1] In the past the term "communal" has been used to refer to religious appeals and religious associations. More recently, it has come to be applied to tribal and caste appeals as well. The term is invariably used as a pejorative. Throughout this study we have used the word "community" to describe groups organized by caste, religion, race, tribe, or cultural-linguistic region, that is, groups whose membership is drawn from communities into which individuals are born.

associations have increased in membership and new ones have been created. Does this development necessarily constitute a threat to the Indian political system?

In order to explore this question, it is first necessary to define the character of community associations. Community associations constitute one type of associational interest.[2] A distinction can be made between associations on the basis of the population groupings from which they recruit their membership, that is, whether the population grouping is joined voluntarily or whether it is one into which an individual is born. Among the former associations are those based upon class and occupational distinctions: trade unions, business associations, peasant organizations—and one might also include refugees and students; among the latter are religious, tribal, caste, and linguistic associations. One is tempted to categorize one group as modern, the other as traditional; but such terminology can be grossly misleading. The so-called modern groups often have ascriptive features. Among business organizations, for example, are associations which are largely Marwari, or Bengali, or Gujarati; and such regional distinctions within the business community may be more important for some purposes than whether a businessman is in commercial or industrial activity, an importer or exporter. Nor are the so-called traditional groups always as traditional as they might at first appear. Indian tribal associations, for example, are not generally built upon traditional tribal structures, as they often are in Africa. Having lost their traditional political structures, the tribes that organize create modern associations whose leaders are more often Cambridge, or at least Calcutta, graduates than traditional tribal chiefs. Then, too, the modern-traditional dichotomy has erroneous predictive consequences; for it suggests that the traditional groupings are temporary and reactionary, and that the modern associations are the wave of the future. On the contrary, as economic growth has occurred in India and political awareness has

[2] Gabriel A. Almond, in *The Politics of the Developing Areas* (Princeton, N. J.: Princeton University Press, 1960), has identified four main types of structures in the articulation of political interests: institutional, non-associational, associational, and anomic interests. In the previous chapter we suggested that a considerable part of interest articulation in India occurs on an unorganized basis, or through what Almond has called non-associational interest groups, and that many interests in India are thus far unorganized and inarticulate—in a sense not interests at all but only potential interests. In chapter viii we will assess the role of anomic interests. Institutional interests within authoritative political structures, e.g., the army, bureaucracy, public corporations, ministries, etc., will not be systematically examined in this study. Such a study or series of studies needs to be undertaken. Here, however, we are concerned primarily with the impact of political demands from society upon government and the problems that such demands raise in a society and polity of scarcity.

increased, the number of community associations has grown. Before 1947 the most prominent division in Indian life was between Hindu and Muslim groups; and after 1947 among the most prominent groups were those that emerged from linguistic-regional sentiments. Tribal and scheduled-caste bodies are now multiplying; and within political parties ascriptive identifications are playing a more prominent role. In a society in which ethnic-cultural identifications are great, such affiliations are likely to play an increasingly important part in the emergence of political groups.

To argue, as some have done, that occupational groupings are specific in their demands and community associations are diffuse, further compounds the confusion. Many of the community associations are quite specific in their demands. The Andhra Mahasabha wanted the central government to agree to the creation of an Andhra state. In West Bengal, the many tribal associations agitate for more concessions—jobs, educational opportunities, government grants—for their communities. Similarly, the Anglo-Indian Association is concerned with specific government policies that protect or injure Anglo-Indians. It agitates, for example, for making English (the mother tongue of Anglo-Indians) one of India's official languages.

On the other hand, not all occupational groupings are specific in demands. Unions and peasant associations may make specific demands, but they may also embrace broad ideological outlooks. In fact, occupational groups are more likely to have an ideological *Weltanschauung* than are community associations.

There are four major types of community associations in Indian politics, based on religion, caste, language, and tribe. In short, the major types of social institutions in Indian life, excluding family and kinship units, have associations that articulate their interests. That is not to say, for example, that all tribes or all castes have their own political associations. Far from it. But increasingly, such social groupings have had their political manifestations.

Many of the political movements present in India are political "overflows" of community tensions. Since India's social system has both hierarchical (caste and class) and horizontal (tribal, religious, linguistic) groupings, political expressions follow suit; and since both hierarchical and horizontal divisions tend to be local or regional in character, there is a multiplicity of local parties and interest groups of an order rarely found in other nations. Therefore, to analyze such associations, the types of communities which they represent, the kinds of demands which they make, the targets of those demands, and above all, the effects which they have, one must look at these associations on the local and regional level.

Tribal Associations

The political activities of India's tribes must be examined in the context of the larger relationship between tribal and Hindu society. For centuries, if not for several thousand years, tribes have gradually been absorbed into the Hindu fold. Many castes were once individual tribes. In some instances, tribes have retained their autonomy, but have adopted many features of Hindu life—the ban on widow-remarriage, vegetarianism, abstention from liquor, and various Hindu rituals. This process of "Sanskritization" [3] (the emulation by one community of the behavior of another) often makes it difficult to draw the line between a tribe and a caste. The 1941 census reports that there were some 25 million tribals in India; the 1951 census (which rejects tribe and caste as appropriate classifications for census enumeration, and lists tribes in the religious category) reports that there are only 1.7 million tribesmen in India. This shift does not mean that all of India's tribesmen have suddenly become Hindus, and that tribes as such are suddenly disappearing; nor has genocide occurred except, in a manner of speaking, through census redefinition. The Indian constitution recognizes certain tribes, irrespective of their religion, in its provisions for the treatment of backward or "scheduled" tribes and castes (so-called because they are listed on a schedule issued by the Government of India upon the recommendation of the state governments). The shift from the 1941 to the 1951 census, however, calls attention to the fact that there has been, in some instances, considerable cultural assimilation, which makes it difficult to distinguish tribes from Hindu castes; this assimilation has often been accompanied by changes in the structure of political authority within the tribe. In other instances, the tribe has remained relatively isolated from surrounding peoples or, having come in contact with other people, has successfully withstood cultural penetration. In either event, new forms of political expression have emerged in recent years. It is these new forms which we shall examine in three Indian states—West Bengal, Bihar, and Assam—all of which have substantial numbers of tribals.

[3] For an examination of this process, see "A Note on Sanskritization and Westernization," by M. N. Srinivas, *Far Eastern Quarterly*, XV (August, 1956), 481–96. See also "The Hindu Method of Tribal Absorption," by Nirmal Kumar Bose, in his *Cultural Anthropology and Other Essays* (Calcutta: Indian Associated Publishing Co., Ltd., 1953), pp. 156–70.

In West Bengal, the tribe as a political entity, capable of dealing as a unit with external government and administration, has largely disappeared, although many features of tribal life—above all, identification with the tribe—continue. Most of the tribesmen in West Bengal have actually migrated from their natural setting in Madhya Pradesh, Bihar, and Orissa to work in Bengal as either agricultural laborers or factory hands. Most are in the districts of Burdwan, Bankura, Purulia, Midnapore, and the tea plantation areas of north Bengal (West Dinajpur and Jalpaiguri). They consist of the Santals (845,000), Oraon (203,000), Munda (83,000), Lepcha (13,400), Mech (10,700), and Bhutia (4,800).[4] The total tribal population is therefore approximately 1,160,000, or a little more than 4 per cent of the population of West Bengal.

Until 1947 tribal organizations in Bengal were virtually non-existent. In the nineteenth century, there had been revolts among the Santals, a tribe that took to agricultural labor, but no permanent organization emerged.[5] A number of the Santals and other tribesmen who came to Bengal reclaimed land; but wealthier and often better educated peoples soon exploited them, took their land, and forced them into agricultural labor. In an effort to arrest this process, the government of Bengal in 1940 appointed government welfare officers; but the program to improve the health, welfare, and education of the tribes was negligible. In 1947, the West Bengal government created a Tribal Welfare Department to protect the tribes and to provide social welfare services. Government officials were appointed to deal with the tribes, to help set up co-operatives, and to provide educational health facilities and other welfare services.

It was only after the government program was launched that tribal associations emerged. After 1947, about fifteen tribal associations were created. These associations have had no finances and little organizational structure, often no more than a president and secretary. The leaders of these associations have generally been non-cultivating tribal landowners, a rural gentry comparable in position to the *bhadralog,* or gentlefolk, found among Hindu Bengalis. These leaders have often utilized the associations to win popularity and to run successfully for the legislative assembly seats allocated to tribals. Most of the fourteen or fifteen reserved seats are held by Congressmen associated with these tribal associa-

[4] Figures from the *Census of India, 1951.*

[5] In 1855, an oppressed group of Santals in Santal Parganas and Birbhum districts revolted against landlords, moneylenders, and government officials. Martial law was established and the rebellion crushed. For a sympathetic account, see Sir William Wilson Hunter, *Annals of Rural Bengal* (London: Smith, Elder & Co., 1897).

tions. Hereditary tribal leaders have little if any power. Among the Santals, for example, a new leadership has arisen based upon wealth, education, and access to outside political authority. The last qualification is measured by the recognition given to a tribal leader by the government tribal welfare officers. These officers may appoint a member of the tribal rural gentry to be responsible for dealing with local conflicts, to represent the government among the tribals, and to present the demands of the tribals to the government. An annual sum of Rs. 100 ($20) may be given to each such tribal leader for performing these services.

Political activity among tribes in West Bengal is probably greatest in the Darjeeling region in north Bengal. Here, unlike other parts of West Bengal, are tribes in their natural setting. These tribes have retained their language, dances, dress, and culture to a far greater extent than other tribes in West Bengal; and they generally have less contact with non-tribesmen than other tribes in the state. On the whole, they are not "scheduled," i.e. listed as depressed communities; the only two scheduled tribes are the Lepchas and the Bhutias. While the Lepchas outnumber the Bhutias in Darjeeling district (13,100 to 4,000), the Bhutias are politically and educationally more aggressive. The Bhutias have their own tribal welfare association, which informally nominates the tribal candidate for the legislative assembly from their locality. The present deputy minister of tribal welfare in West Bengal is a Bhutia.

A substantial number of Bengal's tribals are scattered throughout the state and are organized not as tribals but as landless laborers or factory workers. Santals, for example, are a substantial component of the iron and steel unions in Jamshedpur. In the Sundarban region south of Calcutta, both Congress and the leftist parties are actively attempting to gain recruits for their unions from among the landless laborers (including Santals). One government official in the tribal welfare department estimates that in some demonstrations, particularly those concerned with food, as many as 50 per cent of the demonstrators are Santal landless laborers, largely from the Sundarbun region.

India's best organized tribal party is the Jharkhand in Bihar. It is the second largest party in the state and derives its support from the tribes residing in the Chota-Nagpur region of Bihar, where there are more than six million members of scheduled tribes—largely Munda, Oraon, Ho, Bhumij, and Kharia. Nearby are large numbers of Santals.

Jaipal Singh, founder and leader of the Jharkhand party, is himself the son of a well-to-do family of the Munda tribes. He studied in India and at Oxford, where he obtained his M.A. He was an Olympic player, an official of Burmah-Shell, vice-principal of Rajkumar College, where the sons of ruling princes received their education, and later minister in one of the princely states. In 1938 he organized the All-India Adibasi (tribal) Mahasabha, which worked for the improvement of tribals and for the creation of reserved tribal seats in the legislative assembly. During the war, when Congress leaders in Bihar were in jail for their support of the Quit India movement, Jaipal Singh endorsed the war effort, and successfully recruited countless numbers of tribesmen into the army and found others jobs in the British and American armies situated in Chota-Nagpur. He thereby enormously strengthened his ties and those of his organization with the tribes in the area. Relations between the Adibasi Mahasabha and the Congress party in Bihar were understandably strained. The groups were further separated by the strong antipathy of many tribals for the non-tribal Biharis, a feeling that was nurtured by their better educated leaders, who resented what they felt was Bihari domination of the state, and especially of administration, and Bihari penetration into tribal land.

At the close of the war, Jaipal Singh organized and became president of the Jharkhand party, which adopted as its central plank the creation of a Jharkhand or tribal state out of Chota-Nagpur and the contiguous predominantly tribal districts of Orissa. To help raise the living standards of the tribes and to protect them from Hindu attempts at absorption, the Jharkhand party has argued that the interests of the tribes can best be satisfied in a separate state within the union. The proposed state of Chota-Nagpur would be rich in deposits of iron, mica, copper, coal, bauxite, antimony, and china clay.

In 1952 Jaipal Singh was elected to Parliament to fill the scheduled-tribe seat of Ranchi, Bihar. The Jharkhand party itself emerged in this election as the second largest party in the state; and in the predominantly tribal districts, it tied Congress with thirty-two seats. Although the party has been unsuccessful in persuading the States Reorganization Commission of the central government to look into the demands of various groups for a reorganization of state boundaries, the party's leaders claim they have forced the Bihar government to pay more attention to the development of the Chota-Nagpur region, in particular, to support new educational facilities.

The government's recognition of the special position of scheduled tribes in Bihar has not only facilitated their political organization, but has also been a significant factor in the maintenance of tribal identification. As an anthropologist has written:

. . . the rise of the Jharkhand Party has contributed to a strong new identification with all *adibasi*. In addition it has provided a new avenue of social mobility, i.e., election to public office. Through the Jharkhand Party and other institutions for tribal welfare the Santal who is better educated than his fellows can get status in an area less competitive than that of the wider Indian society. Finally there are significant practical reasons for maintaining their identity as members of a scheduled tribe. Among such benefits are scholarships, special governmental appointments, and preferential industrial appointment.[6]

Assam, the northeasternmost state of India, shares with Bihar the basic problem of dissension from tribals on the border. But in Assam, the tension is doubly great. For one thing, Assam borders on a foreign country, not another state. For another, the agitating tribals are more formidable—they have a much greater measure of traditional tribal autonomy, and they have had the weapons with which to try to extend their autonomy.

Assam is bounded by Tibet, China, Burma, and East Pakistan, and is connected with the remainder of India by a narrow strip of land. Along the Assam-Burmese border lie 3,070 square miles of the Naga Hills, in which reside some nineteen Naga tribes, largely cut off from the mainstreams of Hindu culture. Throughout the nineteenth century, periodic raids into the plains by the Naga highlanders presented problems for the British; and British annexation of the hills did not diminish the Naga efforts to become independent, although part of the Naga territory remained unadministered. When the Simon Commission visited India in the late 1920's, the Nagas pressed their demand for independence. But the most recent independence movement in Assam took shape shortly after the end of the Second World War.

During the war, parts of the Naga Hills were occupied by Japanese troops. A. Z. Phizo, a leading Naga, contacted and collaborated with Subhas Bose's Azad Hind Fouz (the rebel Indian National Army, which supported the Japanese). By the end of the war, Phizo's independence movement had both money and weapons. The sources of these have never

---

[6] Martin Orans, "A Tribal People in an Industrial Setting," *Traditional India: Structure and Change,* ed. Milton Singer (Philadelphia: American Folklore Society, 1959), p. 238. Orans' study is of the Santals in the Jamshedpur steel regions who have come from neighboring districts of Bihar and Orissa. In all, the Santals number close to three million.

been fully uncovered, but it is believed that the Nagas either collected their arms from the Anglo-American arms dumps left during the war or bought equipment from the Karen rebels of Burma across the Tuensang border of India. Part of Phizo's support came from Naga soldiers demobilized from the Indian army. Out of this group Phizo created the Naga Home Guard, the core of his fighting army. It has been estimated that some five or six thousand rebels were in the Naga Home Guard, the majority of whom were demobilized Naga soldiers.[7]

In 1949, the Government of India extended its administrative control into the hitherto unadministered areas of Tuensang. Three Naga chiefs issued a call to the United Nations for intervention against what they described as an Indian invasion of free Nagaland. The government of Assam, which had jurisdiction over the Naga territories, attempted to pacify the Nagas, but without success. The administration of the Naga areas was at first in the hands of the Assam governor; in 1951 control was turned over to the Assam cabinet. Phizo thereupon organized a Naga National Council, which began to function as a parallel government. The state administration was ignored and lawlessness grew. Many of the Nagas felt that the five deputy commissioners who had been appointed in the Naga Hills since Independence were inexperienced men with little knowledge of the customs and language of the tribes. In 1956 a serious rebellion led by Phizo—who had by now emerged as the single most important Naga leader—erupted. Tension between the Nagas and the Assam government grew so great that the Government of India decided to send in a military force to pacify the area. The central government was eager for a political settlement that would fall short of conceding the Naga demand for independence, but would give the Nagas a large measure of autonomy. The Government of India let it be known that it would support the creation of a Naga area directly under the administration of the central government.

Some fifteen hundred delegates from tribes of the Naga Hills and Tuensang Frontier Division assembled at Kohima, Assam, on August 23, 1957. The delegates to this Naga People's Convention, none of whom were Phizo supporters, proposed a political settlement with the Government of India and recommended the establishment of a new territory that would include the Naga Hills District of Assam, the Tuensang Division of the North East Frontier Agency (NEFA), and the reserved forests in the Naga Hills district, which had been transferred out of the

[7] P. N. Dutt, "The Naga Question: A Probe into the Rebellion," *Hindustan Standard,* December 25, 1957.

district in 1921. They proposed that the governor of Assam act as agent of the president of India in administering the territory. The Nagas further said that they hoped for a settlement "within the Indian Union." Their demand, in other words, was for independence from the administrative control of the Assam government. Since the violence had largely been in the Naga Hills District, which was under the jurisdiction of the Assam government rather than the centrally controlled NEFA, their demand clearly reflected upon the policies and administration of the Assamese. In September, 1957, Nehru announced his acceptance of the proposal of the Naga People's Convention, and also declared a blanket amnesty for the rebels. The Assam government was not pleased but reluctantly gave in.

Since Phizo's rebels were not at Kohima, the delegates appealed to "the countrymen in arms to give up the cult of violence." [8] The rebels, however, were not pacified by the government's concessions. In early September, their leader created an international stir with a letter to the *New York Times* reiterating his demand for an independent Nagaland. Phizo said that the Nagas did not share a common tradition or culture with India, and that most of the educated Nagas did not want to have an independent state in India, but wanted to be an independent nation.[9]

In December, 1957, the new administrative unit was created. It was reported that differences had developed among the Nagas, with one section eager to give a trial to the new administration, and another section, under Phizo, ready to renew hostilities. It was also reported that the soldiers in Phizo's group were giving him complete support, but that among the civilians there had been many defections.[10] Throughout 1958, sporadic violence from Phizo's rebels continued.[11]

Although the Nagas represented Assam's most severe tribal problem, and Phizo continued to demand complete autonomy, other tribes also presented difficulties for the state government. In both the 1952 and 1957 elections, several tribal parties participated: the Tribal Sangh, the Tribal League, United Mizo Freedom Organization, Khasi Jaintia Rural Organization, Khasi Jaintia National Federated State Conference, Garo National Conference, and the Hill Peoples' party. In October, 1954, a conference of tribal leaders, meeting in the Garo Hills, proposed the

[8] *Statesman*, August 26, 1957.

[9] *New York Times*, September 2, 1957.

[10] *Statesman*, December 22, 1957.

[11] On July 30, 1960, Nehru announced that the Nagas would be given a separate state within the Indian Union. The new Nagaland would have 6,236 square miles and about 400,000 persons.

unification of all the hill districts, including the Naga Hills District, into a single state. In the 1957 elections, the Eastern India Tribal Union emerged as the strongest tribal party, sweeping the tribal areas on the issue of a separate hill state.

In assessing the reasons for the demand for a separate hill state, the States Reorganization Commission said:

> The problem in the hill areas at this stage is at least as much psychological as political. There is no denying the fact that the demand for a hill state partly reflects the separatist pull of the extremist elements. Other factors, however, appear to have lent support to the demand and these are:
> (i) suspicion and distrust of the people of the plains by the tribal people of this area;
> (ii) the diversity of races and cultures and the different levels of social, educational and political development in the different areas of this region which have prevented the tribal people from coming up to the level of the people in the plains;
> (iii) lack of communication in those areas which has made it difficult for the various tribes to come in close contact with the rest of India; and
> (iv) the economic backwardness of the region.
> It has also been alleged that the Government of Assam has not been as sympathetic and helpful to the tribal people as it should have been.[12]

The Commission noted some of the complaints by the tribal interests: lack of sympathy from the administration, inadequacy of financial resources, interference from above, neglect of the tribal areas by the government, imposition of the Assamese language and culture, and the opening of tribal lands to settlers from the plains.[13] It rejected the various proposals for autonomous hill states (there were a number of alternative proposals by different tribal groups), but recommended that the role of the district councils and of the administrative relations between the tribal areas and the state government be re-examined.

[12] Government of India, States Reorganization Commission, *Report* (Delhi: Manager of Publications, 1955), p. 185.
[13] *Ibid.*, p. 188.

This brief examination of tribal movements in three states, Bihar, Assam, and West Bengal suggests at least three types of tribal associations.

1. Interest-group associations, such as those found in West Bengal, where tribes are concerned primarily with maximizing their economic benefits and employment and educational opportunities by influencing government policy and administration. These limited objectives, expressed by new voluntary associations in West Bengal, are clearly related to the dispersal of the tribal peoples and their separation from a centralized tribal authority that is capable of coping with external political institutions.

2. Political parties, such as those found in Bihar, parts of Assam, and in north Bengal, concerned with affecting state policy and administration, and also with winning power within the existing political system. The demands of these parties for political power center upon the creation of separate tribal districts or, in the case of the Jharkhand party, a separate state in which the tribals would predominate. Their concern is with sharing or controlling political power. They tend to operate in areas with substantial tribal concentration, which lends considerable power to tribal votes. As in the case of tribal interest groups, the tribal parties represent new political structures.

3. Secessionist political movements, such as the Naga National Council in Assam. In that region opportunities for secessionist activities are enhanced by the proximity of the tribes to the international border and by the relatively few ties and lower degree of assimilation with the Hindus on the plains. But here again, the demand for a separate Nagaland is made by a new leadership that is divorced from traditional tribal authority. Among those Naga tribes that have retained their own traditional internal political structures, tribal leaders seem to have associated themselves with the more moderate Naga People's Convention, which has been willing to accept a settlement within the Indian Union. It would seem that the new, younger leadership is seeking to create structures of authority that are free both from Indian domination and from traditional tribal leadership.[14]

In all three types of situation, it appears that new tribal organizations have emerged with new leaders who are divorced from old tribal forms and leaders. The position of tribes in Africa is obviously not analagous,

[14] The evidence for this is not conclusive, but is suggested by research conducted by Marcus Franda for an unpublished Master's thesis in the Department of Political Science at the University of Chicago, entitled "The Naga National Council: A Study in Group Politics" (1960).

since in Africa traditional structures of tribal authority continue both as instruments of internal government and as the basis of external relations. In the situations described here, the tribes have created new forms to deal with external authority. The extent to which traditional political institutions persist in these tribes and provide internal authority, and the kinds of relationships that exist between traditional tribal political institutions and these new forms are areas for further inquiry.

Religious Associations

The hill tribes' fear of being assimilated by the plains people has its parallel elsewhere in India. For example, the movement of the Sikh Akali Dal for a new Punjabi-speaking state in which the Sikh community would be in the majority cannot be understood without recognizing the fears of assimilation within this community. Like many of the movements of various religious and tribal groups for independent or autonomous states, the Akali Dal grew out of a fear not only of being ignored or maltreated by the majority community, but of being culturally obliterated by that majority. A political movement by the community—even when it does not succeed in satisfying its political demands—can be a device for establishing cultural boundaries. Political organization and agitation sharpens distinctions when cultural boundaries are fuzzy and assimilation processes are under way. That the process of cultural assimilation is often accompanied by efforts toward political autonomy is clearly evident in the case of the Sikh community.

The Sikh religion developed in the sixteenth century as a syncretistic religion related to the non-caste, theistic Bhakti (devotional) movement of Hinduism and the tolerant, devotional Sufi movement of Islam, which had spread among north Indian Hindus by the fifteenth century. Guru Nanak (1469–1539), the founder of Sikhism, was by birth a Hindu. He opposed asceticism, caste, worship before images, and elaborate rituals, and won support for his syncretistic faith among Punjab peasants. As time went on, the line between Sikhism and the Hindu and Muslim faiths sharpened. The *Adi Granth*, a compilation of Guru Nanak's writings, became the holy scripture. Gurmukhi, a new script, was developed. New temples of worship, the *gurdwara's*, were erected. Finally, under the leadership of Gobind Singh (1666–1708)—the last of the ten Gurus, or spiritual leaders of the faith—Sikhism became a militant sect with distinctive symbols of its own. Guru Gobind organized the Sikhs against their Muslim rulers and tried, unsuccessfully, to overthrow the Mogul Empire in the north. He created the Khalsa, or "the pure" followers, and initiated them into observing the "Five K's," namely, to wear uncut hair and beard (*kesh*), to wear a hair comb (*kungha*), to wear shorts (*kuchha*), to wear a steel bangle on the right wrist (*kara*), and to carry a sword (*kirpan*).

Gobind Singh's military aspirations were not realized until sometime after his death in the eighteenth century, when Sikh power extended well beyond the frontiers of the Punjab. It was not until 1849, after the Anglo-Sikh wars of 1845 and 1848, that all of the Punjab fell into British hands. Lord Dalhousie ingratiated himself among the new subjects by recruiting the militant Sikhs into his army and by announcing that no Sikh would be required to cut either his hair or beard and that every effort would be made to maintain the integrity of the community. Ironically, however, temporal power had been accompanied by a tendency for Sikhs to return to many Hindu practices, such as caste, Brahmanical ritual, and worship before images.

In the nineteenth and early twentieth centuries, the Sikhs experienced many movements of social reform and cultural revival.[15] Among the most important was the Akali movement, a struggle of orthodox Sikhs to wrest control of the *gurdwara*'s from *mahant*'s, or temple managers, who were no longer subject to the control of the community. The Akali party, successful in this attempt, became the single most powerful political force among the Sikh community. But in spite of attempts at cultural revival, and in spite of the Sikh-Muslim conflicts that preceded and accompanied Partition, the disintegration of the Sikh community continued. Khushwant Singh, a Sikh writing about the future of the Sikh community, argues that even the external forms and symbols of Sikhism are disappearing and that eventually the Sikhs will again be merged with Hinduism.[16]

Since Independence the Shiromani Akali Dal, the foremost Sikh party, has agitated for the creation of a Sikh majority state which could preserve the integrity of the community. Religious, or communal, demands are widely condemned in post-Independence India, and so the Akali Dal has presented its demand in the form of a Punjabi-speaking state. Since Hindus in the Punjab write in the Devanagari script (in which Hindi is written), while Sikhs write Punjabi in the Gurmukhi script, the Akali Dal has declared that the boundaries of the proposed state should

[15] For a description of these movements, including an analysis of modern political movements, see Kushwant Singh, *The Sikhs* (London: George Allen & Unwin Ltd., 1953).

[16] *Ibid.*, p. 177.

include those whose Punjabi is written in Gurmukhi. The States Re-organization Commission rejected the demand on the grounds that Pun-jabi (even in the Gurmukhi script) and Hindi are so intermingled in the Punjab that boundaries drawn along linguistic lines would not be feasible and that substantial minorities, if not a majority, would oppose the creation of such a state.

In an effort to counter the demands of the Sikhs, several Hindu organ-izations, including the Jan Sangh and the Hindu Mahasabha, demanded the creation of a Maha (greater) Punjab so as to diminish the proportion of Sikhs. The States Reorganization Commission offered a compromise proposal, which was accepted by the Government of India, to incorporate PEPSU, an amalgam of former princely states with large numbers of Sikhs, into a new Punjab state. In the new state, the Sikhs number ap-proximately one-third.[17]

Hindu-Sikh tensions have continued in the form of an argument over the relative roles of Punjabi and Hindi in the new state. The state was declared bilingual; and both Punjabi (in Gurmukhi script) and Hindi (in Devanagari script) were recognized as official languages. The state was divided into Hindi and Punjabi regions, with the official government language and the language of instruction in schools to be that of the respective regions. After this agreement was reached, members of the Akali Dal joined the Congress party en masse, although agitation for a Punjabi-speaking state continued among some Sikhs. The major attack against the regional formula, however, came from orthodox Hindu po-litical groups, especially the Arya Samaj, a religious and cultural organ-ization, and the Hindu Mahasabha. These two Hindu groups launched an agitation in May, 1956, for the establishment of only one official lan-guage in the state (i.e., Hindi), for abolishing the separate regions, and for leaving the choice of the medium of instruction in the schools to parents. The Arya Samaj, which strongly supports reconversion to Hin-duism, criticized the regional formula as a concession to communalism.[18] Communal conflicts have continued, even though the Congress party, which is committed to the regional formula, controls the state legislature and the governing committees of both regions. In September and Octo-ber, 1961, tension increased when Master Tara Singh, leader of the Akali Dal, launched a dramatic fast unto death for a Punjabi state. The fast

---

[17] Government of India, States Reorganization Commission, *op. cit.*, p. 155.

[18] For an analysis of the Arya Samaj and Hindu Mahasabha agitation, see Joan V. Bondurant, *Regionalism versus Provincialism: A Study in Problems of Indian Na-tional Unity* (Indian Press Digests Monograph Series, No. 4 [Berkeley, Calif.: Uni-versity of California Press, December, 1958], pp. 116–24.

was terminated when the central government agreed to appoint a commission to look into charges of discrimination against the Sikhs.

Caste Associations

Just as tribal loyalties have been a dominant theme in Assamese politics, and religious loyalties in the Punjab, caste feelings have been central in Madras. The role played by caste in politics is not a simple one. A local caste may be organized to win benefits for itself under the constitutional provisions for scheduled castes; or a caste may form a component of the national Scheduled Caste Federation. It may support a single political party, as a substantial part of the Kamma caste supports the Communist party of Andhra; or it may play an independent political role, as does the Palli caste, which organized the Tamilnad Toilers party and the Commonweal party in Madras. A group of castes may openly identify themselves as being opposed to a particular caste, as does the anti-Brahman Dravida Munnetra Kazhagam in Madras; or a party may conceal its caste loyalties with ideological trimmings, as does the anti-Brahman Marxist Peasants and Workers party of Bombay. Finally, a caste may be politically organized on an *ad hoc* basis, as often happens in village *panchayat* elections, or not politically organized at all; nevertheless, a person's caste may still be a consideration in the selection of candidates for Parliament or state legislative seats. Alternatively, a caste may function as an interest group with limited interests: the fisherman caste of West Bengal, for example, functions like any occupational group concerned with obtaining assistance from the state Department of Fisheries (whose minister, incidentally, was a member of the same caste). Elsewhere, a caste may be powerful enough to seek control of the state government: in Andhra, the Kammas and Reddis are both powerful, and each seeks to dominate the state government. The role of caste is indeed complex. Occupational interests, minority fears, assimilation fears, and political ambitions are all intertwined in caste politics.

Here we shall explore some aspects of caste politics in the state of Madras, where a single caste movement (or, to be more accurate, a group of castes) is as powerful as any to be found in India, and has considerable potential for further growth. The movement is known as the Dravida Munnetra Kazhagam (Progressive Dravidian Association). It is a new organization, but its antecedents can be traced to the time of the First World War when the South Indian Liberal Federation was organized. The federation, known as the Justice party, called upon non-

Brahmans to destroy Brahman power in the administrative services, professions, and religious life. It opposed the Swaraj (Home Rule) movement and gave its support to the Montagu-Chelmsford reforms of 1919.

The Justice party tended to be strong in those areas of south and western India where the influence of Brahmans was great, Madras and the Marathi- and Kanarese-speaking areas of Bombay. In Madras, it was in power from 1921 to 1926. According to the supporters of the movement, the Justice party government helped foster rural education, formed a public health staff, developed demonstration farms, village *panchayat's*, and co-operative credit, and in general furthered rural development.[19] In office it took the position that "where there are candidates for recruitment with proper qualifications the unrepresented or less-represented communities would be selected in the first instance."[20] The effect of this policy was to reduce the number of Brahmans in administrative posts.

In 1926, the pro-British Justice party was defeated by Congress on the national freedom issue; but in 1930, when the Swaraj and Congress parties did not participate in the elections, the Justice party again assumed power. However, in 1934 when Congress returned, the Justice party was again defeated. Although the party declined in strength, anti-Brahman movements continued to exist. In 1936, E. V. Ramaswamy Naicker, a onetime Congressman, started the Self-Respect Movement to dispense with the service of Brahmans in marriage and other ceremonies, and in general to remove caste distinctions. To Naicker, anti-Brahman meant anti-Sanskrit, anti-Aryan, and antinorthern as well.

In 1937, Naicker achieved considerable prominence as a result of his campaign against the teaching of Hindi in Madras schools. In 1938, the Justice party, in an effort to revive itself, elected Naicker as its president. In 1940, at the Justice party convention in Conjeeveram, he proposed the establishment of an independent Dravidian state to be carved out of South India. Naicker then created the Dravida Kazhagam, or Dravidian Association, as a political vehicle for his proposal. In 1949, a split occurred in the Dravida Kazhagam: several of the younger men who opposed child marriage objected to Naicker's marriage to a young girl in the party. It was then that the Dravida Munnetra Kazhagam (DMK) was formed.

Both the Dravida Kazhagam and the DMK refused to recognize the Indian constitution after Independence. Neither would honor the national

[19] A. P. Patro, "The Justice Movement in India," *Asiatic Review*, N.S. XXVIII (January, 1932), 33.
[20] *Ibid.*

flag. Both argued that the five-year plans were partial to the north, and both opposed the use of Hindi in schools and government offices. Both are still anti-Hindu, anti-Brahman, and antinorthern. They picket north Indian merchants, break Hindu images of Rama and Ganesh, and erase Hindi names from railway platforms. Both stress social reconstruction: they favor widow remarriage, oppose distinctions, and advocate the confiscation of temple property. The ideology of the movement is well summarized by G. S. Seshadri:

> The Kazhagam, along with its off-shoot the Dravida Munnetra Kazhagam (Progressive Dravidian Federation) believes that there are two races in India, the Aryans of the North and the Dravidians of the South; that in the Indian Union the Aryans of the North are dominating the Dravidas of the South; that South Indian Brahmins are in fact Aryans and as such basically different from others; that the acceptance of Hindi as the National language is an act of Aryan dominance and imperialism in the South; that the Dravidians of the South, to rid themselves completely from such dominance, should form an independent *Dravida Nadu* or *Dravidasthan.*[21]

While there is agreement on essentials, there are, however, differences between the two organizations. While Naicker's Dravida Kazhagam (DK) works only to unite Tamils, the Dravida Munnetra Kazhagam seeks to unite all those who speak Dravidian languages in India's four southern states (although its strength is limited to Madras). While the DK burns Indian flags and Naicker has advocated the killing of Brahmans, the DMK claims to be more constitutional and also more democratic in its internal organization, with its own local units and an elected governing council.[22]

The DMK is also more energetic as an independent political party than the DK. In April, 1956, when Kamaraj Nadar succeeded C. Rajagopalachari as chief minister of Madras and formed a completely non-Brahman Congress ministry, Naicker gave Kamaraj his support; and in the 1957 elections for the Madras Legislative Assembly, Naicker's organization endorsed the Congress party's candidates. In contrast, the DMK

[21] G. S. Seshadri, "The Dravida Kazhagam in Madras," *Indian Affairs Record*, III (February, 1957), 3.
[22] The material presented here is based upon an interview with C. N. Annathurai, whom I met at the DMK's center in Conjeeveram in January, 1958.

would not reconcile itself with Congress. In 1957 it ran its own candidates for the first time and won 15 of the 117 seats it contested. The DMK has also been organizing trade unions and working in plantations and among peasants, and has created a Dravida Kazhagam Progressive youth group with branches in several universities. In April, 1959, it defeated Congress for control of the Madras Corporation by winning 45 seats to Congress' 37. And in the 1962 elections to the legislative assembly, the DMK increased its seats from 15 to 50, and its popular vote from 13.7 per cent to 27 per cent.

According to C. N. Annathurai, the DMK leader, the movement receives financial support from many Tamils in the film industry, who are attracted to the DMK by its pro-Tamil, anti-Sanskritic orientation. To improve the position of non-Brahmans, the DMK favors improving educational facilities and increasing the number of non-Brahmans in government and administration. There are strong socialist overtones to the movement, which attract many young people and intellectuals. Annathurai says he favors nationalizing big industries, but encouraging small industries under private enterprise. If an independent South Indian state were formed, he would impose tariffs on the products of the northern textile mills to protect South Indian handlooms.

Both DK and DMK support appears to come from middle-income non-Brahmans, and to be strongest in the urban areas of Madras. Both groups draw from a wide variety of castes in Madras.

In contrast, there were in the 1951 elections two smaller parties which drew their support from a single caste, the Tamilnad Toilers and the Commonweal party. These two parties were supported by the Vanniyakula Kshatriya (or Palli) caste, an intermediate caste of field laborers. In 1952 the Tamilnad Toilers won nineteen seats in the Madras Legislative Assembly and polled 783,346 votes, while the Commonweal party won six seats with 193,598 votes.[23] Behind these two parties stood the Vanniyakula Kshatriya Sangham, a caste association started some thirty years ago by a low-caste community that for some time had sought to raise its status by persuading the census commissioners to classify its members as high-caste Kshatriyas.[24]

[23] T. Balakrishnan Nayar, "Madras," in S. V. Kogekar and R. L. Park (eds.), *Reports on the Indian General Elections, 1951–52* (Bombay: Popular Book Depot, 1956), pp. 87–88.
[24] Census commissioners were major targets of caste pressure groups throughout the nineteenth and early twentieth centuries when castes sought to obtain government support for their efforts to change their position on the caste hierarchy. Since Inde-

Increasingly, the community has pressed for greater educational opportunities and greater political power. It has demanded that the proportion of appointments to the civil services reflect the percentage of Vanniyars in the population, and has pressed the Congress party for nominations to elective bodies. Since Congress did not satisfy their demands, the Vanniyars put up their own candidates for district-board elections in 1949. They founded the Tamilnad Toilers party in South Arcot and Salam districts and the Commonweal party in North Arcot and Chingleput districts to compete in the 1951 elections for the Madras state assembly. After the elections, the Congress ministry agreed to bring two leaders of these parties into the cabinet; and the two parties were subsequently dissolved. Their members joined the Congress party. But the Vanniyakula Kshatriya Sangham continues as an interest group to demand fee concessions, scholarships and reservation of seats for Vanniyars in colleges and universities, reserved places for new appointments to the civil services, Congress tickets for district-board and legislative-assembly elections, and government economic assistance for the districts in which Vanniyars predominate—irrigation development, electricity, improved roads, multipurpose water projects, relief for tenants, and land reform that would make members of the caste (mostly tenants and agricultural laborers) owners of the soil.[25] In the 1962 elections for the Madras Legislative Assembly, a large number of Vanniyakula Kshatriyas in North and South Arcot, Trichinopoly, Tanjore, and Salam supported the DMK. It was in these districts that the DMK registered most of its gains.

Since caste as an endogamous unit is relatively small, anthropologists have been somewhat puzzled by the emergence of political organizations based upon large-scale caste solidarity. Srinivas concludes that roads, railways, postage, the telegraph, cheap paper, and printing have enabled castes to organize as they had never done before. "A postcard carried news of a caste meeting, and the railway enabled members scattered in far-flung villages to come together when necessary, while the availability of cheap newsprint facilitated the founding of caste journals, whose aim was to promote the interests of their respective castes."[26] Srinivas notes

pendence, caste has been eliminated as a general census category, and now pressures by low castes are directed toward getting on the list of scheduled castes. Substantial material benefits result from such a listing; therefore some castes are now willing to press for recognition as a low caste so as to maximize their material gain.

[25] Lloyd I. Rudolph and Susanne Hoeber Rudolph, "The Political Role of India's Caste Associations," *Pacific Affairs*, XXXIII (March, 1960).

[26] M. N. Srinivas, "Caste in Modern India," *Journal of Asian Studies*, XVI (August, 1957), 530.

further that in addition to bringing together fellow castemen from widely different areas, railways and factories have served to relax rules of intercaste pollution.

Linguistic and Ethnic Associations

Perhaps no demand upon the Indian government has received more attention than that for linguistic provinces.[27] It was first expressed in the 1920's when many Indians pointed to the fact that existing state boundaries reflected the pattern of British expansion and had little or no relationship to existing cultural-linguistic regions. The Indian National Congress therefore agreed to organize its provincial units on the basis of linguistic regions rather than existing administrative boundaries. Since it had committed itself to the principle of reorganizing states along cultural-linguistic lines, demands for such a reorganization were pressed immediately after Independence. At first, the new national government postponed reorganization so as to cope with the pressing problems that accompanied Partition. Later, the national leadership feared that reorganization would tie up the administrative services and distract the public's attention to the point that the development program would suffer. But with the spread of agitation—first in the Telugu-speaking areas of Madras, then in Bombay, Punjab, Travancore-Cochin, and elsewhere—the national leadership feared that failure to reorganize the states would result in so much disorder that development would not be possible.[28]

[27] There are several convenient summaries of the linguistic agitation controversy. See W. H. Morris-Jones, *Parliament in India* (Philadelphia: University of Pennsylvania Press, 1957), pp. 16–33. Morris-Jones discusses the controversy in the context of cultural diversity in Indian life. Other thoughtful discussions include Marshall Windmiller, "Linguistic Regionalism in India," *Pacific Affairs*, XXVII (December, 1954); and Selig S. Harrison, "The Challenge to Indian Nationalism," *Foreign Affairs*, XXXIV (July, 1956). An interesting case study of the Bombay controversy can be found in Marshall Windmiller, "Politics of State Reorganization in India: The Case of Bombay," *Far Eastern Survey*, XXV (September, 1956). A study of the movement in Andhra can be found in the work by Selig Harrison, *India—The Most Dangerous Decades* (Princeton, N.J.: Princeton University Press, 1960).

[28] There are three relevant "official" documents: the *Report* of the Linguistic Provinces Commission of the Constituent Assembly of India, in 1949; the *Report* of the Linguistic Provinces Committee of the Indian National Congress (1949); and the *Report* of the States Reorganization Commission, Government of India (1955). The Constituent Assembly commission (known as the Dar Commission) rejected the principles of linguistic states. The Congress commission accepted the general argument of the Dar Commission, but conceded that Andhra might be a special case. Thus Andhra state was created in October, 1953; and in December the government

The States Reorganization Commission, appointed by the Government of India, agreed to draw up a proposal for the reorganization of state boundaries. It refused to do so on explicitly linguistic grounds; for to concede such a principle, they feared, would be to perpetuate irredentist arguments, inhibit interstate mobility, and conceivably force reorganization with each population shift. But in practice—Bombay and a few other areas excepted—reorganization tended to coincide with linguistic boundaries. Indeed, the States Reorganization Commission (and the government, which accepted most of its recommendations) acceded to virtually all the major linguistic pressures, while rejecting those of tribe and religion. Although demands for a separate tribal state in Chota-Nagpur and the Sikh demand for a Punjabi state were rejected—and the Akali Dal and the Jharkhand party remain unsatisfied—the central government even agreed in late 1959 to partition Bombay state into Marathi and Gujarati areas.

Political parties capitalized on much of the sentiment for linguistic states. In some areas, Congressmen and Socialists pressed for new linguistic boundaries; and in almost all areas where linguistic sentiment existed, the Communists supported it. In a few areas, especially where the national parties were intransigent, new parties were created to press for linguistic reorganization. In the Tamil-speaking districts of Travancore-Cochin, for example, Congressmen broke away from the parent organization and formed the Tamilnad Congress in order to press for the merger of their area with the neighboring Tamil-speaking state of Madras. In the Marathi-speaking areas of the state of Bombay, a coalition of opposition parties and dissident Congressmen banded together to form the Samyukta Maharashtra Samiti in order to agitate for the organization of a Marathi-speaking state.

In Manbhum district in Bihar, a group of Bengali-speaking Congress Gandhians created the Lok Sevak Sangh in 1948, originally to do Gandhian constructive work in the area; soon, however, it began to agitate against the state's introduction of Hindi into the district schools. The government argued that the language spoken in the area was closer to Hindi than Bengali. In the 1952 elections the Lok Sevak Sangh defeated the Congress candidates in seven out of the twelve assembly constituencies and for two out of four Parliamentary seats. In 1955 it pressed its demand that the district be merged with West Bengal before the States

---

agreed to appoint the States Reorganization Commission. The new commission agreed to a substantial reorganization of boundaries; most of its proposals were incorporated into the States Reorganization Bill of 1956.

Reorganization Commission. A major portion of the Lok Sevak Sangh's demand was accepted; and most of the disputed area was added to West Bengal as Purulia district.

Gradually, the Government of India has acceded to the demands of the various linguistic groups throughout the country. In 1956 India's states were reorganized largely along linguistic lines; and in 1960 the state of Bombay was bifurcated. The Tamilnad Congress returned to the Congress party; Congress dissidents in the Samyukta Maharashtra Samiti returned to the Congress party in Bombay; and in 1960—as the one major unifying issue disappeared—the Communist-Socialist-Peasants and Workers party alliance began to fall apart. In West Bengal, however, the Lok Sevak Sangh continued to function, and in the 1957 elections won most of the seats to the legislative assembly from Purulia district, which had recently been merged with West Bengal. The Lok Sevak Sangh is now a distinct group within the assembly, is part of the opposition, and functions primarily as a district block advocating greater government assistance in the development of the district.

In spite of the reorganization, linguistic minorities remain in almost every state; and in a few states, linguistic movements continue to exist and press for the absorption of districts in neighboring states. For example, districts or parts of districts in Mysore, Gujarat, Bombay, and Bihar are still disputed. The stakes involved in these various demands are considerable. Apart from the historic traditions associated with linguistic-*cum*-cultural regions—many have histories of independent statehood and rich literary traditions—there are substantial material advantages for the residents of unilingual states. Jobs in administration, colleges, and universities are obviously more easily assured for the educated middle classes if the state's political, administrative, and educational affairs are conducted in the mother tongue. In many instances, the reorganization along linguistic lines enhanced opportunities for political office as well for the educated middle classes.

Few states, moreover, are without linguistic minorities who are so dispersed that irredentist movements are pointless. These minorities, therefore, are often organized to protect thmselves and their economic interests against cultural and linguistic assimilation through the school system. For example, in West Bengal, which is a relatively homogenous state linguistically, there are 1,881,000 immigrants from other states of India in a total population of almost twenty-five million. The bulk of these immigrants are from neighboring Bihar (1,109,000) or from Uttar Pradesh and Orissa (497,000), but there are important minorities from

Rajasthan, Madras, Punjab, Madhya Pradesh, Assam, and Bombay, with small numbers from almost all the remaining states. While the Hindi-, Bihari-, and Oriya-speaking peoples from neighboring states are largely in working-class occupations, those from other states, especially from South India and Rajasthan, are often in business or services (i.e., government or mercantile houses). Many of these minority groups are organized by economic interest rather than by linguistic-cultural background; but in practice many of their economic associations coincide with community affiliations. The Marwaris, for example, are a business community from Rajasthan. Both the Bharat Chamber of Commerce and the Bow Bazar Tenants Association of Marwari tenants are Marwari organizations; and the Punjabi Sikhs who run taxis in Calcutta have organized their own association, which rivals the Bengali taxi association.[29]

Most of the minority communities in West Bengal have cultural, educational, and welfare associations of their own with few, if any, political functions. The Tamil Sangha, a cultural and social organization of people from Madras, runs a Tamil school. Wealthy members of linguistic communities have social clubs, such as the Hindustan and the Kerala clubs. Since these minorities are often widely scattered, small, and generally not in a location contiguous to their mother region, none of their organizations represent secessionist movements.

In north Bengal there are substantial numbers of immigrants from neighboring Nepal. One important group, known as the Gurkhas, has its own organization, the Gurkha League, which was started before 1947 as a protectionist association for its members who worked in the tea plantations. It has its own labor section, known as the Sramik Sangh, which works among the tea garden workers of Darjeeling. Soon after its founding, the organization became deeply involved in political activities. The League, unlike other ethnic bodies in West Bengal, runs its own candidates for the state assembly. Until 1955 it worked closely with the Congress party, which supported Gurkha League candidates for the state assembly. In 1955, however, the Sramik Sangh joined with the Communist-sponsored Mazdoor Union in a strike among the tea garden workers.

[29] Political demands of local minority associations are generally directed toward the state government or the state Congress party organization. The Sikh taxi association, for example, maintains a Bengali secretary to serve as a liaison with the state government and the Congress party. In recent years, the secretary doubled as the chief public-relations officer of the Congress party office in Calcutta. Since the voting power of these associations is negligible and their members often scattered, they must rely upon personal influence and personal favors, which are often repaid in the form of financial contributions to the party chest.

The deputy labor minister of the Congress government condemned the strike: A conflict ensued within the Gurkha League. Some members favored a break between the League and the Congress, while others preferred to maintain the existing ties. The feud became so acrimonious that in 1956 the League split into a left and right wing. The left-wing Gurkhas worked closely with the Communists, and in the 1957 election won three out of the four Darjeeling district seats for the West Bengal Legislative Assembly.[30]

Political Parties and Community Associations

In the minds of most national and state policy-makers, the leaders of the major national parties, and the intelligentsia in general, community associations represent a blot on the body politic. "Provincialism, communalism, casteism," in Nehru's words, are discussed as threats to national unity and modernization. Each of the major national political parties, Congress, Communist, Socialist, and Jan Sangh, has affiliated with it certain mass, or "front," organizations, which are created and controlled by the party. Each party views the organization and affiliation of such groups as essential to its political success.

"Mass" is defined to encompass organizations of students, peasants, workers, women, and refugees, that is, groups organized by sex, age, occupation, and economic position. That Indian society should be divided into peasants and landlords, workers and employers, and the like, seems quite natural to the leadership of the major parties. Such groups as caste and religious and ethnic communities are not considered mass organizations. In fact, the national parties have in the past looked upon community (or "communal") associations as their enemy. British democratic theory and Marxist theory both seemed to preclude the organization of a political order on the basis of loyalty to kin, caste, or tribal, religious, or cultural community. Even some Hindu communal parties hesitate to admit openly that they recruit by community. Jan Sangh says it admits non-Hindus. The RSS (Rashtriya Swayamsevak Sangh) and the Hindu Mahasabha have defined the concept of nation in such a way that it includes Hindus, Buddhists, and Jains; Muslims and Christians are included only in so far as they adopt Indian names and dress, and accept the

[30] Communist interest in the area is intensified by its proximity to Nepal, Sikkim, Tibet, and China. In recent years, the Communists have been strong supporters of the creation of a separate hill district with great autonomy within the state of West Bengal.

heroes of the epic literature. But by restricting themselves primarily to Hindus, these two groups are viewed as political outcastes by other national parties. In short, the major national parties do not accept a view of Indian society as one divided by caste, tribe, language, or religion, but look forward to a society that, if at all, is divided by economic class, sex, age, and other such "modern" divisions. This conception of mass has led Congressmen, Communists, Socialists, and, to a lesser extent, members of Jan Sangh to organize peasants, workers, women, and students. Each party has such front groups associated with it.

Since, however, community associations do not generally fall within the definition of mass, they have tended to develop outside the fold of the national parties. The result has been that community parties and interest groups are relatively free from the control of the national parties. However, local party leadership has not failed to sense the great political power wielded by such groups. While ideologically opposed to community groups, in practice the major political parties, and especially their local leadership, have often organized on a community basis or have been willing to collaborate with community associations. Ironically, but —given their sensitivity to questions of power—quite appropriately, the Communists have been particularly active in this arena. Before Independence, the Communists were among the most active supporters of the Muslim League's demand for a Pakistan state; and since Independence, the Communists have actively supported the demand for states reorganization along linguistic lines. The writings of Stalin[31] have done much to reconcile subnational particularisms with a class view of society. The Communists define India as a multinational society (in contrast to the Congress and Socialist parties, which see India as a single nation), and from time to time have redefined the ethnic-religious-linguistic groups that make up the nation.[32] Despite the fact that the Communists have given support to, and have tried to infiltrate, certain community groups, they have not created them as they have trade unions and peasant and student associations. Nationality is viewed by the Communists as a subjective condition, while class is clearly an objective condition; the party may therefore support community groups, but must scientifically initiate class associations.

[31] Especially, *Marxism and the National Question* (Moscow: Foreign Languages Publishing House, 1950).

[32] For a detailed discussion of the Communists and the nationality question in India, see Gene D. Overstreet and Marshall Windmiller, *Communism in India* (Berkeley, Calif.: University of California Press, 1958), pp. 487–507.

Since the community groups have their own leadership, it has often been difficult, and in some instances impossible, for the national parties to gain control of them. In spite of Communist support for the Pakistan movement before 1947, the net gain to the Communists from Muslims was small, and may have been more detrimental to the party among non-Muslims than of benefit among Muslims. The leader of the Jharkhand party in Orissa and Bihar regards his own party identification as more significant than any sentiments he may have for any national ideologies. Both Communists and Socialists have endorsed the movement for states reorganization, but regional linguistic movements were in most instances already well organized. In the Telugu-speaking areas of Madras, conflicts between national parties disrupted the Andhra Mahasabha. But other community groups—the Lok Sevak Sangh and the Jharkhand party in Bihar, the Naga National Council in Assam, the Sikh Akali Dal in the Punjab, and the Dravida Munnetra Kazhagam in Madras—have not fallen under the control of other parties; to the contrary, other parties have often turned to them for support.

In Madras, the CPI allied itself with the Dravida Kazhagam in the 1951–52 elections;[33] but Communist-DK ties did not last much beyond the 1952 elections. By 1957, the DK's ties were largely to the then dominant group in the Congress party in Madras. In fact Kamaraj Nadar, the chief minister of Madras, was endorsed by Ramaswami Naicker, the DK leader. Elsewhere, however, the Communists have maintained their links with community organizations. They work closely with such groups in Darjeeling district and have been active members of the Samyukta Maharashtra Samiti, a coalition of parties in Bombay organized to agitate for the creation of a greater Maharashtrian state.

The Socialists too have made some effort to work with community groups. In the 1952 elections, the Socialist party negotiated electoral alliances with the Jharkhand party in Orissa and Bihar and with the

---

[33] The Communists declared that their alliance was based upon the following points of agreement:

1. The Dravida Kazhagam stands for replacing the Congress Raj;
2. It is a fighter for civil liberties;
3. It supports workers' and peasants' struggles;
4. It is a friend of the U.S.S.R., Peoples' China, and the Liberation Movement in Asia.

The two parties, however, differed on the following basic points:

1. The CPI is opposed to the anti-Brahmanism of the Dravida Kazhagam;
2. It does not agree with the Dravida Kazhagam's theory of Dravidasthan.

Crossroads, December 28, 1951; quoted by Nayar, in Kogekar and Park (eds.), *Reports on the Indian General Elections, 1951–1952*, pp. 89–90.

Scheduled Caste Federation in Bombay. But again, these ties have been in the form of electoral alliances, and have not resulted in extended or prolonged and intimate contacts. Socialist and Communist alliances with community groups have been widely attacked in the press; and within the parties themselves, there have been rumblings of dissatisfaction among party rank and file.

The Congress party, particularly on the local level, has been most adaptable to community interests. Efforts are made to nominate candidates of important local castes and religious and tribal groups. When feasible, Congress has sought to absorb some community interests—for example, their unsuccessful attempt to bring about a Congress-Akali Dal merger in the Punjab, and their attempts to win support from Christian and Nayar organizations in Kerala, to regain former Muslim League support in many states, and to secure the collaboration of the Anglo-Indian Association, Gandhian *harijan* organizations, and many local caste groups. The national leadership of Congress is often embarrassed by such efforts on the part of its local organizations.[34] But as M. N. Srinivas has written: "Caste is so tacitly and so completely accepted by all, including those who are most vocal in condemning it, that it is everywhere the unit of social action."[35] To caste, one might add many religious (especially non-Hindu), linguistic, and tribal groupings.

Local community groups are often more willing to work with Congress than with other parties because Congress is in power. Furthermore, the very flexibility of Congress party ideology is an attraction to community associations, which can work with Congress without being required to adopt the more rigorous ideologies of the Communist, Socialist, and Jan Sangh organizations. Nonetheless, community associations have thus far maintained their independence from all parties, including Congress. To date, sufficient general hostility exists toward community organizations to discourage their merger with national parties.

Functions of Community Associations

Unless one is bound to nineteenth-century Marxian notions about the nature of society and polity, the reasons accounting for the existence of

[34] In early 1960, the national Congress party organization successfully prevented the Congress party in Kerala from forming a coalition government with the Muslim League, with which it had worked earlier in an effort to defeat the Communist government, on the grounds that the League was a "communal body."

[35] Srinivas, "Caste in Modern India," *Journal of Asian Studies*, XVI (August, 1957), 548.

community associations would seem to be the same as those explaining trade unions and peasant, business, or landlord groups. The expansion of the communication network, which extends the network of group affiliations; the growth of government, which stimulates groups to organize and present demands; and the emergence of democratic institutions, which provides greater opportunities for political organization, are factors which affect community groups as well as occupational and class groups. Modernization also strains relations between groups—between workers and employers, landlords and tenants, and also between Sikhs and Hindus, Kammas and Reddis, hills people and plains people. In so far as economic conflicts involve superior-subordinate relationships, there is every reason for competing caste or religious groupings, for example, to organize as do workers and peasants. India's social structure is built upon a plurality of identifications; and there is no reason why her political interest groups should not now and for the foreseeable future mirror her social structure.

It is reasonable, then, that community groups in India should perform a number of different functions and reflect different needs of particular communities. These include:

1. *Boundary-maintenance functions.* As the existence of social groups is threatened by change, the group, or its leaders, may organize politically to preserve or establish the identity of the group. As Adrian C. Mayer has written, ". . . caste becomes a political division of society, at the same time as it is losing its position as a ritual division." [36] Khushwant Singh has argued that the Akali Dal demand for a Punjabi-speaking state represents an attempt by Sikh leaders to prevent the community from being absorbed by Hinduism. Likewise, tribal demands for autonomous political units often represent an attempt to prevent the community from being assimilated into the Hindu fold.

Political organization in itself is a means of preserving the identity of the group, for what is involved is not the creation of a political organization to govern the community, but rather a political organization to deal with the outside world. An internal political organization that includes the entire community (such as an entire caste or religious community) is generally non-existent; but where such an organization does exist (as in some tribes), new political institutions have been created to cope with external authority. The demands which the political organization makes are directed toward preserving the community—from control over the language used in local schools to establishment of a more or less autono-

[36] Mayer, "Local Government Elections in a Malwa Village," *Eastern Anthropologist,* XI (March–August, 1958), 202.

mous political unit. Moreover, the creation of a new community-wide association in itself serves to strengthen loyalties to the community.

2. *Social mobility functions.* Individual leaders of the community may regard politics as an opportunity for social mobility, as noted by Martin Orans in his description of the political leadership of the Jharkhand party. The community itself may be rising or may attempt to rise in status through political activity. The anti-Brahman Dravida Kazhagam and Dravida Munnetra Kazhagam in Madras, and the anti-Brahman Peasants and Workers party in Bombay, represent such efforts by caste groups. As Kathleen Gough described DK appeal in a Tanjore village:

> It is important to notice that the people who oppose the traditional village system are not those who suffer most acutely under it, but those who have partly extricated themselves from it through some change in their economic circumstances. It is not, for example, the very poor Konar tenants in Kumbapettai who support the anti-Brahman Dravidas' Kazakam movement, but rather the somewhat wealthier and more independent "upstarts" of the two new streets, and to a much larger extent, the new, independent non-Brahman landlords of neighbouring villages, who resent the orthodox Brahman's unwillingness to treat them as his ritual equals.

Speaking of the Communist appeal, she continues:

> Communist supporters, again, appear to be stronger among landless, high school educated youths of any caste and among Adi Dravidas who had temporarily left their natal village, tried many jobs and come home to find the *status quo* too conservative for them, than among regular labourers still attached to their traditional masters.[37]

Social conflict may be intensified as distinctions between secular and ritual status increase; *thus, the economic improvement of ritually low status groups is likely to stimulate the political organization of such communities.* If this proposition is correct, then economic growth, particularly as it affects the position of groups within the social structure, is likely to result in an increase of community associations.

[37] Gough, "The Social Structure of a Tanjore Village," in *India's Villages* (Calcutta: West Bengal Government Press, 1955), p. 92.

The presence of community associations and their multiplication suggests that the popular notion of the "revolution of rising expectations" is in reality an explosion of social competition. Rising expectations are not aimed at American, Russian, or British living standards, but are demands by one group for improvement in its economic and social position vis-à-vis another group within India: Telegus in relation to Tamils, hills people to plains people, low castes to high castes, tribals to Hindus. Expectations are directed at seats in local colleges, posts in administration, political office, and new expenditures for local services such as roads, wells, and schools for one's own community.[38] Clearly, for most Indians, the great competition is not between India and the West, or even India and China, but between social groups within India.

The desire to preserve the group against assimilation, and the desire to preserve or further enhance the position of socially mobile groups by political means, may in fact be strengthened by government policy. The constitution provides for separate representation for scheduled castes and tribes in Parliament and in state legislative assemblies. In addition, a 1951 amendment to the equal-rights provision of the constitution states that "(4) Nothing in this Article or Clause (2) or Article 29 shall prevent the State from making any special provision for the advancement of socially and educationally backward classes of citizens or for the Scheduled Castes and Scheduled Tribes." In Mysore only 30 per cent of the seats in medical and engineering colleges are allocated solely on the basis of merit; and Brahmans may apply for only one in five posts.[39] Most states, in fact, have similarly modified the merit principle in order to assist backward communities. Khasa Subba Rao (a leading South Indian Brahman journalist) has even argued that steps taken by the Madras government to give preference to non-Brahmans in administrative and other appointments have assumed the character of an "anti-merit drive." [40] Equalitarian values (often reinforced by political motives) do in fact complicate merit standards.

[38] Some mention might also be made here of the non-political functions of a caste association in providing scholarships for its members, constructing hostels for its students at local colleges, building hospitals, etc. Such activities strengthen identification with the caste association and facilitate the carrying-on of political activities by the association. I am indebted to Professor Bernard Cohn for calling this point to my attention.

[39] Srinivas, "Caste in Modern India," *Journal of Asian Studies*, XVI (August, 1957), 542.

[40] Khasa Subba Rao, "Currents and Cross-Currents in the Political Life of Madras," *The Mahratta*, February 1, 1957, p. 3.

Types of Demands and Their Impact on Government

Demands upon government by community associations are of two types:
1. For changes in political boundaries, or the status of political entities. These may range from a demand for complete independence (Nagas, Dravida Munnetra Kazhagam) to one for regional autonomy (Akali Dal, Jharkhand, and perhaps the Dravida Kazhagam).
2. For greater opportunities from the existing government—more seats in the legislative assembly, more posts in administrative services, more seats in the colleges, or in the economic sphere, greater state investment in the areas in which the community predominates. Such demands are made by tribal organizations of West Bengal, Kamma and Reddi castes in Andhra, Lingayat and Okkaliga castes in Mysore, Nayar, Christian, and Izhava communities in Kerala, Rajput, Bhumihar, and Kayastha castes in Bihar, the Scheduled Caste Federation, the Anglo-Indian Association, the Gurkha League in West Bengal, the low-caste Shoshita Sangh in Uttar Pradesh, and the Lok Sevak Sangh in Purulia district of West Bengal.

Assessments of community associations by both Indians and Europeans often exaggerate the extent to which they and their demands are likely to impede national unity. The 1947 Partition experience intensified fears of Balkanization. Partition is, however, far beyond the demands of most groups. Moreover, the central government is militarily capable of preventing the success of secessionist movements. The many groups placing pressure on state governments for favors and special opportunities play a role not unlike that of various ethnic groups in American politics. Candidates are selected on the basis of their vote-getting ability with major communities in their constituency. In so far as a single caste, or religious group, or region of the state, dominates the ruling party and the government, that community often receives advantages in administrative and political appointments. Expenditures by the state departments of public works, ministries of community development, cottage industries, fisheries, and so on, are often influenced by the political power of various community groups within the governing party.

Many Indians look upon attention to such considerations as an Indian failing that demonstrates the incapacity of Indians to run representative institutions. Central government officials, senior administrative officers, and many intellectuals decry such behavior as a violation of democratic principles. There is in their minds an image of the British democratic process as they believe it operates—rational and public interest-oriented, with conflicts between economic classes rather than ethnic groups.[41] Few Indians have had direct contact with British political practices, and even fewer with American politics. The Indian intellectuals' appreciation of democracy is thus largely derived from the theoretical writings of the nineteenth century or descriptions of institutions by British scholars. Not until recently has British scholarship systematically described either voting behavior or the role of interest groups in the making of policy decisions. Moreover, although American political science scholarship has drastically changed earlier conceptions about the nature of democracy, such literature has not been widely read by Indians; in so far as American politics is known to them, it is interpreted through critical British eyes.

It is assumed by many Indian intellectuals that the Indian population is particularly susceptible to having its passions and loyalties exploited; and indeed there is some truth to this. In the eyes of these intellectuals, the existence of community associations, and the demands made by them, result from the exploitation of community sentiments by politicians, as if politicians in "truly" democratic societies do not behave in such a way. But the presence of a democratic framework, and especially of universal adult suffrage, requires that the local politician seek to organize interests, sentiments, and loyalties in such a way as to maximize his political opportunities. In the process, he may appeal to caste, religious, linguistic, and tribal identifications as well as to secular identifications, such as peasant, worker, refugee, student, woman, and so on. Representative government is the catalyst for all kinds of organizations that bespeak a greater involvement in politics by the population.

Do the demands of community groups, in fact, represent a threat to the

[41] The papers by Indian political scientists printed in *Reports on the Indian General Elections, 1951–52*, ed. Kogekar and Park, illustrate this naïveté concerning the supposed rational character of the democratic process and the extent to which Indians deviated from that ideal. The writer from Assam: "As a consequence [of considering the chances of success of the candidates by the party selection committees], such factors as integrity received secondary consideration" (p. 7). The Bihar correspondent: "The election further revealed the strength of the mediaeval caste organisation which played a decisive role in some of the constituencies" (p. 28). The Madhya Pradesh correspondent: "The methods adopted by various party candidates and independents for canvassing votes were often impeachable. Evidence of communalism, casteism, parochialism and linguism was available" (pp. 77–78). From West Bengal: "The elections were not altogether free from the influence of casteism, communalism, and provincialism. In many places candidates were given nomination by different political parties chiefly in consideration of their caste, religion, or place of birth" (p. 174).

objectives of India's national leadership; and if so, how? The most pressing fear has been that community groups may, by stressing particularistic
loyalties, weaken the development of a sense of national citizenship on
the part of the population. This problem appeared to be most serious during the agitation for the creation of linguistic provinces. Some writers have
expressed the fear that unilingual states will strengthen regionalism as
opposed to central power; and that although the central government may
be able to maintain unity, representative institutions may be injured in
the process.[42]

It can be argued, however, that the creation of linguistic states added
few problems to an already difficult situation; a number of states (including Orissa, Bihar, West Bengal, Uttar Pradesh, and Mysore) were
already largely unilingual, and the States Reorganization Commission
only enlarged the number. The effervescence of regional languages since
Independence has resulted in the partial displacement of English in public life. This undoubtedly complicates the problem of interstate communication, but that problem would have existed even if some states were
multilingual. Nor does the growth in regional literatures and loyalties
necessarily intensify provincialism. Though the Bengali-, Marathi-, and
Tamil-speaking areas have had a cultural renaissance since the mid-nineteenth century, these regions may boast of some of the most distinguished
cosmopolitans to be found anywhere in India.[43]

The fact is that reorganization has occurred, and India is still united.
In the 1957 elections Congress maintained its position in most states, and
on the whole did not suffer from the decision to reorganize the states.
Only in Bombay, where Maharashtrians continued to clamor for the
creation of a Marathi-speaking state with the city of Bombay as its capital,
was Congress substantially weakened. And in the 1962 elections, after
Bombay state had been bifurcated, Congress substantially increased its

[42] Selig Harrison, "The Challenge to Indian Nationalism," *Foreign Affairs*, XXXIV
(July, 1956). Fears of the divisive effects of language and caste are more fully expressed by Mr. Harrison in his *India—the Most Dangerous Decades.*

[43] Conceivably, conflicts between the states and the center are intensified when
loyalties are oriented around linguistic regions rather than around the nation as a
whole. However, central-state conflicts are clearly built into any federal system. The
very fact that Indian states direct so many demands toward the center suggests that
they recognize a central authority with which they must bargain. There is no reason to
believe that regional loyalties seriously impede efforts by the states to seek satisfactory
resolutions of their demands with the center. One must remember that in India states
are not trying to prevent central intervention in state affairs (as in mid-nineteenth
century United States), but rather are eager to encourage greater central participation in state development through infusion of central government funds.

hold in the new state assemblies of Gujarat and Maharashtra. As the states-reorganization issue recedes into the background, the issues that remain are those which involve conflicts of interest between community organizations *within* the states. In Kerala, the Christians, Nayars, and Izhavas, with their respective ties to Congress, Socialist, and Communist parties, have been locked in struggle. In Andhra, the Kamma-Reddi conflict continues. In Mysore, the Lingayats and Okkaligas are still feuding. However, in the 1962 elections, separatist movements within states did not do particularly well. In Punjab, where agitation for the state's bifurcation was particularly intense before the elections, the parties which favored bifurcation—the Akali Dal, Communist, and Praja Socialist— won only 20 per cent of the vote, while Congress and Jan Sangh, which opposed bifurcation, won over 53 per cent of the vote; in the districts which contain a Sikh majority, Congress and Jan Sangh won by 19 per cent. In Bihar, the Jharkhand party won only 19 seats in the legislative assembly compared with 32 in the 1957 elections; and in Vidarbha, a section of Maharashtra where there has been agitation for a separate state, the separatist movement, the Nag Vidarbha Andolan Samiti, won only 4 seats though it put up 21 candidates for the assembly. In Madras and in the hill areas of Assam, however, separatist movements continued to thrive.

In choosing between the values of "responsibility" and "responsiveness," state governments are increasingly demonstrating their responsiveness to community demands. At the moment, two upper castes often stand alone in vying for control of a state government. Since politicians, on the whole, respond most readily to demands of the group to which they themselves belong, state governments are often accused of being dominated by a particular caste or religious community. But when community associations increase, the possibility that any single community will dominate a state government is likely to decrease. As more caste and tribal groups, trade unions, and peasant associations emerge, those who wish to win power will have to turn to the interests of communities other than their own.

The reader is likely to detect here the Madisonian argument concerning the role of factions in representative government. Madison's analysis has proved to be correct in the history of the United States; and there is reason to believe that, with some variations, the analysis applies to India as well. Its application in the United States has differed, perhaps, from Madison's expectations, for when Madison wrote, the problem of ethnic minorities was a minor one in the United States. But in the twentieth century, the arrival of a large number of ethnic groups, particularly in urban centers, resulted in the development of party machines concerned with balancing their tickets in order to win elections. So long as no one ethnic group predominated, the party machines could not afford to represent any single ethnic interest alone.

These machines played an important part in integrating immigrants into American life. They sponsored Americanization programs, facilitated contact between communities, and opened channels between the citizen and his government. Most important, the new, potentially revolutionary citizens were given the feeling that government was not intractable, unlike many of the European governments from which they had fled. Admittedly, much was done through a patronage system that often overlooked merit, and there was considerable corruption. But looking back to the late nineteenth and early twentieth centuries, it is apparent that this may have been a small price to pay for acculturating immigrants into a democratic society.

This is not to argue that India should give up her merit system for recruitment into the administrative services or colleges and universities, but only to suggest that patronage—and even corruption when widely applied and involving many individuals from many communities—may facilitate an adjustment to democratic institutions. There are difficulties in applying this approach to India: first, because of the key role that administration and government play in the country's development, India cannot afford the inefficient system of administration that characterized late nineteenth-century America; second, since the opportunity for rewards in the private sector of the economy are not as extensive in India as they were in nineteenth-century America, the failure of individuals to gain access to government jobs through a widespread patronage system is likely to be politically far more devastating; and third, ethnic minorities in India are more likely to agitate for the creation of new political units, since the precedent for creating new units as a consequence of political agitation has already been established, whereas no such tradition was created in the United States. It is also important to note that ethnic minorities in the United States were not so concentrated as they are in India, where there has been less geographic mobility. In the United States, moreover, the popular emphasis on cultural assimilation made it less likely than in India that a minority would press for cultural autonomy.

To summarize, if the Indian people are to accept democratic institutions, some of the community associations' demands must be met. It will require considerable political skill to satisfy these demands without destroying the merit system. In the long run, favoritism to particular communities is likely to decrease when enough local groups are organized that office-seeking politicians find it politically unprofitable to associate themselves closely with any single group. In short, the greatest protection against the demands of powerful community groups is the multiplication of community and non-community associations.

Until such a dispersion of community organizations takes place, however, there is considerable danger that the government's modernization programs will be injured. Successful particularistic demands for seats in colleges and civil service positions not only threaten the quality of educational institutions and administration, but also affect popular attitudes toward the state's capacity and willingness to provide equity. A sense of equity with regard to the government's distribution of its largess can have a profound effect on the extent to which loyalties to governmental institutions develop.

The argument of this chapter can be put in the form of the following propositions:

1. *Social changes accompanying modernization are facilitating the development and not the diminution of community interests in Indian politics.*

2. *The threat of community associations to orderly state government and to merit standards in recruitment is most pronounced when the number of associations within a given state is small.*

From the first proposition, we have concluded that the number of caste, religious, tribal, linguistic, and ethnic associations is likely to increase as the pace of social change increases. From the second proposition, we have concluded that the increase in such associations is likely to have a stabilizing effect. It may very well be that India, now and perhaps for a short time to come, is experiencing its most severe crises with community organizations. The moral problems which they raise for Westernized public figures, the threats which they pose to merit systems, the intensity of conflicts between two or three antagonistic groups in many Indian states, constitute severe problems now but are likely to diminish—not as community associations disappear, but as they increase.

IV. TRADE UNIONS

Nowhere is the conflict between the productive requirements of the state and the consumption requirements of organized groups seen more clearly than in the relations between government and trade unions. The demands of Indian trade unions are more or less those of trade unions elsewhere: higher wages, improvement in working conditions and hours, protection against retrenchment, and safeguards for their unions. These demands and many others are, of course, directed at management. But in India, to an even greater extent than in late nineteenth- and early twentieth-century Great Britain and the United States, unions are bound up in government and politics. Why and how this is so, and what are the consequences, will be dealt with in this chapter.

According to the 1951 census, the total number of workers in modern manufacturing industries in India numbered about 2.5 million. The addition of those employed in plantations, mining, construction, utilities, transportation, and communication brings the total to around 7 million. In 1959 the government reported that union membership in the four national federations was 1,863,290. The total membership of all unions was reported in 1959 as 3,647,148. The most heavily unionized industries in India are iron and steel (60 per cent), chemical (49 per cent), cotton textiles (47 per cent), publishing and printing (40 per cent), and railways (40 per cent); these are followed by food and tobacco (35 per cent), jute (32 per cent), post and telegraph (27 per cent), coal mining (26 per cent), and insurance and banking (19 per cent). Most unions are plant-wide or firm-wide; craft unions are rare. Individual unions tend to be small (65 per cent have fewer than three hundred members each), badly financed (the average union has an annual income of less than Rs. 2,000), and poorly organized (to have so much as one full-time officer is the exception).

Limitations of size, finances, and organization, however, do not prevent Indian unions from being vocal. Every year since 1947, there have been from 500,000 to 1,800,000 workers on strike—the latter number in 1947. Around 700,000 is a typical annual figure. Indian industrial workers have won wages which are low by western standards, but which are substantial when compared with those paid to workers in agriculture. Much of what the workers gain is achieved through the activities of the government—sometimes as a result of prodding from one or more of the four national trade union federations. In its 1954 report,[1] the Indian National Trade Union Congress (INTUC) summarized its effects on government policy for the previous year. They had, or so INTUC claimed, successfully persuaded the central government to prevent the rationalization of textiles, to subsidize the handloom and *khadi* (hand-spun, hand-woven cloth) industries by raising a cess on the cloth mills, and to levy a duty on machine-made *bidi's* (indigenous cigarettes) in order to protect hand manufacturers. On the state level, INTUC persuaded the government of Bengal to intervene and prevent further retrenchment in the jute and textiles industries, which were undergoing rationalization. INTUC successfully opposed tea garden employers in Assam, and persuaded the government to retain the law that forbade recruitment of labor from outside the state. In Mysore, INTUC convinced the government to increase dearness (cost-of-living) allowances in government industrial concerns by five rupees per month, extend the Payment of Wages Act to transport workers and enlarge the inspectorate staff for implementing the Factories Act. INTUC, along with other trade union federations, worked to abolish the managing-agency system, urged labor participation in industrial management, supported ceilings on incomes and profits, and advocated an across-the-board 25 per cent increase in wages in all industries, to be paid with money accrued from increased production.

The explanation of why so many union demands are directed at the state may be found partly in the history of Indian trade unions. As we have noted earlier (chap. ii), Indian trade unions were largely organized by nationalist militants concerned with directing the working force against the British regime. While many trade union leaders were genuinely concerned with the lot of the workers whom they organized, the

[1] Indian National Trade Union Congress, *Annual Report*, November, 1953, to October, 1954 (New Delhi: Indian National Trade Union Congress, 1955).

fact is that many of the strikes, demonstrations, and agitations were political and were directed against the government.

Another explanation—and perhaps a more important reason today— is that so much of what unions do and want is determined by government legislation and administration. The British government in India, prodded partly by industrialists at home, partly by the International Labour Organization to which it subscribed, partly by its own humanitarian and paternalistic notions, and partly by a desire to minimize opportunities for nationalist agitators, introduced welfare legislation dealing with conditions in factories, employment of women and children, hours of work, and the like. This legislation was maintained and enlarged by the new government after 1947. Today, India's labor legislation is—on the books —among the most advanced to be found anywhere in the world.

The most important addition after Independence was the Industrial Disputes Act, passed in 1947; this act created conciliation and arbitration machinery for the settlement of industrial disputes.[2] Under the provisions of the act, a labor commissioner in each state appoints conciliation officers to meet with labor and management to settle a dispute; in the event conciliation fails, the labor commissioner may recommend to the state labor minister that a tribunal be appointed. If a tribunal is appointed, its decisions are binding on both parties; and during tribunal hearings as well as after a decision is rendered, it is illegal to strike over the issues under consideration. Since the government determines which disputes are placed under arbitration, trade unions are obviously concerned with exerting pressure upon the government to appoint—or not to appoint— a tribunal, depending upon whether the union believes it can get more from a tribunal or from the threat of strike.

Legislation often allows considerable discretion to ministers, and this makes ministers as well as legislators the objects of trade union pressure. For example, whether the Minimum Wage Act (a central government act) should be extended to additional industries is a matter to be determined by each state's labor minister. In West Bengal, representations from unions persuaded the minister to extend the act to the *bidi* industry.

---

[2] For a description of this law and other labor policies pursued by the new government, see Charles A. Myers, *Labor Problems in the Industrialization of India* (Cambridge, Mass.: Harvard University Press, 1958). Myers' work is the most complete study that has been made of the problems of labor in economic development. The volume also contains useful appendixes, including the labor-policy section of the first and second five-year plans and the important trade union agreements with the Ahmadabad Millowners' Association and the Tata Iron and Steel Company. For a thoughtful critique of Myers, see the review by Richard D. Lambert, "Labor in India," in *Economic Development and Cultural Change*, VIII (January, 1960).

The implementation of laws, particularly factory acts, is another area in which unions seek to influence government. Union leaders will visit the chief inspector of factories to call his attention to non-enforcement of the Factories Act in particular plants; and efforts by an employer to recruit without working through the government employment exchange are likely to spur a union leader to visit the director of the Employment Exchange.

Union leaders may run for public office to improve their capacity for influencing government policy and its implementation. As one Calcutta trade union leader frankly explained:

> . . . some of the United Trade Union Congress unions supported me personally in my campaign for the assembly. They didn't support me officially with union banners or union funds, since other party people are in the same unions. I was strong in engineering, the mercantile houses, government, and printing press workers. I could get support from these unions on an individual basis, with men and money. The workers like to see me in politics, even if they support other parties. They like to see their office bearers in the assembly since it gives the union more prestige and it helps them. [How does your being in the assembly help them?] When I was not an M.L.A. I found it hard to get a hearing with a minister. I could call, and they might give me an appointment for next week. Now as an M.L.A. I can see the minister immediately, and if I don't get results I can speak up in the assembly. [What do you see the minister about?] The appointment of tribunals and the implementation of laws, such as the factory acts . . . .[3]

The involvement of government in labor-management relations presents many difficulties for the party in power. An unpopular tribunal decision turns workers against government, not employers. In one instance, the government chose to overrule a tribunal's award to bank employees, with the result that the threat of an illegal strike was directed at the government rather than at the employers. Why, then, does government involve itself in industrial disputes?

Cessation of production through lockouts or strikes means a slowing-

[3] Based on an interview.

down of national economic development;[4] and increased production in India is seen not simply as the need of individual entrepreneurs, but as a national need. The Indian government thus acts as if it were in a perpetual state of war, intervening in all disputes which affect the national interest. The Indian government's policy is obviously much more analogous to a wartime policy than, for example, to prewar industrial policy in the United States. Prior to the 1930's, government in the United States was sympathetic with management, as were other governments in the West. In the 1930's, a government more sympathetic with labor took steps to equalize the conflict. Thus, in the United States the government sought not to eliminate labor-management conflict, but to balance it. Not until the Second World War did the United States government take steps to prevent strikes and to make sure that the behavior of neither labor nor management resulted in production losses. The aim of the Indian government is similar to the American wartime attitude; that is, not to balance the two forces, but to ensure that they do not collide. The Indian government leadership is fully aware of one obvious consequence of such a policy: it makes both labor and management dependent upon government conciliation officers and arbitration tribunals for the settlement of disputes, so that collective bargaining becomes the exception rather than the customary method for handling labor-management relations.

While publicly labor and management often chaff at the system of compulsory arbitration, privately they support it. V. V. Giri, an INTUC leader, strongly opposed compulsory arbitration until he became minister of labor. He then became convinced of the necessity of the policy, and became aware of the extent to which both management and labor actually found the government's program satisfactory.[5] For management, it offers the hope of ensuring labor peace. As in other societies that have undergone the early phases of industrial development, management in India tends to be unsympathetic to unions—viewing union leaders as political exploiters of the workers, and treating unions as impediments to increased production and rationalization and as unnecessary limitations of the prerogatives of management. Government conciliation and

[4] The similarities with current thinking in the West are apparent; and this makes current Indian thinking on industrial-relations issues acceptable to many Western economists. Charles Myers, for example, accepts compulsory arbitration as a necessary, though perhaps unfortunate, concomitant of economic planning.

[5] See V. V. Giri, *Labour Problems in Indian Industry* (Bombay: Asia Publishing House, 1958). For a critique, see S. D. Punekar, "The Giri Approach to Labour Problems," *Economic Weekly*, X (April 19, 1958).

arbitration obviates the necessity for management consultations with labor (in fact, conciliation officers often meet separately with management and union leaders because of the unwillingness of management to meet with union men) and guarantees that a settlement made by government tribunals, if not always satisfactory to management, is at least not completely unacceptable. Then too, in the event labor refuses to accept tribunal judgments and resorts to a strike, the strike is illegal and the government is brought in as a protector of management.

On the labor side, union leaders recognize the weak position from which they must bargain and their incapacity to lead a successful strike when labor surpluses offer management an open field for recruiting strikebreakers. They therefore find the tribunal a device through which something, at least, can be gained. Since tribunals make decisions based upon an assessment of both the needs of labor and the capacity of management, the weakness of the union does not become a factor in the settlement. It is often possible to bring a dispute before conciliation officers and then to a tribunal long before a union that is just being organized would by itself have the strength to negotiate with management. The union leader can then point to early successes, and thereby strengthen his appeal to the workers to join the union. INTUC, which as a federation endorses the principle of arbitration, argues that "unfettered reliance" on collective bargaining would give "free handle [*sic*] to unscrupulous employers and disruptive elements in the trade union field." [6]

For the same reason that the government tries to prevent strikes, it is also eager to build responsible trade unions—that it, unions whose demands will be moderate, and who will support arbitration proceedings and obey them, minimize strikes, and encourage workers to increase productivity. The Indian National Trade Union Congress—in reality, the labor wing of the Congress party—is organized along these principles, and supports the basic program of the present government. Its leaders proudly declare that their demands are in the national interest, not in behalf of sectional interests. Their first loyalties are to the Congress party, then to the present government, to the nation, and last of all to the workers who belong to their unions. [7]

[6] Indian National Trade Union Congress, *Annual Report*, November, 1952, to October, 1953 (New Delhi: Indian National Trade Union Congress, 1953), p. 208.

[7] This harsh description of the loyalties of INTUC leaders is from "Politics of Trade Unions in India," by Ralph James, *Far Eastern Survey*, XXVII (March, 1958), 43. Actually, INTUC leaders would endorse such a description of their hierarchy of loyalties with a sense of pride in their capacity to break loose from parochial sentiments. The argument can be phrased another way from INTUC's point of view: the

How successful has INTUC been in winning the support of the working force? How successful has Congress been at winning workers' votes? And how successful has the government been in minimizing strikes? To answer these questions, one must take a closer look at the politics of Indian trade unions.

Trade Union Politics

The number of unions registered with the government and the total membership of unions have skyrocketed since Independence. From 1,087 registered unions in the year preceding Independence, the number jumped to 2,766 in 1947, to 3,150 in 1948, to 3,766 in 1950, and 6,658 in 1954 and 8,713 in 1959. Claimed union membership jumped from 864,000 in 1946 to 1,331,000 the year of Independence and to 3,647,148 in 1959. The changed political environment was one factor in this growth, but another was the breakup of the All-India Trade Union Congress (AITUC), a more or less unified federation of trade unions.

After Independence, four national trade union federations, each associated with one or more political parties, began to compete for worker loyalties, or more precisely, for membership. The formation of conflict between the four federations—INTUC (Congress), AITUC (Communist), HMS (Socialist), and UTUC (Marxist-left)—was closely related to the conflicts between the major political parties.[8] In general, the non-Communist trade unionists were eager to break their ties with the AITUC, which had fallen under Communist control during the war. But to understand the direction taken by each federation, one must study the political forces in each area. In Ahmedabad, for example, the unions were among the strongest in the country; but in comparison with trade unions elsewhere, their traditions and orientation were moderate. Ahmedabad is a cotton textile city built upon indigenous capital; and nationalist trade unions had not antagonized the Indian employers as a means of opposing the British. A tradition of harmonious relations has been built

interests of workers can best be satisfied by national growth, and national growth depends upon strong government and a strong Congress party. In a given economic dispute, it is best for INTUC to encourage a peaceful, if sometimes unsatisfactory, settlement rather than resort to a strike; in a political dispute (such as the states-reorganization controversy), it is best for INTUC to support the view of the Congress party and government rather than what may locally be more popular.

[8] The political background of this trade union struggle is described by Myron Weiner in *Party Politics in India* (Princeton, N.J.: Princeton University Press, 1957), chap. vii. For a brief summary of the development of the major federations, see chap. ii of this volume.

by the Gandhian-oriented working force and business leadership. In contrast, Calcutta trade unions were aggressively anti-employer as well as anti-imperialist. For in Calcutta, the capitalist Indian Jute Mills Association, the Bengal Chamber of Commerce, the Indian Tea Association, and the Indian Mining Association—all powerful groups—were British. Class struggle was as much a part of the nationalist creed among Calcutta unionists as class harmony was the nationalist creed among Ahmedabad unionists.

After an unsuccessful effort by non-Communists to regain control of AITUC, the non-Communist group broke away to form INTUC. In West Bengal the driving force of the new federation was two men, Deben Sen and S. C. Bannerjee. No sooner had the new federation been founded than conflicts arose in leadership. In part, these conflicts, like many others in Indian political parties, involved personal differences among various factions and leaders within the organization. But there were also substantial policy differences. Both Deben Sen and S. C. Bannerjee were associated with a faction of the Congress party in West Bengal that had lost a struggle for control of the party organization and the government. In 1949 a group of Congressmen, including these two leaders, had broken with the party to form the Krishak Praja Mazdoor party (Peasants and Workers Peoples party). These two trade unionists remained hostile to the government and to other INTUC leaders. Sen and Bannerjee had no qualms about advocating strikes, while Congress INTUC leaders supported compulsory arbitration in the event that collective bargaining failed. Deben Sen was instrumental in calling a strike of twenty-five thousand Calcutta Corporation workers in 1948, a strike which lasted about eight days. And in 1950 Sen called a general strike of three hundred thousand jute workers.

The Congress-oriented INTUC leadership further resented having in their presence two trade unionists who so clearly and openly opposed the existing government; they argued that Deben Sen's presence compromised the position of INTUC. For one thing, Sen and the Krishak Praja Mazdoor party willingly collaborated with the Communists in trade union disputes, a policy which ran counter to official INTUC policy. The Bengal Congress INTUC leaders asserted that Sen and the Communists kept anti-Congress signs in the Calcutta headquarters of INTUC. Under no circumstances, they argued, could INTUC tolerate within its ranks officials who collaborated with the Communists, who were so clearly against the Congress government in the state, and who wanted to pursue a program of strikes.

The national INTUC leadership, however, wanted to keep Deben Sen, Bannerjee, and the Socialist group within the organization. The 1953 annual INTUC report discussed the situation frankly.

> There was continued insistence on the part of one section [in West Bengal] that people who are connected with political parties rival to the Congress should not occupy responsible positions within the INTUC. The INTUC working committee was not prepared to concede such a position. We have always held that the INTUC is a working class organization based on democratic ideals, having its own constitution and objectives and that as long as a person pledged loyalty to the fundamental principles of the INTUC and acted within the framework of its discipline, no discrimination could be made against him on political grounds.[9]

But ultimately the Bengal Congress INTUC group won out. The death of Hariharnath Shastri, general secretary of the national INTUC and a strong supporter of a non-partisan federation that would unite trade unions of all parties (Communists excepted), removed from the scene a strong hand which had restrained the Congress INTUC leaders in West Bengal. The central labor minister, Khandubhai Desai—a powerful figure in INTUC—wanted to throw Sen out, partly because he wanted an all-Congress trade union group, and partly because he held different views from Sen regarding strikes and arbitration. In 1956, Moitriya Bose, an energetic woman and the leader of the Bengal Congress trade union group, announced that she had formed her own Bengal Pradesh National Trade Union Congress (BPTUC); the national INTUC soon gave it official support, and so did the West Bengal Pradesh Congress Committee.

Sen and Bannerjee were also under pressure from their own political group, the Praja Socialist party (a merger of the Krishak Praja Mazdoor party and the Socialist party) to join the Socialist-sponsored trade union federation. Pressed by both Congress and their own party, Sen and Bannerjee joined the Hind Mazdoor Sabha in 1956, bringing their own unions and trade union workers with them.

One major area of Communist trade union activity was among the white collar unions in Calcutta. As elsewhere in the world, office workers

[9] Indian National Trade Union Congress, *Annual Report*, November, 1952, to October, 1953, p. 93.

were reluctant to organize, but after 1946 the number of white collar unions multiplied. The Communists were the most active in organizing middle-class workers; by 1952 it was clear that the major groups of white collar workers were either affiliated with AITUC or were controlled by Communist party members; bank employees, life insurance employees, tramway workers, mercantile employees, and teachers were all, or in large numbers, associated with the CPI. Engineering workers, particularly the skilled or semiskilled, belonged to Communist-dominated unions. Unlike the workers in the other industries of West Bengal, this work force was largely Bengali. Among the non-Bengali workers in Calcutta, who constitute the bulk of the manual laborers in the state, the Communists have, on the whole, been weak, while Congress and the Socialists have been strong.

If moderation is the keynote of Congress unions, militancy is the keynote of all others. Non-Congress union leaders view their main tasks as those of making inroads into industries, such as jute, that have undergone little unionization; of building labor membership in existing unions; and of competing successfully against rival unions. All these objectives necessitate a militant policy: high and often irresponsible demands, radical slogans, and strikes. While INTUC is in principle reluctant to press for strikes and hesitates to embarrass the Congress government (epecially after Deben Sen and S. C. Bannerjee left), other trade unions feel no such restraints. Tribunals, they believe, are to be used not so much as a means of settling disputes, but as an instrument for furthering union organization. The challenge this presents to a more moderate, responsible unionism, such as the INTUC seeks to build, is apparent. In no industry has the challenge been more dramatic than in iron and steel.

Jamshedpur is a large steel town located in Bihar, the iron-coal-power center of northeast India, if not of south Asia.[10] Relations between the Tata Iron and Steel Company, the paramount industrial concern in Jamshedpur, and the Tata Workers Union is often referred to as a model for other industries. The union is an independent union; but its president, Michael John, has been an official of INTUC, and in general the union adheres to the moderate INTUC line. For a period before 1956 a break-

[10] This account of the 1958 strike in Jamshedpur is from "Order and Disorder in the Labour Force: The Jamshedpur Crisis of 1958," by Morris David Morris, in *Economic Weekly*, X (November 1, 1958), 1387–95. Morris based his account partly upon the official analysis published by the Tata Iron and Steel Company and partly upon interviews with union and company officials before the strike began. Morris' account is the best attempt to describe the dynamics of trade union leadership, membership, and company relations for a single industry in India.

down in relations between union and management seemed possible when controversies arose over the effects of building a new plant in Jamshedpur, programs to rationalize labor in the existing plants, and wage problems in general. But in 1956 a settlement was arrived at which emphasized union prerogatives, such as the right to participate in certain types of plant decisions, recognized the union as sole bargaining agent, and established a dues check-off, instead of providing immediate wage benefits of a substantial nature. In short, the union had mitigated its worker-oriented demands for the sake of consolidating its own position in the industry. The agreement was heralded as a responsible solution to difficult problems. Michael John, as president of the union, sought to placate those workers who demanded more substantial increases in wages; indeed, he often seemed to defend management to his union members. Communist trade union organizers proceeded to agitate among the steel workers, arguing that Michael John was a tool of the management and that demands for higher wages should again be made. In May, 1958, much to the surprise of Michael John, the industry, and the government, a Communist-led strike broke out in Jamshedpur of such proportions that it appeared that virtually the whole work force was involved. The Tata Iron and Steel Company was paralyzed, police were called out to protect plant property, a police firing occurred, 4 died, and 114 persons were injured. Property worth 1,115,000 rupees (about $230,000) was destroyed, 335,000 man-days of work were lost, and the company failed to produce 45,000 tons of steel. The strike was eventually broken, but meanwhile the Communists had made an inroad into the steel industry.

Morris concludes that at this early stage of industrialization great attention has to be paid to workers' short-term wage demands, and that as rational as a long-term settlement might appear to both union and management, the tension associated with annual settlements serve as a catharsis for workers who constantly need to be reassured that their leadership is vigorous.[11]

> It should be recognized that any great industry or firm is destined to face periodic difficulties with its work force. No matter how disciplined the labour, how strong and democratic the union, how reasonable the relation between union and management, how generous and sophisticated the wage and social welfare benefits provided by a company, periodic upheavals are inevitable. In fact, occasional strikes may be

[11] *Ibid.*, p. 1395.

necessary cathartics to release the tension of urban-industrial life, as festivals and village brawls release the tensions of rural-agrarian existence.[12]

Arbitration and Industrial Relations

If, as it appears, a kind of Gresham's law operates in which militant unionism drives out responsible unionism, how has the Indian government fared in its efforts to restrain militant unions by legal means? Do conciliation and arbitration proceedings in fact minimize the number of work stoppages? Statistically, there is little evidence for or against the effects of the legislation. The number of strikes, the number of workers involved in strikes, and the number of working days lost have varied from year to year since the passage of the legislation. Although on all three counts the numbers are higher now than during the era before legislation, the work force is also larger, and there are more unions. However, an index of industrial relations indicating the number of man-days lost in relation to the number of man-days actually worked shows that, proportionally, losses have been slightly lower from 1947 (when the Industrial Disputes Act was passed) to 1954 than from 1939 to 1947 (see Table 4). However, there has been a substantial increase in the number

TABLE 4

INDEX OF INDUSTRIAL RELATIONS*

Year	M Estimated Man-Days Actually Worked (In Hundred Thousands)	L Man-Days Lost Owing to Industrial Disputes (In Hundred Thousands)	M/L	Index of Industrial Relations (M/L for 1939 = 100)
1939....	5,358	49	108	100
1940....	5,644	71	79	73
1941....	6,599	29	228	210
1942....	6,984	56	124	115
1943....	7,455	23	328	301
1944....	7,720	32	238	219
1945....	8,087	40	204	188
1946....	7,083	120	59	54
1947....	6,961	158	43	40
1948....	7,222	75	96	88
1949....	7,448	49	152	140
1950....	7,663	118	64	60
1951....	7,762	28	275	253
1952....	7,856	21	382	351
1953....	7,736	26	301	277
1954....	7,924	27	292	268

* Taken from V. V. Giri, *Labour Problems in Indian Industry* (Bombay: Asia Publishing House, 1958), p. 92.

[12] *Ibid.*, p. 1389.

of man-days lost since 1954: 5.7 million in 1955, 7 million in 1956, 6.4 million in 1957, 7.8 million in 1958, and 5.6 million in 1959.[13]

The fluctuation in the number of work stoppages since 1947 does, however, indicate that factors in addition to the role played by government officers are at work. The number of disputes in which conciliation officers participated, and even the number of disputes settled by arbitration tribunals, are also obviously no index of the success of the legislation. There are no official figures on what proportion of all labor disputes are referred to arbitration. Kennedy reports that several conciliation officers with whom he spoke estimated that approximately 10 per cent of the disputes that were under conciliation in their areas were eventually arbitrated.[14] How many of those disputes would have been settled by collective bargaining if the government had not intervened can only be conjectured. Many of the disputes might not even have occurred, since, as we have noted, weak unions might not have undertaken to press demands if they had felt that they lacked the capacity to organize a strike. In fact, one can argue as has Bernard S. Cohn in the field of land-rights litigation,[15] that Indians use tribunals to further and not to settle disputes.[16]

Those unions most willing to accept the decision of tribunals are often either too weak to do otherwise or unlikely to resort to a strike even if legislation should permit them to do so. Strong unions are prepared to, and often do, resort to strikes if the tribunal decisions run counter to what they feel they deserve. The latter situation is well illustrated in the 1956 coal strike in West Bengal.

A dispute between the Colliery Mazdoor Congress, under the leadership of Deben Sen, and the coal industry in the Ranigang area of West

[13] *Indian Labour Statistics, 1960* (New Delhi: Labour Bureau, Ministry of Labour and Employment, Government of India), p. 135; and *India 1961* (New Delhi: Publications Division, Government of India, 1961), p. 379.

[14] Van Dusen Kennedy, "The Conceptual and Legislative Framework of Labor Relations in India," *Industrial and Labor Relations Review*, No. 10 (July, 1958), p. 492.

[15] Cohn, "Some Notes on Law and Change in Northern India," *Economic Development and Cultural Change*, VIII (October, 1959), 79–93.

[16] It is also easier for unions to raise funds during conciliation, and especially arbitration, proceedings than usual. Union officials receive payment from their unions—from 50 to 100 rupees for handling arbitration cases, and this becomes an opportunity for general union fund raising. This is not to argue that conciliation and arbitration proceedings actually increase union-management conflict, for to argue this would be to reverse the argument of those who say it decreases conflict; and both positions are without evidence. Arguments can, it seems to me, be presented on both sides; all I am arguing is that the claim made by supporters of arbitration, that it is necessary in an "operation bootstrap" situation such as exists in the new states, lacks empirical support.

Bengal was brought before a tribunal. In May, 1956, a decision was rendered. A few months later, in September, the Colliery Mazdoor Congress called for an increase in wages to certain categories of workers, the payment of a bonus, and a program for the distribution of free rice by management to protect workers against increases in the price of their food staple. To what extent political consideration motivated these demands is difficult to say. Deben Sen had just left INTUC and was in the process of transferring his unions, including coal, to the HMS. Elections to Parliament and to the state legislature were pending; and Deben Sen, along with other union leaders, was a candidate. In any event, spokesmen for the coal industry argued that a strike at this time would be illegal for three reasons: (1) The tribunal award of May was binding on all parties for a year unless appealed within a month; Sen's Colliery Mazdoor Congress had not appealed within the stipulated time and must therefore be presumed to have accepted it. (2) Certain other parties to the dispute before the tribunal—including the Communist-controlled unions—had appealed against various terms of the award, and these appeals were now before the appellate tribunal. Since several managements were party to these appeals, any strike during the time they were pending was illegal. (3) Conciliation proceedings, which had been started by the government in early September, were still effective. The government, agreeing with at least some of these arguments, declared that any strike at this time would be illegal.

On September 18 some 38,000 coal miners went on strike. Deben Sen and twenty other organizers were immediately arrested by the West Bengal state government. Several police firings occurred, but the strike continued. Many union officials and some management people felt that the arrest of Deben Sen had made a settlement more difficult, for no responsible official was available with whom management and government could negotiate. Several leaders of the BPTUC (the INTUC federation in West Bengal) visited the coal areas and urged the central government to intervene. The Socialists, who supported the strike, continued to demand the release of their leader from jail.

By the end of the month, the strike was still on, although some 30 per cent of the work force, apparently feeling the financial pinch, had returned to the mines. Finally, on October 1, Deben Sen was released. B. C. Roy, the chief minister of West Bengal, intervened and negotiated directly with Sen. On October 14 he announced that he had told Sen that the strike was illegal, but that if it were called off he would persuade management to discuss the union's demands. Simultaneously with B. C.

Roy's announcement, and nearly a month after the strike had begun, Deben Sen called off the strike and the miners returned to work.

Although the government was instrumental in ending the strike, it had been unable either to enforce the original tribunal award or to prevent the strike in spite of its legal powers. Another important aspect of this crisis was the penetration of Communist workers into Deben Sen's union. Although Deben Sen had many union organizers of his own, he was very willing to co-operate with Communists, both on union and on party fronts—which was one of the reasons he and the INTUC had parted ways. Communist union organizers were very active in the coal industry; and some argued that Deben Sen's union, although a member of the Socialist federation, was virtually controlled by the Communists. Many Socialist HMS trade unions were reluctant to work with him because of his collaboration. The question of Communist collaboration with non-Communist trade union workers is closely associated with the controversy over militancy versus moderation in trade unionism. So long as the BPTUC is pro-Congress, and so long as it urges moderation to the point of avoiding strikes, non-Communist unionists are under pressure to work with militant Communist organizers as a means of strengthening their own position vis-à-vis Congress unions. Although anti-Communists in the Socialist HMS have rightly argued that collaboration with the Communists, even on specific issues, is an asset to Communist trade union workers, Deben Sen and his supporters have argued that only through militancy can the trade union movement be built. They claim that INTUC's antistrike policy is a blow to labor, and that every effort should be made to stymie the growth of INTUC—including collaboration with the Communists. In such industries as jute where union rivalry is intense, even anti-Communist Socialist workers have been unable to work with Congress union leaders despite their shared anti-Communist sentiments.

The Communists—who view Congress trade union workers as their main competitors—attribute their expansion in West Bengal to several factors: (1) In the major issues of concern to labor—wages, rationalization, and unemployment—workers have not been satisfied with the results INTUC has achieved by relying on government machinery. (2) While INTUC doesn't oppose strikes in principle, but only argues that a union should not resort to strikes unless all other methods have failed, in practice it rarely permits unions to strike. (3) AITUC's efforts to join with other unions on issues of common interest have left INTUC increasingly isolated.[17]

[17] Based on interviews with Communist trade unionists in West Bengal.

AITUC's freedom to sponsor antigovernment demonstrations is another asset. AITUC calls out workers to protest nuclear tests, the Suez crisis, and the food situation in the state. Apart from the political benefits the party may receive, such demonstrations are devices employed by AITUC to increase the commitment of the workers to its unions. While AITUC probably is not as large as INTUC, it is perhaps more successful in calling out workers for demonstrations and strikes than any other federation. In short, AITUC is as much concerned with building solidarity as in building membership. AITUC union leaders also claim to be more effective in collecting dues from their members than other unions. The presence of a committed trade union force is in itself an asset in the drive toward further expansion. The ability of AITUC unions to keep the support of their workers means that AITUC is better able to carry out agreements with the employers than other unions which in some plants may have a larger, but less committed, membership. Therefore, as one Communist official has noted, employers in engineering firms are increasingly more willing to work with AITUC than with other unions in the industry, in spite of their political differences.

While the degree of commitment cannot readily be measured, it should be possible to estimate union membership with some ease. Unfortunately, the figures on union membership are notoriously inflated. When unions register with the labor commissioner in each state, they declare their membership. However, since there are no union elections and there is no check-off system, neither government nor management can themselves verify the number of members in a particular union. In West Bengal, according to the claims made by each of the federations in 1956, INTUC had 442,000 members, AITUC was second with 226,000, HMS third with 130,000, and UTUC last with 35,000. Privately, Congress trade unionists put their membership at about 200,000 (after Deben Sen withdrew an estimated 60,000 workers), and estimated the AITUC membership as about 150,000. In 1957 the HMS leadership privately claimed that its membership was about 150,000. But these figures are at best rough estimates. The only point on which the four federations agree is that INTUC is probably still the largest, followed in order by AITUC, HMS, and UTUC.

The votes given by laborers to candidates for parliament and the state legislative assembly are susceptible of more precise description and analysis. INTUC candidates did not do well in the 1957 national elections. Leading INTUC workers—the general secretary of the Bihar TUC, the Congress trade union candidate in Jamshedpur, D. G. Ambedkar in the city of Bombay, Khandubhai Desai in Ahmedabad, and G. Tewari in the textile center at Indore—were defeated. INTUC head-quarters, however, claimed that its candidates won 75 per cent of the parliamentary seats they contested and 70 per cent of the assembly seats. In West Bengal, where the AITUC, HMS, and UTUC united behind labor candidates against the Congress candidates, the opposition did fairly well in labor constituencies. In Howrah, Bauria, Garden Reach, Asansol, Burnpur, and the plantation areas of north Bengal, the Com-munists and their allies won new seats or received more votes than they had in 1952. Of greatest concern to Congress was the inroad made by op-position candidates in the jute belt of West Bengal, where the working force is made up primarily of non-Bengalis, and where all the major unions were vying for support.

Why has INTUC suffered losses both in elections and in its control of particular unions and industries? To what extent are forces at work which constitute a threat to responsible unionism in general and to INTUC in particular?

As we have already indicated, INTUC's policy of moderation is a liability in the struggle to control a working force which has a relatively low commitment to factory work and which tends not to calculate the costs to itself of work stoppages. It is difficult for INTUC to win new members among workers where other, more militant, unions are en-trenched; but it is not impossible for other unions to break into INTUC strongholds, as the Communists did in Jamshedpur. Responsible union-ism could conceivably win out, however, if the state were so solidly behind responsible unions that the government forcefully intervened on their behalf. Some commentators fear that Indian unionism is moving in the direction of a state-controlled pattern, comparable to that in the Soviet Union or, perhaps, Egypt.[18] But in spite of the powers available to it, the Indian government—at the moment at least—is incapable of acting in the authoritarian manner that such a policy would require. It has been argued, for example, that Congress unions are more likely to obtain tribunals appointed by the state ministry of labor than are non-

[18] This point of view is argued by Ralph James, *op. cit.*, and Morris David Morris, "Trade Unions and the State," in *Leadership and Political Institutions in India*, ed. Richard L. Park and Irene Tinker (Princeton, N.J.: Princeton University Press, 1959). Morris fears that Indian unions will become instruments of the state aimed at ensur-ing the discipline of the work force on behalf of efforts to industrialize the country. His own—later—study of Jamshedpur is, I think, a telling argument for the position argued here: that extremist if not totalitarian (i.e., Communist and Marxist-left) control of unions is more likely and in the long run a greater threat.

Congress unions. But although there is some truth to this, the government's hand is often forced by Communist, Socialist, and other non-Congress unions. One leftist trade union leader reported that leftist unions will often threaten a strike so as to force the government to appoint a tribunal. Many state ministers of labor have hoped that by appointing tribunals they would, in effect, be reducing the militancy of leftist unions and would thereby reduce strikes, even if one result of their acquiescence were a multiplication of leftist unions.

Where the state government is clearly pro-labor, it is possible for INTUC to argue with some conviction that moderation is more likely to bring returns than militancy. But INTUC leaders in West Bengal complain that they are handicapped by the absence of a pro-labor state government and ministry of labor, such as they believe exist in Bombay and other states. They maintain that although other states have generally recruited their labor ministers from the ranks of INTUC, in West Bengal the government has hesitated to appoint a man who would be unacceptable to the business community. INTUC leaders had, in fact, hoped that Moitriya Bose, their president, would be appointed after the 1957 state elections. INTUC has pressed for the appointment of a state labor advisory board, composed of labor, management, and government representatives, to consider industrial relations policy for the state. The state government did not agree until 1957. INTUC officials have also pressed the government for various study boards to inquire into industrial conditions in each industry, but only in jute—and then only after much agitation—has such a body been appointed. Finally, INTUC leaders have felt that the chief minister is basically probusiness and that he believes an employer has the right to hire and fire as he sees fit. They note that some Congress officials in the state, including the president of the West Bengal Congress, feel that the only justification for the existence of INTUC is to prevent other political groups from organizing and using workers to their advantage. The notion that workers need to be organized to protect workers' rights is, in fact, rejected by many government and Congress officials. While such attitudes are not reflected in any outright antilabor policies of the state government, they do make INTUC's task more difficult.

Radicalism and Outside Leadership

Even if government were more sympathetic to INTUC and took steps to strengthen INTUC unions against others, responsible unionism would still be faced with the challenge of pervasive militancy. Some Indian industrialists, and observers of labor relations in India, have argued that militancy is a quality of the "outside leadership" that controls Indian unions, not of the work force itself. They claim that if the power of "outsiders" could be broken, militancy would disappear. No issue has been more discussed in the literature on Indian industrial relations than the role of the outsider; and we will dwell only briefly on this phenomenon.

The outsider, that is the labor leader drawn from outside the ranks of labor, seemed at first appearance to be the product of the nationalist movement. It was national leaders seeking to win labor participation in the struggle against the British who first entered union work. But the reasons why workers have accepted outside leaders and have rarely produced their own, and why the phenomenon persisted after Independence, have been the subject of much conjecture. The hypotheses suggested are many: (1) The use of English in tribunals and the presence of complicated labor legislation calls for skills—administrative, linguistic, and legal—that workers do not have, and forces workers to turn to a more educated outside leadership. (2) Many of the politicians in trade union work have been active for twenty to thirty years, and their leadership persists although their original intent in entering trade union work —winning support for the nationalistic struggle—has disappeared. (3) Unions lack the finances for supporting full-time professional union workers, and must therefore rely on financially independent outsiders who live off their private incomes and legal work. (4) Status considerations— the unwillingness and inability of people on the bottom of the social ladder to communicate directly with those of higher caste, economic standing, and power—make it difficult for factory workers to deal directly with management or government; hence an intermediary leadership of higher status is needed. (5) In some industries the status gap is enhanced by a linguistic and ethnic gap: British management versus Indian workers, or Marwari management versus Bihari or Oriya workers, or Gujarati management versus Maharashtrian workers, or Tamil management versus Telugu workers, and so on.

Some of these hypotheses prove to be irrelevant when one considers that other types of interest groups, such as peasant organizations and refugee groups, are also largely controlled by outsiders. Those groups which have an inside leadership—such as caste, tribal, religious, and linguistic bodies—turn for leadership in external relations to men who are in many respects similar to those who control unions: full-time professional politicians, frequently with private incomes from the land, who are college- or at least secondary-school graduates. Generally by reason of their income, education, family background, landownership, or caste, they are of higher social status than the groups that they lead. Of the various hypotheses, status is perhaps the most persuasive, and most adequately explains the general phenomenon. Although India has a hierarchical social system in which subservience to authority and acceptance of one's role, no matter how onerous, are important values, people have not been reluctant to protest through political organization. But in organizing politically, they turn to those of higher status for their leadership (or at least are organized by them). To argue that the use of English in labor tribunals, the need for familiarity with complicated labor legislation, and the hostile character of many employers toward workers are responsible for the workers' unwillingness to deal with authority does not account for the equal dependence of peasants upon outsiders. In the countryside, the middle-class rural gentry has, perhaps always, been the intermediary between low caste, low status peasants and those in authority. Today, both in the countryside and in the cities, political organization of the poor and low in status is progressing faster than any breakdown in the hierarchical social system. It is even questionable whether any such breakdown in the concept and practice of hierarchy has occurred at all. The continued need of workers and peasants for a leadership with which they can communicate and which in turn can speak boldly to authority is no less important than the readiness of politicians to fill this intermediary role.

Furthermore, militancy in the work force—the making of extreme demands often associated with millenarian and messianic visions, and the readiness to resort not only to strikes, but to sabotage and various forms of coercion—appears to be a phenomenon characteristic of countries in which peasants are first entering factory life. High rates of absenteeism, high turnover, and other manifestations of low commitment to industrial occupations are not uncommon. Family dislocation (many workers leave their families behind when they come to the city to work in factories, as evidenced by the high male to female ratio in urban working class constituencies), combined with the fact that workers do not own any urban property (such as a home, vehicle, or appliances), facilitates belief in the slogan, "You have nothing to lose but your chains." The act of joining a trade union—sometimes the worker's first voluntary participation in an organized group concerned with making demands upon authority—is often accompanied by exaggerated notions about the capacity of group organization to influence authority and even to change the very character of the system. There is often a sense of exhilaration that is more attracted to the millenarian claims of ideologies than to the voice of moderation.

The Indian trade union movement is one of the most maligned in the world. Unions are poorly organized, membership turnover is great, dues-paying is limited to a few and is irregular, and union activities are limited to strikes, demonstrations, and election work. Only rarely does a union provide services for its members. Rival unionism is rampant, unions are led by outsiders, and control of unions is often in the hands of political parties seeking to use them for their own ends.

Unions have had some success in agitating for higher wages, improved working conditions, and diminished rationalization of industry. But much of what unions have won has come through conciliation and arbitration procedures, or through demands upon government legislators, rather than through collective bargaining. Proposals to strengthen unions through compulsory collective bargaining, union shop, a check-off system, or the designation of a single union as the exclusive bargaining agent for employees within an industry are generally not supported by unions, management, or government. Employers, political parties, trade union leaders (with the exception of Communists), and government officials all lament the politicalization of trade unions; but the trend has been toward a more fragmented trade union movement, paralleling the fragmented party system of India.

These characteristics of Indian trade unions are defects, if one uses British or American trade unions as a model. But given the purposes of employers, political parties, trade union leaders, and government, the trade union movement in India functions as well as it can.

The government wishes the unions to exercise discipline so that the work force may contribute its maximum potential to the nation's economic development. Perhaps the strongest pressures against new legislation to provide for compulsory collective bargaining and exclusive bargaining rights for majority unions come from the cabinet ministers, who are, in effect, among India's largest employers. Ministers in charge of railways, defense establishments, and post and telegraph services have opposed efforts by the central labor ministry to write new legislation that would affect these ministries. V. V. Giri, in his letter of resignation as India's labor minister, reported that "there is a growing feeling among the employing ministries that each can have its own way and its own labour policy, thus rendering the Labour Ministry almost super-fluous. . . ." [19]

Business, although for different reasons, shares government's concern for maintaining industrial harmony. Opposition political parties and union leaders associated with them want to strengthen trade unions as weapons against the existing government. Indian workers, like workers elsewhere, want to maximize their own well-being. But the notion of unions as autonomous bodies, free from government, management, and party control and concerned with protecting their own interests within the national interest, is an American and British conception widely supported in India in the abstract, but far removed from the actual purposes of the major participants in the development of trade unionism. [20]

The critical questions in the development of a trade union movement are not whether workers will be dissatisfied, whether they will make demands, or whether they will organize—for all three are inevitable in an industrial society in which individuals have the right to organize—but rather who will lead the organization of workers' protests and for what purposes.

Today the Indian trade union movement is divided by three conflicting political pulls. The government, the Congress party, and the INTUC hope to see the growth of responsible unionism. They see responsible unionism as the most satisfactory means of safeguarding the workers' interests, while at the same time contributing to the nation's economic growth. The Socialists and their federation, the Hind Mazdoor Sabha, and many of the unions not affiliated with any federation view militant unionism as the direction toward which the movement must head. [21] Demands are high, there is a readiness to participate in strikes,

[19] *Deccan Herald* (Bangalore), Sept. 9, 1954, quoted by Kennedy, *op. cit.*, p. 496.

[20] After noting that the first five-year plan calls for the development of a system of collective bargaining, Kennedy concludes: "Existing legislation . . . [has] a negative influence on collective bargaining . . . the legislation, in effect, grants labor relations rights of a sort to all unions, no matter how small, but concedes no preferred status to majority unions; it permits two or more rival unions to represent workers and make demands on employers in what would in the United States be single bargaining units, without providing a means of settling representation disputes; it provides for works committees in establishments regardless of whether unions already exist in them; it requires employers to institute standing orders covering certain terms and conditions of employment by a procedure which, in effect, bypasses bargaining; it does not make bargaining compulsory and does provide alternative government machinery for dispute settlement. These are a far cry from the collective bargaining objectives announced in the First Five Year Plan." (*Ibid.*, p. 493.)

[21] For an exception to this view among Socialists, see Asoka Mehta, "The Mediating Role of the Trade Union in Underdeveloped Countries," *Economic Development and*

and HMS sees the interests of the workers as paramount; for unlike INTUC members, there is no need for HMS trade union workers to choose between their loyalties to the party and their loyalties to the union. Finally, there are pressures from Communists for the creation of a trade union movement which is not only militant, but which, more importantly, can be used as an instrument by the party for winning power and for destroying the institutions of representative government.

If one perceives threats to production as the greatest danger of the trade union movement in a society undergoing planned industrialization, then the moderate policies of INTUC and the procedures of conciliation and arbitration advocated by government are understandable. Whether moderate unionism can win out, and whether arbitration does in fact minimize losses in production, is, as we have noted, open to question. But the strategy is, at least, understandable. If, however, one sees as the greatest danger the possibility that totalitarian parties may gain control of the trade union movement, with resultant threats not only to production but to the institutions of representative government, then an alternative strategy might be required. Militant unionism committed to the democratic framework can compete more successfully with totalitarian militant unionism than can the responsible unionism of INTUC. Conceivably, the triumph of militant unions could mean greater production losses or a larger labor bill than the triumph of responsible unions, but can responsible unions win out in the struggle with the Communists? And can one assume that in the long run strong trade unions concerned with bread-and-butter issues will result in a less productive work force? Or that all claims on consumption necessarily limit investment? Finally, were the choice simply between responsible unionism and militant unionism, there would be little to lose; but if the choice should narrow to responsible unionism versus totalitarian unionism, there is great danger that the non-Communist unions would be squeezed out. If government's objective were to permit the creation of a strong militant trade union movement committed to the democratic framework in the hope that in time militant unions would become responsible, the INTUC's policies

---

Cultural Change, VI (October, 1957). Mehta, onetime general secretary of the Praja Socialist party and a leading Socialist unionist, argues that "the major question for unions is subordination of immediate wage gains and similar considerations to the development of the country" (p. 16). Whether this means a continuation of arbitration Mehta does not say, but he does warn against "heavy reliance on Government machinery." Mehta stresses the need for voluntary restraints on consumption by trade unions and the important role unions might play in cushioning the urban shock for new members of the industrial work force.

and that of government in the field of industrial relations would be somewhat different. Legislation might then provide for compulsory collective bargaining, majority unions with exclusive bargaining rights, and the elimination of compulsory arbitration except in a few essential services. And INTUC itself would make workers' demands paramount, even if it entailed a more militant policy toward management (including government management), which might result in more frequent work stoppages.

The tasks faced by leadership in the field of industrial relations in underdeveloped economies were well summed up by Walter Galenson when he wrote:

> . . . development planning under democratic auspices must accept as a major variable the growth of labor unions. These organizations are likely to be highly political and imbued with a radical ideology. They will inevitably impose some costs upon the community and reduce the practicable rate of investment. However, if properly handled, they perform the vital function of channeling worker protest into socially useful forms, and help prevent the subversion of democracy. The role of the statesman is to minimize the cost and maximize the positive attributes of nascent unionism.[22]

[22] Galenson (ed.), *Labor and Economic Development* (New York: John Wiley & Sons, Inc., 1959), p. 18.

V. ORGANIZED BUSINESS

In underdeveloped countries the position of business has often been an ambiguous one. In the era before Independence businessmen had to choose between collaborating with a colonial regime that often had the power to make or break an enterprise and identifying themselves with the nationalist movement. With the achievement of Independence, business communities have had to adapt themselves to governments that are concerned with developing the public sector and often critical of private enterprise. In India, which has the largest private business sector to be found in the underdeveloped world today, we have an opportunity to observe the way in which business communities have adapted themselves to socialistic policies and to the system of representative government that has given rise to these policies.

Until 1959 no political party in India of any importance could be said to be a strong supporter of private enterprise. But in that year the Swatantra (Freedom) party was established. The circumstances under which this party developed and the attitude of the business community toward it give us some insight into the political attitudes and position of India's business communities.

When the Swatantra party entered the political scene, it was universally derided by the other national parties. Its leadership was too distinguished or too popular for the party to be ignored. But other parties and most Indian intellectuals found the party's program too nineteenth century for their taste, for the Swatantra party declared itself unabashedly sympathetic to the private entrepreneur in business and agriculture. It opposed proposals for joint farming in agriculture and ceilings on landholdings, as well as further nationalization and the continued imposition of controls over business. Indeed, its cardinal principles were derived from the liberal past: it saw virtue in private profit-making and economic growth through free use of market mechanisms; it favored a greater role for the private sector and greater freedom by limiting the role of government.

The Swatantra party's greatest support came from the Forum for Free Enterprise, which was started by a group of businessmen in Bombay, especially those associated with the Tata enterprises. Some say the party is, in fact, the Forum's political arm. The Forum claims support from businessmen in cement, textiles, shipping, insurance, and many medium-sized enterprises which resent government controls or which, according to the Forum, have been hurt by government enlargement of the public sector. Unlike the business chambers, the Forum's aim is to educate the public, particularly the educated middle classes, to be more sympathetic to the ideals of free enterprise. Concentrating in New Delhi and Bombay, the Forum has sponsored public lectures and circulated its brochures. Outside of these two cities, the Forum attracted some support in the textile industry in Ahmedabad and sugar mills in Madras. Of the many business chambers in India, only the All-India Manufacturers Organization, a group of small businessmen and small manufacturers, supports the Forum.

Associated with the Forum, and some say its intellectual leader, has been Minoo R. Masani, onetime public relations official of the Tata enterprises, and a founder-president of the Congress Socialist party. Masani, a Parsi like the Tatas, broke from the Socialists in the late 1930's and became a leading independent politician, a mayor of Bombay, India's ambassador to Brazil, and a leading independent member of the Constituent Assembly.[1] Masani ran and lost as an independent in the 1952 elections to Parliament, but won in 1957 with the support of the Jharkhand leader, Jaipal Singh, in a heavily tribal constituency in Ranchi, Bihar. Masani's militant anticommunism, his opposition to Nehru's non-alignment policy, and his criticisms of government planning policies did not endear him to many intellectuals. Nor were his immaculate English speech (his mother tongue), his dress (European), and his secular mannerisms likely to endear him to the masses. Nonetheless, there clustered around Masani a small group of younger intellectuals, some of whom had earlier been associated with M. N. Roy's Radical Humanist move-

[1] In a brief pamphlet, *Socialism Reconsidered* (Bombay: Padma Publications, 1944), Masani justifies his ideological break with socialism.

ment and some of whom had, like Masani, defected from the Socialist movement. While associated with Tata, Masani was able to extend his influence to several Bombay businessmen who have provided support for two Masani-supported enterprises: the Democratic Research Service, an anti-Communist research and propaganda body, and the Congress for Cultural Freedom, an anti-Communist, prodemocratic body of intellectuals associated with the International Congress for Cultural Freedom.

While the Congress for Cultural Freedom successfully attracted the support of intellectuals in various cities in India and won considerable support from leaders of the Praja Socialist party, such as Asoka Mehta, and from Gandhian leaders, such as Jayaprakash Narayan, support for the Forum for Free Enterprise was largely confined to Bombay. Furthermore, efforts of the Forum to build a popular movement were not successful; several candidates for Parliament sympathetic to the Forum were defeated in the 1957 elections.

In Madras and Andhra, however, movements developed which coincided with the Forum's activities in Bombay. In Madras, the elder statesman, C. R. Rajagopalachari, onetime governor general of India and former chief minister of Madras state, led a movement against the adoption of Hindi as the country's official language. "C.R." had for some years been critical of both the state and central governments' economic policy, but had not tapped any popular support until he turned against Hindi. C.R.'s public speeches were then well attended, and press coverage, both in Madras and elsewhere, was great. Meanwhile, in neighboring Andhra state, N. G. Ranga, onetime Socialist—a founder of the Kisan (peasant) Sabha, and a popular figure in his state—broke with the local Andhra Congress organization. He nationally expressed his opposition to the Congress party's decision to support large-scale co-operatives, and attacked joint farming, which he considered a threat to the ideals of private, individual farming.

Masani, Rajagopalachari, and Ranga shared a distrust of the expansion of state power at the center; and on this platform the Swatantra party was built. It was formed in the legislatures before it was organized in the constituencies. In the Parliament, it began with a vocal opposition bloc organized by Minoo Masani; it had legislative backing in Bombay, Madras, and Andhra. A few newspapers greeted the organization of a conservative party as one which might challenge the Socialist proclivities of India's four national parties (parties with more than 3 per cent of the national vote to Parliament are declared "national"; these include Congress, the Communists, the Praja Socialists, and Jan Sangh); Nehru and a few Congressmen criticized the new party for its outdated Victorian outlook. But the stir one might have expected from the creation of a business party did not materialize. One reason is, perhaps, that the party appeared to threaten no one. Organizationally it had yet to prove itself; and there was no evidence that it had popular support. Furthermore, the business community itself seemed reticent to back it; and except for a few businessmen in Bombay, Madras, and Delhi (but none in Calcutta), it was hard to find any business support for the party. Business chambers remained silent; and many businessmen privately expressed their concern that the new party might either cause a loss in support for Congress and increased threats from the left or set off a reaction against business within the Congress party. But there was no evidence that the smaller businessmen in the towns, or for that matter even the larger businessmen in the big cities, were withdrawing their financial support from the Congress party.

The aloofness of the business community was certainly not a result of its sympathy for government policy. The nationalization of the airlines, the Imperial Bank, and the life insurance industry, the establishment of state trading, the imposition of high taxes and especially of a wealth tax (a kind of capital levy), and innumerable regulations of business had made many businessmen critical of what they saw as undue government control.[2]

[2] The point of view that Indian business is not merely regulated but state controlled was argued by W. H. J. Christie, president of the (largely European) Upper Indian Chamber of Commerce. "We see prospects and the fact of a rising standard of living around us; and inflation, for the time being held in check. We are told that we have a full scope in the expansion of economic activity and we are encouraged, even commanded to take part in it. We earnestly desire to do so, and moreover, we are sincerely at one with the objectives of increasing the general level of prosperity, reducing inequalities of wealth, expanding employment and improving conditions of labour and relations between employer and workmen. We admit the need for a measure of regulation and direction. We should bend to our task with courage and confidence, and face the future jubilantly.

"What prevents us from doing so? In a few words, it is this. . . . There is scarcely a thing we can do in our business without government's permission, and the delays attendant on it. We cannot start or close a business, expand or contract a factory without government permission. We cannot raise capital or distribute to shareholders the reserves which are their property without permission. We cannot appoint a new Director, a Director cannot retire, without Government's consent. Much that we buy and much that we sell is subject to official controls. In some industries, for instance sugar, the price of 75% of all that enters into the cost of production is controlled by the Government. We are dependent on State controlled electricity for our power and State owned railways for our transport, of our fuel, our raw materials, our finished goods. We cannot pay our staff at our discretion, though certain members of our staff have to be employed and paid at Government's discretion. We cannot reduce our

Some Indian intellectuals have argued the reverse position—that business wields undue power in India. They speak of the Birlas, Dalmias, and Mundhras much as American intellectuals in the late nineteenth and early twentieth centuries spoke of the Fords, Rockefellers, and Carnegies —not as foundations endowing research and scholarship, but as evil influences on democratic institutions and as vested and powerful private interests. Socialism, they say, is a political language, honored in party manifestoes and in the speeches of government ministers, but not followed in practice. What socialism exists at the policy level is often nullified at the administrative level where business is exceedingly influential.[3] Taxes are high, but unpaid; import restrictions are great, but unobserved; the public sector expands, but private businessmen receive contracts and make high profits. Licenses are needed to open a business or operate a bus or taxi, but local businessmen can in effect buy licenses through the local Congress party and the local administration. If business in Calcutta is least interested in the Forum for Free Enterprise and the Swatantra party, it is because the West Bengal government is in fact controlled by businessmen.

Is the Indian government socialist or bourgeois government? Or is it socialist at the center, and bourgeois in the states? Or does Indian business operate within a basic value framework which limits its political role, and which, perhaps paradoxically, is accepted by the business community? To answer these questions, one must look at the political organization of Indian business and the ideology it propounds, and only then, at its interconnections with government.

The Political Effects of Organized Business: West Bengal

While few Indians will argue that the national government is the tool of the business community or, for that matter, of any particular interest, many point to the state governments as the repository of capitalist influence. In West Bengal, intellectuals have noted that while the state is populated predominantly by Bengalis, economic power is in the hands of non-Bengalis: factory workers from Bihar, Orissa, and Uttar Pradesh,

---

labour force without Government's consent and without severe penalty. About the only thing we are free to do without consent is to pay a bonus to our labour, provided of course we pay enough. All this—and taxation too" (*Statesman*, February 27, 1956).

[3] A rather typical view is expressed by D. D. Kosambi, a leading Indian mathematician and historian: "The class that rules India today, the paramount power, is the Indian bourgeoisie" (Damodar Dharmanand Kosambi, *An Introduction to the Study of Indian History* [Bombay: Popular Book Depot, 1956], p. ix).

and Marwari industrialists and commercial entrepreneurs. Even many of the shops, buses, and taxicabs, as well as the important rice trade, are in the hands of non-Bengalis. On the basis of economic facts, many Bengalis conclude that the state government is controlled by non-Bengalis, and especially by Marwari businessmen.

In terms of personnel, there could be no doubt that Bengalis control the state government; the cabinet, the bureaucracy, the legislative assembly, and the leadership of political parties are all Bengali. Indeed, the Oriyas, Biharis, and other non-Bengali groups are not represented within the governmental framework in spite of their substantial numbers and their economic power. In 1957 there was only one non-Bengali in the cabinet—a Marwari in charge of the ministry of local government. All of the thirty-man executive committee of the West Bengal Congress party was Bengali. Of 221 members of the legislative assembly for whom occupational information was available, only 18 were businessmen. If any single group predominates in the cabinet, in the state legislature, and in the executive committee of the Congress party, it is the professional politicians and, to a lesser extent, landholding members of the rural gentry.[4] Political power in Bengal, as elsewhere in India, is largely in the hands of those who have devoted their entire lives to politics. To speak of this group as being coincidental with the middle class, or the bourgeoisie, or the Westernized, or the intelligentsia, is to overlook and oversimplify the particular outlook and role of this group.

Political power need not, of course, rest in the holding of office, for offices can often be controlled from outside. But it is difficult to discover the extent of such outside control by examining legislation to see if specific pieces reflect the viewpoint of a controlling group; in practice, one cannot separate the pressures of the business community from the inherently sympathetic attitudes toward business of those directly responsible for formulating policy.

One can point to specific pieces of legislation in West Bengal in which the government was sensitive to the rights of private property: the Estates Acquisition Act, which confiscated *zamindari* landholdings in the state, was careful to exclude urban property and to provide substantial compensation; the Eviction Bill (later renamed the Refugee Rehabilitation Bill) was clearly aimed at protecting property owners against squatting refugees. One can also point to specific aid in industrial rela-

[4] For a more detailed discussion of political personnel in West Bengal politics, see Myron Weiner, "Changing Patterns of Political Leadership in West Bengal," *Pacific Affairs,* XXXII (September, 1959).

tions given by the ministry of labor in West Bengal to the business community, such as the efforts of the ministry to avoid strikes and the quick application of arbitration proceedings so that, pending a government settlement of the dispute, strikes are illegal. One can cite instances in which law enforcement agencies were reluctant to prosecute for illegal hoarding of food or for the misuse of government permits to run price-controlled food shops. All these signs indicate that the state government is sympathetic to the business community.

Indeed, while businessmen are critical of policies in New Delhi, they speak generously of B. C. Roy, the chief minister of West Bengal, and of some of his associates in government and in the Congress party. Both Bengali and non-Bengali business communities have the ear of the chief minister. The chief minister constantly exhorts Bengalis to enter business activities and has personally encouraged many former *zamindar*'s to invest earnings in business. B. C. Roy publicly criticized the second five-year plan for emphasizing big industry and for neglecting consumer goods and small-scale industries—a point of view which endeared him to the small-business Bengalis and to those politicians who saw unemployment as a growing political liability. The government has also gone to some effort to replace Punjabi-owned and -operated taxis with taxis owned and operated by Bengali refugees by giving more licenses to refugees from East Bengal and granting new permits only to small taxis. The government's decision to nationalize buses (largely Punjabi-owned) also provided additional employment for Bengalis.

If the West Bengal government appears to be more sensitive to the needs of the business community than other state governments, the reverse is also true—the business community of West Bengal tends to give more support to the state government than business communities elsewhere. This support takes two forms. It involves direct financial support for the Congress party organization and for Congress candidates to the state legislative assembly and to Parliament. The Representation of the Peoples Act limits candidates for the legislative assembly to an expenditure of Rs. 5,000 (about $1,000), and candidates for Parliament to Rs. 25,000 (about $5,000). Since there are 221 members of the legislative assembly (M.L.A.'s), it is possible that as much as Rs. 1,105,000 is spent by Congress candidates for the state assembly and another Rs. 1,475,000 for the 59 parliamentary seats from West Bengal. Actually, since few candidates stay within the legal limit, it is quite likely that expenditures during an election year would be two or three times this amount. During a non-election year, the *pradesh* (state) Congress committee office in

Calcutta has an annual budget of Rs. 250,000–300,000, of which Rs. 73,000 is raised from dues and the remainder from donations. The district Congress committees also have substantial yearly budgets. However, neither the Congress party nor the other political parties publish a budget or any information concerning other sources of income.[5]

Apart from direct contributions to the party or to party candidates, the business community supports Congress by contributing to the many emergency funds created by the party and by government officials to meet famines, floods, and other natural disasters. The Congress party organization in Bengal, as elsewhere in India, has been in part a famine-relief organization. Emergency relief activities are generally not conducted by the party organization directly, but rather by eminent Congress leaders acting as individuals on special relief committees created on an *ad hoc* basis. Natural catastrophes have often been a political asset to the Congress party. In 1957, for example, a pre-election flood and famine in Midnapore district (an opposition stronghold) occasioned a rapid dispersal of funds, medical aid, food, and clothing by both the government and business-financed, Congress-dominated relief committees. The result was a considerable increase in the Congress vote in the district.

The Congress party of West Bengal is largely built on rural votes and business finances.[6] With these two elements on its side, it has been possible for the Congress party to lose Calcutta and the urban vote in general without losing power. It has also permitted the state government to resist many of the demands made upon it by organized urban groups.

[5] In March, 1957, the Calcutta High Court approved an application of the Indian Iron and Steel Company, Ltd., a Martin Burns enterprise, to change its Memorandum of Association to allow it to divert some of its funds to political donations. Justice P. B. Mukherjee, who ruled on the request, urged legislative enactments prohibiting such contributions or requiring the company to list such contributions on its annual balance sheet; but in spite of an initial flurry in Parliament, no such legislation was passed. The only public information concerning the size of any individual businessman's contribution to the Congress party is a statement by Mundhra, a leading Marwari businessman in Calcutta who had been accused of successfully influencing officials of the Life Insurance Corporation to buy shares of his enterprises at higher-than-market prices. Mundhra said that he had contributed Rs. 100,000 to the Congress party chest and that other businessmen had donated even more.

[6] Considerations of the needs of the economy may have led B. C. Roy to criticize the second five-year plan for its emphasis on "the development of heavy industries and the urban areas to the neglect of consumer goods industries and the rural areas," but it is also a fact that these last two sectors are sources of Congress strength in West Bengal.

The Political Organization of Indian Business

The political role played by business in India—whether at the state or national level—is inextricably tied up with the development and role of organized business associations. Business associations in India date back to the early nineteenth century—as early as 1801—when British indigo planters created their own associations.[7] The first major and lasting business association was a chamber of commerce founded in Calcutta in 1834—one year after the East India Company severed its trade connections with India in order to devote its entire energies to the task of governing. The ending of the monopoly of the East India Company in 1823, when trade was opened to British commercial interests, and the severance in 1833 of the company's trading connections opened India's doors to the diversification of British commercial interests in India and gave rise to the need for organized effort on the part of those interests. It was thus in the European-created centers of European commercial activities—Bombay, Madras, and Calcutta—that the first European chambers were created. Some Indians have argued that the Calcutta chamber symbolically marked the transition of economic power from one British organization to another. But while the East India Company constituted the government, the newly created chambers had to operate as interest groups—powerful ones no doubt—seeking to influence government policy in competition with other interests.

Toward the latter part of the nineteenth century and early in the twentieth century, organizations of Indian businessmen developed. Of these, there have been and continue to be five types:

1. *Trade and industrial organizations.* The association of indigo planters of Bihar was followed by other British organizations in specific trades and industries. In 1830 several European traders and merchants organized the Calcutta Traders Association. Toward the latter part of the nineteenth century, with the promotion of the tea, jute, and coal industries by Europeans in India, new trade associations developed in each of these fields. When Indian business expanded into the field of cotton textile manu-

---

[7]A good account of British chambers can be found in Geoffrey W. Tyson, *The Bengal Chamber of Commerce and Industry, 1853–1953: A Centenary Survey* (Calcutta: Bengal Chamber of Commerce and Industry, 1952). Tyson quotes with approval a statement by the French scholar André Siegfried, which might very well describe the current view of English businessmen in independent India. "In life in general and in political life in particular the Englishman acts like an old-time sailor; he manoeuvres in an unstable environment, and he accepts that instability as a fact which cannot change and which it would be folly to resent" (p. 5).

facturers, European and Indian businessmen joined together in 1918 to form, among others, the Bombay Millowners' Association.

Since Indians were active in trade and banking rather than in industry before the First World War, it is not surprising that most of the early Indian associations were in these fields. Associations of piece-goods merchants, grain merchants, sugar merchants, and spice merchants were founded in the latter part of the nineteenth and early twentieth centuries. But not until after the First World War, when Indian interests expanded into industry on a substantial basis, did Indian industrial associations enter the scene. In the 1920's and 1930's associations were formed of jute mill owners, steamship owners, colliery owners, glass manufacturers, soap makers, paper mill owners, and chemical manufacturers. The Second World War gave another spurt to industry, which was accompanied by the growth of associations in the fields of engineering, and the manufacture of paint, fans, woolens, textiles, cycles, plywood, non-ferrous metals, tin cans, sheet containers, lanterns, and automobiles. Many of the associations paralleled similar associations of European businessmen.

2. *Regional organizations.* In the latter part of the nineteenth century, there emerged associations representing a number of diverse trades and industries in a given region, usually a city or province.[8] As we have noted, such chambers were organized by the British in the port towns of Calcutta, Madras, and Bombay. The first such Indian chamber was established at Cocanada in South India in 1885, the year in which the Indian National Congress was formed.[9] Two years later, the Bengal National Chamber of Commerce was organized with thirty-five members in Calcutta "to aid and stimulate the development of commercial enterprise in Bengal and to protect the interests of all persons trading therein; to promote unanimity of practice among members of the commercial community; to represent their views and requirements to authorities; to arbitrate when occasion arises between parties willing to submit their differences to the decision of the association; and generally · to do all such things as may be conducive to the interests of the commercial classes of Bengal." The articles of association of the chamber specified that no

[8] Histories of regional chambers can be found in the following: L. R. Das Gupta, *Indian Chambers of Commerce and Commercial Associations* (Calcutta: Eastern Chamber of Commerce, 1946)—in addition to a brief history of Indian chambers, this booklet contains a list of chambers represented on public and semipublic bodies, including provincial legislatures; and *Fifty Years, 1907–1957* (Bombay: Indian Merchants Chamber, 1958). The line between regional associations and community associations is a difficult one to draw. Some of the regional associations encompass many different communities, but others are confined to a single religious or ethnic group.

[9] This body still exists as the Godavari Chamber of Commerce.

firm could be a member unless at least one-half of the directors were Indians and not less than one-half of the capital was owned by Indians.

The close ties between the first regional chambers and the nationalist movement are evidenced by two facts: first, prominent Congress leaders were elected honorary members of the Bengal National Chamber by its first executive committee; and second, from 1905 on, business groups sponsored an annual Indian Industrial Conference to be held simultaneously with the Indian National Congress meeting. The organized Indian business and commercial community gave its blessings to the *swadeshi* movement, which urged the boycott of foreign manufacturers and the development of indigenous industry. The *swadeshi* movement thus merged the economic discontent of the business community with the political discontent of the rising middle classes.

After the Bengal National Chamber was formed, two other important regional chambers developed: the Indian Merchants Chamber of Bombay (1907) and the Southern India Chamber of Commerce (1909).

3. *Community associations.* Both the trade associations and the chambers of commerce are similar in principles of organization to their counterparts in the West. That business should organize along lines of industry, trade, and region is not unusual and is not peculiar to India. What is peculiar to India, and to other plural societies, is the third pattern of organization—the organization of industrial and commercial interests along "community" lines, that is, in accordance with the linguistic, cultural, or religious groups to which the members belong. To understand why such community organizations for businessmen have developed, one must keep three facts in mind. First, loyalties to kinsmen, village, caste, and religious sect or community are important in Indian social organization. Large-scale territorial loyalties, or loyalties to specific economic interests, are more recent phenomena, which sometimes, but not always, compete with these other more particularistic loyalties. Second, the response to the Western commercial impact was partly in terms of these existing communities. To a large extent the modern commercial classes, and later the industrial classes, grew out of communities that had historically been involved in commerce as communities.[10] Particular communities in western India, for example, were associated with the trade from

[10]A complete history of the origins and developments of entrepreneurial communities in India has yet to be written, but there are several preliminary and very useful accounts. The two most active writers in this area are Helen Lamb and D. R. Gadgil. See, for example, these articles by Helen Lamb: "The Development of Modern Business Communities in India," *Labor, Management and Economic Growth: Proceedings of a Conference on Human Resources and Labor Relations in Underdeveloped Coun-*

across the Arabian Sea and with the caravan routes from the sea to the Gangetic valley. Marwaris (from Marwar [Jodhpur] State in Rajasthan), Jains (members of a heterodox offshoot from Hinduism), Parsis (Zoroastrian refugees from Persia), and Gujaratis in general were among the most active in commercial and industrial life. In other areas, traditional moneylending and trading castes adapted themselves to new forms of commercial and industrial activities. In the south, for example, the *chettiar*'s became a powerful commercial class.

As some of these communities scattered throughout India, they formed chambers of commerce to represent their interests. There were ties of sentiment which bound these communities together, and their interests sometimes conflicted with those of indigenous capital. In the linguistic states-reorganization controversy, for example, those business communities whose economic activities cut across linguistic lines were unsympathetic to states reorganization, while those whose interests coincided with linguistic divisions often favored reorganization.

To illustrate the wide variety of community business associations one finds, we might look briefly at the major chambers in West Bengal. West Bengal has four major Indian chambers and one, the Bengal Chamber of Commerce, composed primarily of Europeans. As we have indicated, the Bengal National Chamber was started by Bengali businessmen in 1887 as a commercial counterpart of the Indian National Congress. Although this chamber is open to all, there is a preponderance of Bengalis among its members. Since relatively few Bengalis took to business activity in comparison with those entering civil service, medicine, and law, and because a great number of non-Bengalis are involved in commercial and industrial activities in Bengal, the political influence of the chamber has never been very great.[11]

---

tries, ed. R. L. Aronson and J. P. Windmiller (Ithaca, N.Y.: Cornell University, Institute of International Industrial and Labor Relations, 1954); "The Indian Business Communities and the Evolution of an Industrialist Class," *Pacific Affairs,* XXVIII (June, 1955); "The Indian Merchant," *Traditional India: Structure and Change,* ed. Milton Singer (Philadelphia: American Folklore Society, 1959), pp. 25–34; and "Business Organization and Leadership in India Today," in *Leadership and Political Institutions in India,* ed. Richard L. Park and Irene Tinker (Princeton, N.J.; Princeton University Press, 1959). D. R. Gadgil, who is now engaged in a larger study of entrepreneurial communities in India, has published two preliminary reports: "Origins of the Modern Indian Business Class" (New York: Institute of Pacific Relations, 1959), and "Notes on the Rise of the Business Communities in India" (New York: Institute of Pacific Relations, 1951). Max Weber's views can be found in his *The Religion of India: The Sociology of Hinduism and Buddhism* (Glencoe, Ill.: Free Press, 1958).

[11] It is generally argued that the Permanent Settlement in Bengal (which fixed payments by proprietors to government irrepective of rising land values) encouraged

In 1900 the Marwaris in Bengal created an association of their own called the Marwari Chamber of Commerce (later renamed Bharat Chamber). Marwaris had settled in Bengal as early as the sixteenth century, and during the nineteenth century emerged as the most important trading community. The community was particularly active in the textile trade; and Burrabazar in Calcutta was the principal market in eastern India. The new organization claimed that it was open to all communities in the piece-goods trade of eastern India. Nonetheless, the organization has always been predominantly Marwari.[12]

In 1950, the membership of the Bharat Chamber was 632. The composition of the membership has changed somewhat from what it was in 1900, when it was created mainly as an association of piece-goods merchants. Some 30 per cent of the association's membership is now in industry (jute, textiles, chemicals, engineering, and shipping), another 30–35 per cent are in the import-export business, and the remainder are in distributive trades (for example, wholesale merchants and suppliers to government). Textile distribution is still, however, a major interest of the association. Small- and medium-scale industries are not particularly

---

investment in land rather than business, so that it was largely non-Bengalis, especially Marwaris, who entered commerce and industry in Bengal. Today there are relatively few large Bengali-owned businesses; Bengalis tend to be active in the smaller firms, and consequently the Bengal National Chamber of Commerce is largely an association of Bengali small businesses. The chamber now has fourteen hundred members, largely owners of rice mills, dealers in fertilizers, and owners of other small industries.

[12]After Independence, the chamber, "with a view to removing any possible misunderstanding," changed its name to the Bharat Chamber of Commerce. K. N. Katju, who was then governor of West Bengal, made the following remarks, which typify much of the current reinterpretation of India's past, before the annual general meeting of the chamber in 1949: "Our ancient caste system, though popularly supposed to be based on birth, was in fact founded upon avocations in life and naturally as professions tended to become hereditary, those who were engaged in business and industry, generation after generation for centuries acquired a special aptitude for such a calling. Just as the Brahmins were regarded as learned people proficient in literature, religious and secular, and philosophy and sciences because of their association with learning and teaching for thousands of years, similarly the great Vaisya Community became traders and bankers and industrialists because they had been pursuing that calling for tens of centuries. The caste system, however, was never restrictive and in recent times the ancient principle that the entire system was originally based not on birth but on profession is becoming increasingly stronger and it is a matter for gratification that people of all communities and all castes are taking to business and becoming successful businessmen if they possess the necessary experience and foresight and aptitude for it. There was, therefore, nothing objectionable in your old name. Nevertheless, I am glad that you with the concurrence of the Central as well as the Provincial Government, changed it" (*Golden Jubilee Souvenir, 1900–1950* [Calcutta: Bharat Chamber of Commerce, 1954]).

well represented in the Bharat Chamber as they are in the Bengal National Chamber.

A third major chamber—and now clearly the largest of the Indian chambers in West Bengal—is the Indian Chamber of Commerce, founded in 1926. Although the first president of the Indian Chamber was a Marwari, G. D. Birla, the chamber was organized to bring together businessmen of all communities, particularly those with an all-India interest. Today the chamber has 340 members, 21 of whom are trade or industrial associations, mostly of an all-India character, which represent sugar, chemicals, engineering, non-ferrous metals, paper, paint, automobiles, and cycles. Of the various Indian chambers in West Bengal, the Indian Chamber is probably the least community-centered. While Parsis and Marwaris are the most active of its members, other communities are also represented. If there is a bias, it is more toward big industry than toward any community. The chamber is most outspoken on behalf of the large industrial firms and managing agencies.

The fourth and newest chamber in Bengal is the Muslim Chamber of Commerce. It was founded in 1932 as an organization of Muslim businessmen, mostly traders. Like the Marwari Chamber, the Muslim Chamber changed its name after Independence to avoid the communal overtones associated with its name; it is now called the Oriental Chamber of Commerce. Adamjee and Ispahani, the two major founders of the chamber, were Muslim League supporters and financiers. Before Partition, the chamber had some three hundred members, many of whom, including its two leading spokesmen, left for Pakistan. Most of its present members are in export-import businesses.

4. *"Peak" associations.* There are three major national federations of Indian business chambers, of which the Federation of Indian Chambers of Commerce and Industry (FICCI) is paramount. It is made up of 123 chambers of commerce and trade and industrial associations throughout the country.[13] At least three of its constituent members are themselves substantial organizations with memberships in the thousands: the Indian Merchants Chamber of Bombay, with a membership of 2,716 (of which 123 are themselves associations); the Indian Chamber of Commerce in Calcutta, made up of 21 industrial and trade associations; and the Southern India Chamber of Commerce, in Madras, comprising 41 district

[13] The FICCI has published an official history, which contains a useful description of the early history of commercial organizations as well as a description of the development of the federation (Federation of Indian Chambers of Commerce and Industry, *Silver Jubilee Souvenir, 1927–51* [New Delhi: FICCI, 1952]).

chambers and associations. Some idea of the magnitude of commercial and industrial organizations in India can be obtained from the fact that the 123 chambers which make up the FICCI have a total of 32,702 members. Many of these member-chambers are themselves federations of associations, so that there are more than 32,702 individual members.

European business is largely brought together by the Associated Chambers of Commerce, with affiliated branches in Bombay, Madras, and Calcutta. The Bengal Chamber is the largest and dominant affiliate of the Associated Chambers. Its president is simultaneously the president of the national body, while the vice-presidents of the Associated Chambers are from the Bombay and Madras chambers. Connected with the national organization is the Central Commercial Organization, which was started by the Associated Chambers as its lobby for dealing with the New Delhi government after Independence. The Central Commercial Organization has about five hundred members.

We have already referred to the small All-India Manufacturers Organization, which was started in 1941 by a South Indian engineer concerned with giving voice to the smaller industrialists in India. The AIMO has its head office in Delhi, with branches in Bombay and Calcutta. It has a national membership of 2,250 individual enterprises.

5. *Employer associations.* Associated with the national "peak" organizations are two major employer groups that are concerned primarily with matters of industrial relations. The All-India Organization of Industrial Employers is an Indian group associated with the FICCI, which has offices in the same building and employs the same secretary. The other, the Employers Federation of India, was originally exclusively European. While it now includes Indian members (as do most other predominantly European organizations today), it is still heavily occidental.

Organized Business in the Nationalist Era

Though business elements have generally supported nationalist movements in Asia and Africa, control of those movements has not been in the hands of nationalist leaders. The great figures of India's nationalist movement from 1885 to 1947 were almost never men of commercial or industrial backgrounds; they were men of landed wealth or from the professions of law, journalism, medicine, education, or administration. The men who financed the Indian National Congress—men like Jamnalal Bajaj and G. D. Birla—had a negligible influence on the basic policies of the movement.[14] Only rarely does one find a man like the late Nalini Ranjan Sarkar in Bengal, who successfully combined work in party politics and business.

Indian business organizations actively sought to influence government policy from the very beginning. They demanded higher tariffs to protect infant industries and to encourage the creation of new industries, called for more credit facilities, lower taxes, a more satisfactory sterling-rupee exchange rate, and in general urged the creation of conditions that would facilitate the growth of internal industry. The Indian chambers demanded and received representation on government bodies. The FICCI, for example, was represented on the Central Banking Enquiry Committee, the International Labour Conference, the Central Tea Board, the Industries Conferences, the Export Advisory Council, and many more government bodies. Each of the various local chambers also obtained representation on provincial government bodies.

But although the chambers did receive some recognition from the British government and occasionally did affect government policy, on the whole the Indian chambers remained dissatisfied, and increasingly turned their attention toward the nationalist movement in the hope that an independent India would adopt policies more sympathetic to the growth of the Indian economy in general and Indian business in particular. The Indian chambers were thus active supporters of the Indian National Congress. Prominent Congress leaders were made honorary members of the Bengal National Chamber of Commerce, including the famous Surendranath Banerjea. Speeches of business leaders redounded with bitter denunciations not only of specific British policies but of British rule itself.[15] The FICCI's representatives to the Round Table Con-

[14] Both men have described at some length their associations with the nationalist movement and more particularly with Gandhi. See G. D. Birla, *In the Shadow of the Mahatma* (Bombay: Orient Longmans, Ltd., 1953), and *To a Gandhian Capitalist: Correspondence between Mahatma Gandhi and Jamnalal Bajaj and Members of His Family,* ed. Kaka Kalelkar (Bombay: Hind Kitabs, Ltd., 1951).

[15] The tone of these speeches is illustrated by the comments of Debi Prasad Kaitan, president of the Indian Chamber of Commerce, in his annual address to the chamber in February, 1928: "1927 is a momentous year in the realm of finance—but not for India. A study of the tendencies and events of Indian trade and finance in the past year and their underlying causes and inner forces in comparison with the tendencies and events of international trade and finance and their underlying motifs will form the most poignant commentary on the painful fact that is, day in and day out, rubbed into us—the fact, namely, that India is only a subordinate branch of the British administration; that we can have no rights apart from what suits British interests, no prerogatives except when graciously tolerated by the benign secretary of state; that in a word, we are but hewers of wood and drawers of water in the much-vaunted

ferences in London were instructed to follow the guidance of Mahatma Gandhi. Throughout the 1930's and 1940's, the chamber issued statements criticizing the government for failing to accept the proposals of the Indian National Congress. When Churchill declared that manufacturing and financial interests were behind the Congress, G. L. Mehta, then president of the FICCI, proudly said that "they were an integral part of the national movement and were fully in accord with the essentials of the Congress demand for freedom and transfer of power.[16] As far as is known, however, the chambers themselves made no direct financial contributions to Congress, although many chamber leaders, as individuals, did participate in and finance the organization. Most of these individuals were followers and leaders of the nationalist movement. There was one notable exception in Bengal, N. R. Sarkar.[17]

Indian business, in its representation before both the Congress and the British, was not interested in pressing for a laissez faire policy. On the contrary, Indian business was eager for greater government participation in the economy. They felt that Indian economic policy was being guided more by interests in London and Lancashire than by the needs of the Indian economy or Indian business. Labor legislation, too, they felt, was

British Commonwealth of Nations." Kaitan also added that "the interests of India are to us, who are connected with Indian business, the sole considerations; the interests of India are, so it seems to me, to the Government of India a subsidiary consideration, as the Secretary of State and through him the powerful British commercial interests have always a strong say" (Indian Chamber of Commerce, *Annual Report of the Committee for the Year 1927*, pp. xxxix and xlv). The speech of Faizulla Gangjee as president in 1929 is even stronger: "1928 is dead and there need be no regret that it is dead. It has been an extraordinarily arduous year for all interests concerned, arduous alike for the aggressor and the aggrieved. If I may refer to the Indian mercantile community as the aggrieved, surely the aggressors are the Government, because there has been unfortunately for us not one gesture of policy or action on the part of the Government, which could show anything but callous indifferences to the interests which we represent" (Indian Chamber of Commerce, *Annual Report of the Committee for the Year 1928*). It is an interesting comment on British respect for civil liberties that such speeches were tolerated.

[16] Federation of Indian Chambers of Commerce and Industry, *op. cit.*, p. 120.

[17] A leading industrialist, president of the Hindustan Cooperative Insurance Company, president of the Bengal National Chamber of Commerce from 1931 to 1935, and president of the FICCI in 1934, Sarkar worked closely with C. R. Das in building the Swaraj party. Sarkar served Das not only as his party secretary and chief whip, but as party organizer and financier. In 1935 Sarkar became mayor of Calcutta. In 1937 he temporarily broke with Congress to become the first finance minister of Bengal in Fazl-ul-Haq's coalition ministry. But at the beginning of the war, Sarkar returned to Congress. Almost immediately after Independence, in January, 1948, he was made finance minister in B. C. Roy's cabinet, and continued his work not only as a policy-maker in the state government (he was acting chief minister in B. C. Roy's absence), but as party organizer and financier for Congress.

guided by Lancashire's desire to raise the costs of production in India in order to minimize competition; and existing tariffs and duties were believed to be attempts to protect British interests.

The socialist statements made by the Congress leadership in the 1930's did not alarm the business community. Talk of class struggle by the Congress Socialist group was overshadowed by Gandhi's notion of trusteeship, i.e., that business was a trustee of the nation's wealth to be used for the good of all, and therefore need not be confiscated by the public. Then too, Socialist emphasis on high tariffs and the role of the state in economic development, the improvement of transport and communications, the development of the rural sector (and rural markets), were all appealing. As early as 1933, the Indian Chamber of Commerce issued a lengthy report to the government of Bengal recommending ways in which the government might develop the province. Birla frequently criticized Gandhi's "antiquarian" anti-industrial outlook, but nonetheless was attracted to his political program and deeply moved by his religious outlook. Bajaj, like many other Marwaris, often seemed more interested in Gandhi's program of cow protection than in his long-range program for the country's economic growth. In any event, so long as Congress was not in itself formulating policy, hardheaded businessmen worried little about the vague socialist biases of the movement. Then too, on the provincial level the socialist biases were less apparent.

Policies pursued by Congress ministries from 1937 to 1939 hardly alarmed the business community. The powers of the provincial ministries granted by the Act of 1935 were limited. Socialist opposition to taking office under the new constitution resulted in a voluntary self-denial of public office by many of the leftists inside Congress. Then too, those in government were eager to avoid policies that would divide Congress, accentuate class struggle, and dry up the financial resources of the party. And finally, many of the provincial governments were controlled by rural interests who were themselves concerned with protecting the rights of private property.

Before India achieved independence, organized business had to deal with two conflicting institutions, the British government and the Indian National Congress. The British government pursued policies which to Indian businessmen seemed biased in favor of their competitors; on the other hand, the British government in India welcomed the participation of Indian business in a host of consultative bodies.[18] Apart from the

[18] Indian business complaints against the British were summed up by Gurusharal Lall in his presidential address before the FICCI in 1947. "Looking to the achieve-

nationalist loyalties that drew Indian businessmen to the Congress, the Congress program of *swadeshi* and its general promise of a regime concerned with the country's economic growth were attractive to them, and served to counterbalance talk of socialism, handicrafts, and cottage industries. Furthermore, the limited experience which business had with the Congress regimes between 1937 to 1939 gave them no reason to be apprehensive about what was to come.

On the eve of Independence, G. D. Birla and other businessmen in the Bombay region proposed a plan for economic growth to be pursued by the new government.[19] The principle of planning by government was clearly accepted. G. D. Birla, speaking before the annual conference of the FICCI in 1947, sounded like a socialist when he said: "It may be a harsh thing to say, but I would not be doing my duty if I did not tell clearly and candidly our Government what the Indian mercantile community thought of the achievements of the new Interim Government. There is no doubt there is a lot of planning. But we are still planning to plan, we are not planning to act. I feel the time has come when planning and action should go together. The time has come when we should talk less of planning and more of action." [20]

Organized Business under Congress Raj

While the new regime was thoroughly committed to the notion that the state had to play a positive role in the country's economic development,

---

ment of the Indian private enterprise during the British administration of this country for over 150 years, it must be admitted that in spite of Government's policy of laissez faire, in spite of their policy of Imperial Preference, in spite of currency manipulations and in spite of administrative discriminations against indigenous private enterprise, it has served the country well in not only improving the economic condition of the masses but in preventing, for generations, a continuous drain of the country's material resources in money and in kind to foreign countries" (*Proceedings of the Twentieth Annual Meeting, Federation of Indian Chambers of Commerce and Industry*, III [1947], 10).

[19] *A Brief Memorandum Outlining a Plan of Economic Development for India*, by Sir Purshotamdas Thakurdas, J. R. D. Tata, G. D. Birla, Sir Ardeshir Dalal, Sir Shri Ram, Kasturbhai Lalbhai, A. D. Shroff, and John Mattai. Part I was published in January, 1944, and Part II (by the same authors with the exception of Sir Ardeshir Dalal, who had joined the government) in December, 1944. Part I focuses on problems of increasing production, and Part II deals with questions of distribution. A summary of the Bombay Plan and comparisons with other pre-Independence development plans can be found in D. S. Nag, *A Study of Economic Plans for India* (Bombay: Hind Kitabs, Ltd., 1949).

[20] *Proceedings of the Twentieth Annual Meeting, Federation of Indian Chambers of Commerce and Industry*, p. 41.

and indeed, to the belief that in the absence of an active government there would be stagnation, the requirements of sheer survival dominated the thinking and activities of the government for the first few years after Independence. Partition of the subcontinent involved an enormous adjustment of government finances, administration, and the military apparatus. The threat of war between Pakistan and India led the government to give increased attention to problems of military development. The need to absorb the princely states, the attempt by the Hyderabad government to establish itself as an autonomous government, and the threat of war in Kashmir turned the government's attention to questions of national survival as a political entity. In so far as attention was given to economic problems, rehabilitation and adjustment necessarily received more attention than programs of growth and long-term planning. Millions of Hindu and Sikh refugees trekked across the borders into West Bengal and the Punjab and squatted in the streets of Delhi and Calcutta. The partition of natural trading units, accompanied by the breakdown in trade relations between India and Pakistan, meant that the new nations had to develop alternative markets for their raw materials and new sources of raw materials for their industries.

There could have been little doubt, however, that the Nehru government would turn as quickly as possible to the longer-range problems of planning for economic growth. For at least three reasons, the government was committed to pursuing such a policy. On ideological grounds, nationalist leaders saw economic growth as necessary to their program of modernizing independent India; they could not conceive that any agency other than the state would provide the initiative. Their experience under a positive, if somewhat authoritarian, colonial government provided them with the institutional environment for such a conception, and the training of many nationalist leaders in Fabian Socialist and Marxist ideas provided them with the ideological justification. Secondly, the demands for greater development that were made by nationalist trade unions, peasant organizations, and student and voluntary associations presented a political imperative to the government; stagnation was therefore politically intolerable. And finally, the new government viewed economic growth as a necessary prerequisite for minimizing particularistic loyalties and "fissiparous" tendencies, which threatened to Balkanize the subcontinent. Only as there was economic growth, they reasoned, would loyalties to caste, religion, and linguistic-cultural regions be replaced by more material ties to economic interests. Then too, the people would give a greater degree of loyalty and support to the national government as they realized that a larger unit of territory under a single government would in fact satisfy their demands.

While the business community approved the development programs that emerged with the five-year plans in general, it had much to complain about regarding specifics. The first five-year plan was criticized at chamber meetings for what industrialists felt to be inadequate provisions for industrial expansion, for its tightening and extension of controls, and for the high level of taxation on the private sector. The Industrial (Development and Regulation) Act was attacked as a source of rigorous regimentation. Also subjected to business attack were the "burdens" imposed by labor legislation, the government's willingness to support inefficient cottage industries but failure to give adequate assistance to small-scale enterprises, the decision to nationalize the Imperial Bank and life insurance, the lack of uniformity in sales taxes levied by state governments, the government's decision to amend the constitution to make compensation for confiscated property non-justiciable, the low (by business standards) government investment in transportation and communication, the decision to set up a state trading corporation to handle certain commodities in foreign and internal trade, and the many rules and regulations associated with the undertaking of new enterprises. When the second five-year plan was inaugurated, the chambers further criticized the government for modifying the 1948 Industrial Policy Resolution and incorporating additional spheres of the economy into the public sector. The new plan was also criticized for being too large, and the taxes it required too high. In the early stages of the third five-year plan, the FICCI criticized the central government for failing to pursue adequate measures to remedy the serious shortages in transport, power, and coal.

In spite of these criticisms the business community in general continued to support the Congress government. It felt that the government had successfully maintained law and order and had provided an atmosphere for economic growth in which the private sector was, in fact, expanding and profits were rising. Privately, the business community also felt that the socialist bark of government was louder than its bite, and that at certain points critical to individual businesses the government did not yield to ideology. And finally, business felt that as long as the most serious opposition to Congress was from the left, it was best to continue to support the present government.

Techniques and Targets of Organized Business

Both British and Indian business organizations had, before Independence, direct legal access to the government through two channels: representation in consultative bodies and representation in legislative assemblies. The system of appointed representation from business chambers to the state legislatures and to the central legislative assembly in New Delhi disappeared with the new constitution, although many of the chambers had requested that the system continue. With Independence, however, the system of business representation on government consultative bodies did continue. This practice was itself, as were so many other policies pursued by the British in India, the extension of a principle which the British government applied at home. The port trusts, tariff commissions, railway boards, and telephone boards, among countless others, included representatives of the business chambers. In addition, the chambers were—and are still—given the opportunity to present their points of view before government (formerly royal) commissions, such as the Taxation Enquiry Commission, the Official Language Commission, and the Rural Credit Enquiry Commission.

But direct personal contact of an informal sort is the most frequent means by which businessmen have access to government officials. The extent of contacts between the government and the business community can be judged by looking at the contacts between government and the Bengal National Chamber of Commerce in two representative years, 1954 and 1955. The annual reports of the chamber for these two years report conferences between officials of the chamber and the chairman of the Central Board of Revenue (which handles taxation), the collector of customs of Calcutta, a member of the Railway Board, the general manager of the South Eastern Railway, the high commissioner for the United Kingdom in India, the minister in charge of refugee relief and rehabilitation in West Bengal, the deputy minister of co-operation, cottage, and small-scale industries, the chief controller of imports, the general manager of the Eastern Railway, and the chief minister of West Bengal. These were, it seems, years of low-level contacts, for the annual report of the previous year describes meetings with Prime Minister Nehru and the central finance minister, C. D. Deshmukh.

Many of these meetings were informal, but some contacts have been ritualized. Most chambers go to some effort to invite high government officials to attend their annual meetings or to meet with their executive boards. The FICCI invited the viceroy as its chief speaker every year;

and in the event of his unavailability, they asked the highest government official obtainable. Even when ties between Indian business and Indian nationalists were many, the FICCI preferred to have British government personnel address their annual meetings. Since 1947 the prime minister or members of his cabinet have delivered the opening address at FICCI annual conferences.

Direct correspondence between the chambers and government officials on specific issues is extensive. Most of the chambers forward to the government all resolutions passed by executive committees. Each year the major chambers publish annual reports, which often include (sometimes as a second volume) their entire correspondence with members of the government. An examination of this correspondence shows the number of points at which specific difficulties encountered by business are ameliorated through government, particularly through administrative action.

Lobbying, in the sense of attempting to influence members of Parliament or the state legislative assemblies, plays a part—but by American standards only a negligible part—of pressure group activities. The Central Commercial Organization, the lobby of the European Associated Chambers of Commerce, claims some success at influencing government policy, especially on such matters as "Indianization" of foreign concerns, reducing taxes on foreign personnel, and freeing from taxes employers' contributions to provident funds. However, the CCO works with cabinet members, ministers, and secretaries to ministries in New Delhi, and rarely at any lower levels of government. Although contact with M.P.'s increased in recent years, it is still largely limited to those times when the select committees are meeting and matters of interest to business are before Parliament.

So long as the business chambers can have only a marginal effect on basic government policies, they direct most of their attention to the amelioration of specific cases. Although individual businessmen manage to obtain licenses for imports, licenses to open businesses, and other assistance from local bureaucrats, much of the negotiation between individual businessmen and government is done through chambers, whose contacts are often better than those of individuals. Although the European chambers deal on the highest levels—in the center primarily with cabinet members, and on the state level only with the chief minister—the Indian chambers also work at lower levels of government and especially with administrators.

Businessmen in India, as elsewhere in the world, have an acute awareness of how the political system operates and what the points of greatest access are. Policy, they believe, is made on the very highest levels and rarely, if ever, reflects cumulative pressure from below. If they neither conduct public relations campaigns nor deal directly with legislators, it is because they recognize that neither the public nor members of legislative bodies have much influence on government policy and administration. There are various estimates as to how many M.P.'s, for example, are friendly to business—anywhere from one hundred up. But the Congress party whip requires that M.P.'s vote as they do, and while the M.P.'s may privately chaff at having to vote for a high tax budget, or for a wealth and expenditure tax, or for nationalization of a particular industry, they have little opportunity to express their viewpoint publicly.

Since they have no effective influence on lawmakers, Indian businessmen establish highly particularistic relationships with individual administrators, who are appealed to on the basis of blood relationship (when it exists), personal friendship, or most often, financial rewards. Mrs. Jhabvala, in her novel on Punjabi business life in New Delhi,[21] describes the attempts by a Punjabi businessman to persuade his son, a rising young administrator, to destroy the father's correspondence with the government since it might cast an unfavorable light upon his attempt to win an important government contract. But blood ties are generally less important than the established system of fees. There is often associated with each administrative act involving a client a non-legal fee for the performance of duties. Indian businessmen know that local administrators often have the power to deny, or at least delay, their requests for the enormous number of permits and licenses needed to operate a business. Bakshish[22]—the word given to the fee paid—has generally been recognized as the oil that makes the administrative machinery operate quickly. Indian businessmen do not consider these fees unjust unless the rates are exorbitantly high for the service rendered, or unless the businessman is denied the right to make payment by the administrator when others are obtaining similar services. European businessmen, unaccustomed to the procedure of paying administrators and often unfamiliar with the rate structure (or sometimes concerned with the fact that they are required to pay more than their Indian counterparts) will often use their Indian personnel to conduct these transactions.

The multiplication of government regulations is a bane to businessmen, not only because of the obvious annoyance, but because regulations

[21] R. Prawer Jhabvala, *The Nature of Passion* (London: G. Allen and Unwin, 1956).
[22] The word comes from the name of the paymaster in the Mogul army, the *bakhshi.*

effectively increase the costs of operation in both time and money. In addition, new regulations raise uncertainties as to administrative fees. Thus businessmen oppose new regulatory acts; but as the acts operate over the years, the fees are often stabilized and businessmen learn how to work through and around the regulations. Indeed, the bakshish system is not as disruptive as might at first appear. It lends to the administrative system discretion and flexibility (which admittedly are provided by other means in other systems) without which many businesses would find it difficult to function. Indeed, some businessmen have argued that if the government enforced all the regulations provided for in industrial relations acts, industrial regulations acts, import and export controls, and the like, economic growth would come to a grinding halt.

In specific instances it is difficult to say whether the demand of the businessman and the subsequent action of the administrator are illegal. Vast numbers of decisions fall into that nebulous realm, the "discretionary." And many administrative acts involve the allocation of a legislatively (or administratively) fixed number of licenses. In Calcutta, for example, as in many other cities, government-appointed shops—a fixed number in each locality—sell rice and grains at controlled government prices. Shopkeepers vie for the licenses; and while there are some general principles guiding the selection of shops (they must be of a certain size, in a convenient location for consumers, of good reputation, and so on), administrators have enormous discretion in their selection. Likewise, most Indian cities fix the number of licenses for buses, taxis, rickshaws, and other forms of transport; and since the demand for licenses is generally greater than the supply, those who make decisions have considerable power. Discretion is also involved in the allotment of import licenses; and although there are principles which in theory determine what shall and shall not be imported, in practice administrators have a great deal of flexibility. On grounds of general principle—often persuasion, and sometimes financial remuneration—the administrator may rule that a manufacturer may import certain raw materials or machine parts without which his factory could not operate, thereby avoiding a reduction in employment.[23]

The point is that in India, as in other societies, businessmen are more concerned with the distribution of wealth than with the distribution of power; they are concerned with the latter only when control of power is

[23] During the second five-year plan, India's imports far exceeded those anticipated by the planners; the result was a more serious foreign exchange shortage than anticipated.

essential to their survival as successful businessmen. Since it is on the administrative level that so many of the distributive questions are decided, it is on that level that businessmen in India tend to work.

Since 1947 access to administration has been complicated by the accession to power of the Congress party. Before Independence, the businessmen dealt directly with an administrative officer; in recent years, he has often had to work through a party official. The president of the *pradesh* (state) Congress committee and, at the local level, the president of the district Congress committee are important links to administrative personnel. In West Bengal, the party organization also makes use of its public relations officer, a post explicitly created to assist the public in making contacts with the government. This officer may attempt to find jobs and financial aid for "political sufferers," i.e., those who can prove that they were jailed by the British and are now in need of aid; and he may also help businessmen obtain permits of one kind or another.

Many Indian intellectuals complain that the standards of administration have declined since the British withdrew, by which they mean that administrators are more susceptible to payments, or to use the pejorative, bribes. It is probably true that businessmen now spend more money to get what they want from government than they did before 1947. But this is perhaps not because the British were better able to maintain standards than the Indians, but rather because (1) the number of regulations, permits, and controls has increased, thereby forcing an extension of the system of payments; and (2) the creation of representative government has injected another receiver into the transaction. Even before Independence, the Congress party was able to use its control of many municipal governments to strengthen party finances; "donations" to the nationalist movement were readily forthcoming from businessmen who received contracts from Congress-controlled municipal governments.

Certainly not all of what businessmen seek is obtained through this system of payments. The chambers also try to persuade policy-makers and administrators. Senior administrators and politicians pride themselves, as we have noted earlier, on their willingness to make decisions on the basis of national goals, needs, and resources without regard for family ties, personal financial rewards, caste relationships, and other factors that they consider irrelevant to the rational allocation of resources. The more interest groups move into the realm of the technical planners—the personnel of the Indian Statistical Institute, the Planning Board, the Panel of Economists, the Finance Ministry, the Central Statistical Organization—the more they must demonstrate that their demands are relevant to successful planning. It is in the operational ministries and agencies, both on the state and national levels, that discretion is more likely to operate.

The pressure groups most effective in influencing planners and policy-makers are those that can provide information and the results of research. The Bengal Chamber of Commerce (the European chamber) has always maintained a large research section, both for the benefit of its own members and to influence government. In recent years, all the Indian chambers have substantially enlarged their research divisions. Detailed critiques are published on the five-year plans, on the managing-agency system, and on specific pieces of legislation. Commenting on the political importance of research, a staff member of one influential chamber said: "The principal role of our chamber before 1947 was to criticize government. Now the chambers are more constructive. The Government of India wants specific statements, 'brass tacks,' as you would say. What do you want to change in government policy and why, they ask. As a result, we now have a greater need for research bodies. We gain a hearing from government and a consideration of our point of view if we present it in a logical and convincing way."

While it is difficult to ascertain how the business chambers have af-fected broad government policy, if indeed they have, one can point to many instances in which the chambers have persuaded the government to reverse or modify specific actions: the Commerce Department's deci-sion to enlarge the Tariff Board, the abolition of a sales tax on hand-loomed cloth, specific export duties such as those on oilseeds, the abolition of the capital gains tax, and a host of other policies that affect substantial numbers of businesses.

Public Opinion and Business

Thus it is clear that Indian business might, for good reasons, avoid with-holding support from Congress and might even give it enthusiastic sup-port. Congress is, after all, not as threatening to business as its resolutions sound, and the alternatives to the present government are far more threat-ening. The attitudes of the public toward the business community further prevent any large-scale attempt to win support for a separate business viewpoint. The one major attempt to reach the educated public—a public relations campaign by the Forum for Free Enterprise—received a cool reception from business. Neither in public statements nor in the annual meetings of the chambers is the welfare state or socialism in general attacked. Only specific regulations and the restrictions that accompany planning are criticized. The reason for this caution lies in the prevalent attitudes toward business; the point of view of many educated Indians was cogently summed up by A. D. Gorwala, one of India's most distinguished civil servants:

> . . . With honourable exceptions, the picture they [businessmen] have presented to the public gaze during the war and after is unattractive in the extreme. Among their leaders today are to be found not a few who can best be described as the "blackmarketing princes of tax evasion." With their ill-gotten hoards, such men have acquired power over well-run businesses, using them solely for personal aggrandizement without any thought of public weal . . . . They render the collection of taxes a farce. Said a Finance Minister: "Half as much tax is evaded as is collected." Taking advantage of every loophole, they use their wealth to buy brains in legal and technical spheres and thus protect themselves from the enforcement of the laws. They set moreover a very bad example to the young who, seeing their success, are led to believe that in blatant aggression combined with the suppression of every honest impulse lies the path to success. Is it any wonder that so long as this class flourishes the rest of society and the instrument of organized society, its Government, look upon the business world with dislike, regard without concern the heaping of unjustified burdens upon it, and consider it desirable neither to consult it nor to listen to its views when put forward unasked.
>
> . . . Why should the honest citizen, who earns his bread by the sweat of his brow, hand over such small amounts as he is able to save to the industrialists, when so many concerns are managed with such little honesty that the profits, or at least the bulk of them, pass in devious ways into the managers' pockets while the shareholder is shown only leases or, at the utmost, gets a very meagre dividend. . . . The large emoluments industrialists so readily allow themselves and their senior personnel would scarcely seem to be in accord with the commonly accepted social objective toward the achievement of which they in conference expressed

so strongly a desire to help. They cannot have forgotten that one such objective is the reduction of substantial inequality. It merely does not help forward the trend to equalitarianism to fix emoluments out of all consonance with the conditions of the country. . . . Committees considering the failure to invest in private enterprise and industrialists cogitating over their sad lack of influence and fall in public esteem are likely to find it profitable to concentrate on all these factors before dilating on the grievances which ordinarily fill their minds.[24]

A study of "popular attitudes toward the private sector" was conducted in 1956 by the Indian Institute of Public Opinion.[25] The survey, made in West Bengal and Delhi, reports that the greatest hostility to the business community comes from individuals in service occupations (e.g., clerks) and professions, from students, and from unemployed and urban workers. Hostility was generally correlated with level of education, the illiterate being less hostile than university graduates. Antagonism to business was also greater in Calcutta and the district towns of West Bengal (46 and 48 per cent) than in the rural areas (38 per cent); the number of "don't knows" was also much higher in the rural areas (39 per cent) than in the urban centers (24 per cent in Calcutta and 22 per cent in the district towns).

Although Indian businessmen are accused of behaving like bazaar merchants, of carrying forward pre-industrial attitudes, and of being socially irresponsible—all of which accusations carry some element of truth—one finds it hard to account for the attitude of educated Indians toward business solely on the basis of this behavior, which can hardly be considered unique. Indian businessmen have probably been no more reprehensible and irresponsible than were the owners of sweatshops and

[24] Gorwala, "The Popular Attitude to Private Enterprise," *Statesman*, January 19, 1954, p. 4. For a brief but sensible critique of stereotyped images about Indian business behavior, see George B. Baldwin, *Industrial Growth in South India* (Glencoe, Ill.: Free Press, 1959). In assessing similar attitudes in France, Henry Ehrmann in his recent study of French business in politics writes: ". . . convinced that public opinion feels antagonistic towards it, French organized business despairs of altering existing attitudes by an open and frontal attack" (*Organized Business in France* [Princeton, N.J.: Princeton University Press, 1957], p. 207).

[25] *Monthly Public Opinion Surveys of the Indian Institute of Public Opinion*, I, Nos. 10, 11, and 12 (May, June, and July 1956). The survey is called "The Measurement of Attitudes to the Private and Public Sectors and the Socialistic Pattern of Society."

coal mines, the producers of patent medicines, and the union-busting businessmen only a few decades ago in the United States and Great Britain. In fact, government regulations compel Indian businessmen to be far more humane to their workers than were nineteenth-century English and American factory owners.

As Edward Shils has written, one difference between modern India and nineteenth-century America and Great Britain lies in the power of those classes that hold antibusiness attitudes.[26] Nineteenth-century intellectuals in the United States and Great Britain could match Gorwala's image of the "blackmarketing princes of tax evasion" with images of the pot-bellied robber barons; and many English bureaucrats and aristocrats shared with the intellectuals a contempt for the new men of wealth. But the gradual spilling-over of the established social classes into industrial activities, and of industrial activities into the bureaucracy, mitigated many of the complaints. In India, as in many other plural societies of Asia and Africa, there have thus far been few mitigating factors. There has, for example, been relatively little movement between Indian business classes and other occupations. The business communities have provided few recruits for the administrative services or for professional party work, and the high-caste rural gentry, which provides so many of the recruits for both politics and administration, has not, on the whole, entered business. There are occasional families with one son in business and another in politics or administration,[27] but among the larger industrialists one is more likely to find entire families in business.

Much of the antibusiness sentiment in India is associated with cultural antipathies. Many of the larger commercial and industrial activities in India are in the hands of entrepreneurs culturally alien to the region in which they conduct their activities; Tamil *chettiar*'s operate throughout South India; and Marwaris, Parsis, Gujaratis, and Jains from western India have businesses throughout the country. In Bengal one rarely hears criticism of Bengal businessmen, but a great deal against the Marwari. In Andhra the popular image of the businessman is a Tamil, and in

---

[26] Shils, "Intellectuals, Public Opinion and Economic Development," *World Politics,* X (January, 1958), 232–55.

[27] The comparatively sharp line separating business and bureaucracy may intensify antipathies, but it also mitigates large-scale corruption. The professional standards of bureaucrats are not often compromised by the corrupting demands of relatives; the bureaucrat will accept a bribe, but it is on a universalistic basis—he is likely to accept money from all who will pay, not simply cater to his kith and kin. Indian businessmen may chaff at the bureaucracy, but they have a much greater expectation of fair play from bureaucrats than one would have found, for instance, among Chinese businessmen in the pre-Communist era.

Maharashtra, a Gujarati. It is perhaps not a coincidence that in Gujarat, where capital is largely indigenous, there is little antibusiness sentiment, and businessmen have a sense of pride in their occupation.[28]

But if Indian businessmen refrain from public relations campaigns on behalf of free enterprise, it is not only because of attitudes prevalent in the public but also because of attitudes held by the businessmen themselves. Few Indian businessmen will argue that their wealth results from their individual initiative; and few will argue for the rights of private property on ethical grounds. In 1957, for example, the Government of India —following the recommendations of a British tax specialist—proposed the adoption of a wealth tax that included a tax on corporate wealth. The proposed tax was low, but nonetheless it had the character of a capital levy and could theoretically have exceeded an entrepreneur's annual profits. Business chambers throughout the country rallied to oppose the tax; resolutions were passed, deputations visited New Delhi, and chamber presidents testified before the select committee of Parliament appointed to examine the proposed legislation. But although chamber resolutions opposed the tax as a whole, businessmen privately conceded that the tax would be imposed and that their best strategy would be to seek modification in the bills, for example, reduction of the size of the levy, certain exemptions, and so on. In an incisive comparison of the attitude of Indian businessmen and American businessmen, a high representative of the Federation of Indian Chambers of Commerce and Industry said:

> No one objected to the wealth tax in principle. Everyone is aware of the great disparity of wealth in this country, but businessmen felt that wealth used for productive purposes should be excluded from the tax. The FICCI argued that no productive capital should be subject to a wealth tax. There was a great deal of protest, but no one was emotional, no one felt it so terrible, because no one looked upon the tax as unethical. In the West, with its concept of self-made men, this taking of property is viewed as unethical, but not so in India. Then too, everyone, including businessmen, accepts the idea of the state playing an active role in economic development. State development of roads, irrigation, and so on, has been accepted for centuries in India. The state has always played a large part in the economy. Com-

[28] Sardar Patel, the *doyen* of probusiness politicians, was a Gujarati.

pare the Indian acceptance of the government's role in the economy with the long struggle which took place on this question in the West. The only grounds on which business opposes any taxes is on the grounds that it discourages production or further investment, never on moral or ethical grounds as in the West, particularly the United States. Businessmen in India accept the idea that taxes are both to raise money for the exchequer and to equalize wealth. It was only on the ground that productive wealth should not be taxed that the wealth tax was opposed.[29]

This attitude toward wealth and how one obtains it is reinforced by a widespread corporate sense. Economic growth in India is seen in national, not personal, terms. Rural development, for example, is thought of in terms of village development, co-operatives, and joint farming, and less often in terms of the individual agriculturalist. The expansion of a public corporation is praised, but the meteoric rise of a private entrepreneur is likely to be viewed with suspicion. Indian intellectuals, politicians, bureaucrats, and vocal middle classes view the desire to do service as the antithesis of the profit motive and as an intrinsically higher form of human activity. The notion that those who seek personal profit may be providing a national service, or alternatively, that those who seek only to provide service—such as the bureaucrat who seeks no profit and takes no risks—may be making no contribution to economic growth, is not widely understood or believed in India. It is important to note here that it is not simply the inequalities of wealth that are condemned, but rather the wealth-seeking motives of the entrepreneur as opposed to the higher motives of the government servant. Although all businessmen in India do not hold an equally low view of profit-seeking, and business chambers defend the profit motive in their discussions, it is rarely argued vigorously. Indian business operates in the framework of the government's ideology. It accepts the idea that government must build an equalitarian society through high taxes and public ownership of many industries; it only argues that socialism must be sufficiently modified to allow free enterprise to contribute to development. There is little notion that private wealth is good, that enterprise should be rewarded, or that the private interest of the businessman is in the public good. These attitudes, which

[29] Interview with G. L. Bansal, secretary-general of the Federation of Indian Chambers of Commerce and Industry, New Delhi, October, 1957.

the business community shares with other Indians, help determine its modes of adjusting to the Indian political situation.

While business in India is politically well organized, its influence on central government policy is negligible. The attention of the business community has therefore been directed to the administration of policy and to the more accessible state governments. West Bengal has been described as a state in which business influence on both policy and administration has been considerable. Because it has been able to obtain many of its demands from the government and because leftist parties remain as potential threats, the business community has kept close to the Congress party. Given popular attitudes toward the business community —attitudes which are in part shared by businessmen—little effort has been made to create a more sympathetic public. But the favors that business receives from the government may not be nearly so important politically as the financial support which the Congress party receives from business. While the business community has a stake in the Congress party, the businessman's ready access to the administration would probably make him tolerant of a change in government. The rise to power of a military dictatorship, the victory of the Praja Socialist party, or even of the Communists, would not drive the business community to the barricades, actually or figuratively. Indian business has learned to adapt itself under different regimes; and in all likelihood it would be prepared to adapt itself again should it become necessary. Indian industrialists are not in the position of English industrialists of the nineteenth century, who saw the expansion of representative government as a necessary step in wresting power from the landed aristocracy. Nor are Indian businessmen in the same position as those of early twentieth-century Japan, who opposed the expansion of representative government as increasing the power of agrarian-supported landlord elements. On the contrary, Indian business is in a silent partnership with the rural hinterland. It has seen representative government work and is not fearful of it. Most probably it could survive without it, and may take no steps to save it; but on the other hand, Indian business is not likely—in the foreseeable future—to take steps to destroy the institutions of representative government. That is of no small importance.

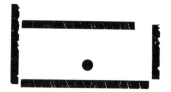

VI. AGRARIAN MOVEMENTS

Modernization, as visualized by state and national leadership in India, requires fundamental changes in the rural areas—in social relations, religious outlook, land tenure systems, and agricultural techniques. Agricultural savings, they believe, could be an important contribution to capital investment. Increased agricultural food production will be essential both for the maintenance of the urban sector and to minimize the drain on foreign exchange. Also, a prosperous countryside could provide a vast market for urban goods.

The state and central governments in India have accordingly developed legislation and services for "reconstructing" rural areas, such as the Community Development Program and National Extension Service, irrigation programs, land reform legislation, social welfare and educational services, and various social reform measures affecting untouchability, divorce, and inheritance rights. The rural population has, meanwhile, developed an almost incredible capacity to resist and even negate many of these. The evaluation reports of the Community Development Program are revealing for the light they throw on the resistance of villagers, and especially poorer villagers, to many features of the programs. Landlords, large and small, have found ways to resist land reform legislation. For instance, *benami* transactions—transfer of title to a friend or relative to circumvent ceilings on land holdings—have prevented any large-scale redistribution of land in many parts of India. Land settlement operations are so affected by landowners through their influence on the administration of land settlement and by the pressures they can put on tenants that existing tenure systems have not succumbed to legislative fiat. Credit facilities created by government co-operatives are often administered in such a way as to benefit few of the tenants and poor peasants, who continue to rely upon village moneylenders.[1] Thus far, government policy has neither sparked the productive capacity of the wealthier high-caste rural classes, nor has it sufficiently broken the hold to spark the enthusiasm of the poorer classes.

Our focus in this study, however, is less on the impact of government upon various groups than upon the influence of groups upon government. We have suggested that rural influence is most effectively exerted upon the government at the local level. This influence is not so much that of concerted and organized group action, as of individual influence exerted by men of power and prestige in the community. A few large landlords, especially *zamindar's*, have reached out into state politics and attempted to shape state legislation; but peasant organizations have been less effective. For example, the various landlord associations and individual landlords who could influence the chief minister, the land revenue minister, or other powerful figures in the West Bengal government and Congress party successfully delayed land reform legislation in that state for many years. Only after the central government (where landlord interests have less influence) had exerted pressure on the state government, did West Bengal proceed with any major land reform bills; and even those were carried through in such a way as to protect, in some measure at least, the interests of landowners.

The success with which landlord groups have influenced state legislation calls attention to the weakness of peasant movements in India. Peasants (a general term by which we mean all those tillers of the soil who do not rent their land to others—that is, peasant proprietors, tenants, sharecroppers, and agricultural laborers) are not well organized. Not only has their influence on state legislation been slight, but they have often lacked the local power necessary to ensure proper enforcement of the law. So long as the wealthy gentry are so closely related, often by family and almost always by interest, with the local bureaucracy, enforcement of legislation is dependent upon vigilant local organizations—political parties or peasant associations. And since the Congress party is often controlled on the local level by those who are hurt by land reform legislation, the party organization cannot and has not played such a role.

[1] See *All-India Rural Credit Survey*, II (*General Report*), (Bombay: Reserve Bank of India, 1955).

The Development of Agrarian Movements

To understand why the peasants have not developed organizations which could effectively articulate their interests, one must first explore the history of such associations. There were many peasant agitations in the nineteenth century—the famous Santal and indigo revolts in Bengal, and others in the Punjab and Maharashtra—but none of these survived in the form of organized groups that could continue to exert influence on administrators or legislators. Gandhi and his supporters organized the peasants of Champaran, Bihar, against the exactions of indigo planters in 1917; and in Gujarat, Gandhi led the famous Kaira *satyagraha* against the realization of land revenue in 1918. In 1928 the Bardoli *satyagraha* against the enactment of land revenue was organized by Sardar Patel. In fact, throughout the 1920's Congressmen penetrated the countryside to win peasant support for "Swaraj"—freedom, defined by Gandhi in the broadest sense as freedom from deprivation as well as freedom from the British raj. Finally, at the 1936 Lucknow session of the Congress, an agrarian program was adopted which said that

> the most important and urgent problem of the country is the appalling poverty, unemployment and indebtedness of the peasantry due fundamentally to antiquated and repressive land tenure and revenue systems and intensified in recent years by the great slump in prices of agriculture produce. The final solution of this problem invariably involves the removal of British imperialist exploitation, a thorough change of the land systems and a recognition by the State of its duty to provide work for the unemployed rural masses.

That same year, a group of Congressmen, some members of the Communist section, some from the newly-formed Congress Socialist party, and some of Gandhian persuasion, formed the All-India Kisan Congress.[2] Many sections of the Congress party criticized this attempt to form a peasant movement distinct from the Congress organization. Their uneasiness grew into antagonism in some states when the Kisan Congress became critical of the agrarian policies of the new Congress-controlled state

[2] These included N. G. Ranga and Swami Sahajanand Saraswati—the first general secretaries—Kamaladevi, Iftikharuddin, Dutt Mazumdar, J. P. Narayan, Indulal Yajnik, Bankim Mukherjee, S. Tagore, Muzaffar Ahmed, Z. A. Ahmad, Sajjad Zaheer, and Acharya Narendra Dev.

governments. In 1937, the Kisan Congress dropped the word "Congress," renamed itself the All-India Kisan Sabha, and adopted the Red Flag, then the symbol of all leftist groups in India.

In a presidential address before an AIKS national convention in 1939, Acharya Narendra Dev explained why a separate *kisan* group was necessary, even though the Congress membership was predominantly peasant and many of the peasants' demands had been incorporated into the Congress agrarian program of Faizpur and the economic rights resolution of Karachi.[3] Congress was, he argued, a multiclass organization within which the peasants were not fully able to exert their influence; many Congress resolutions could not be implemented because *zamindar*'s controlled parts of the Congress organization. A separate *kisan* organization could exert greater pressure on Congress to adopt and carry out the demands of the peasants. The Kisan Sabha, he concluded, should not be in rivalry with Congress, but should complement it.

The new *kisan* organization was a federation of state peasant movements, the largest of which were in Bihar, Andhra, Punjab, and United Provinces.[4] In the Punjab and Bihar, the Kisan Sabha launched mass movements against the government—in the Punjab, it opposed a new system of tax assessment; in Bihar, it pressed the government to abolish the *zamindari* system, reduce rents, pass new tenancy legislation, place a moratorium on debts, and guarantee higher sugar cane prices.

The fortunes of the Kisan Sabha were clearly tied to the price of rice and other agricultural commodities: a rise in agricultural prices as the Second World War approached was accompanied by a decline in the membership of the movement. The movement claimed 572,300 members in 1939, but by March, 1942, the membership had dropped to 225,781. This decline might also be attributed in part to the Kisan Sabha's break with Congress over the issue of national struggle. In 1940 the Kisan Sabha joined the Forward Bloc to support an immediate struggle against the British; but when Congress launched its struggle, the Kisan Sabha reversed its position, and supported the Communist program of backing

[3] Acharya Narendra Dev, *Presidential Address* (Gaya: All-India Kisan Conference, 1939).
[4] The following membership figures were reported for 1938 in *History of the Kisan Movement*, by N. G. Ranga and Swami Sahajanand Saraswati (Madras: All-India Kisan Publications, 1939):

Bihar	250,000	Gujarat	3,500
Punjab	73,000	Central Provinces	4,000
Andhra	75,000	Maharashtra	1,300
Bengal	34,000	Malabar	5,000
Surma Valley	15,000	Karnatak	2,500
Tamilnad	25,000	Delhi	1,500
Utkal	20,000	Hyderabad	2,500
United Provinces	60,000		572,300

the British and the war effort. The result of this shift in policy was a gradual withdrawal of non-Communists from the Kisan Sabha. The Congress Socialist party group, the Ranga Andhra group, and Indulal Yajnik's followers in Gujarat withdrew, leaving behind the Communists and a dissatisfied and confused Bihar group led by Swami Sahajanand Saraswati.

Many Congressmen were imprisoned in late 1942 for opposing the British, and the Kisan Sabha then had an open field for peasant organization. In 1944, the Kisan Sabha claimed a membership of 553,000, with the largest group in Bengal (177,000), followed by Andhra (101,000), Punjab (100,000), and Bihar (67,000). These figures represent the official claims of the All-India Kisan Sabha and, therefore, may minimize the losses in Andhra, where Professor Ranga had defected earlier. Toward the close of the war, further dissension took place within the Kisan Sabha. Swami Sahajanand Saraswati, a long-time peasant leader, a leading founder of the movement, and the single most important peasant leader in Bihar, broke with the Kisan Sabha in 1944. His grounds were that the Communists supported the Muslim League demand for Pakistan, opposed peasants' or workers' strikes and agitations during the "Peoples War" period, were dedicated to maintaining their own party organization at all costs, and were using the Kisan Sabha for party propaganda. Swami Sahajanand then proceeded to form his own All-India United Kisan Sabha, which attracted some of the dissidents who had earlier resigned from the Communist-controlled Kisan Sabha.

With the achievement of independence, the Communist party launched an insurrectionary movement to overthrow the newly independent government. When the Communist party was banned in several states, so was the Kisan Sabha. The ban continued until 1950–51. In 1950 the Kisan Sabha made an effort to bring the non-Communist Marxist-left *kisan* workers (particularly those in the United Kisan Sabha) back into the fold, but with little success.

The AIKS claims to have reached a high point in 1954, when membership figures totaled 1,087,000; in 1955 they dropped to 1,086,000, and in 1956 the total was reported to be 736,000. These figures may suggest a relative consistency and durability of organization which is quite misleading. The state figures published by the Kisan Sabha reveal an enormous yearly variation even when national totals remained relatively constant. In 1954, for example, Andhra had 110,000 members, but in 1959 no membership was claimed at all, since *kisan* workers were reportedly engaged in the state general elections. Bihar, with 56,000 members in

1954, doubled this figure to 100,000 in 1955, then dropped again to 54,000 in 1956. Membership appears to depend largely on the activity of Communist party workers in recruiting during any particular year. Today the All-India Kisan Sabha remains as the major peasant front of the Communist party of India; other parties have developed their own peasant organizations.

Agrarian Movements in Bengal

In Bengal much of the leadership in organizing the peasants was undertaken by those who later became members of the Communist and Marxist-left parties.[5] The movement began slowly; a peasant and workers party with Marxist orientation was organized in the late 1920's; in 1931 a few Congressmen organized the Bengal Krishak Sabha, but its activities were confined to limited parts of Bengal. Actual *kisan* organization was not undertaken until 1932, when political workers in north Bengal began to organize the peasants growing jute and cotton, who had been badly hit by price fluctuations. In August, 1936, a conference of peasant workers was held at Albert Hall in Calcutta for the purpose of organizing the entire province. About two hundred delegates from twenty districts of Bengal attended; and organizing committees were formed for Burdwan, Bankura, Hooghly, Jessore, and Dacca. Organizations were already under way in Tippera and Noakhali; the following year, peasant conferences were held in the districts of Bankura, Jessore, Burdwan, Khulna, and Murshidabad. *Kisan* committees were organized in Mymensingh, Rangpur, Dinajpur, and Rajshahi. In the all-Bengal elections of 1937, the groups in Tippera and Noakhali set up their own candidates; in other districts, the Kisan Sabha supported either the National Congress or the newly organized Praja party—a predominantly Muslim organization that was particularly active among Muslim tenants in East Bengal. By April, 1938, the Kisan Sabha of Bengal could report a membership of 35,575.[6]

[5] For descriptions of the peasant movement in Bengal, I am indebted to Bankim Mukherjee and Abdullah Rasool of the All-India Kisan Sabha, Ram Krishna Bathok and Ramayan Singh of the United Kisan Sabha, Bimal Chandra Sinha (revenue minister of the government of West Bengal), Asoka Mitra (ICS), and H. D. Malaviya, K. K. Chatterjee, and B. Chatterjee of the Congress party. For a thorough study of the movement in Bihar, as well as for a more detailed history of the All-India Kisan Sabha, see Walter Hauser, "The Kisan Sabha Movement in Bihar, 1919–1947" (Ph.D. thesis, Department of History, University of Chicago, 1961).

[6] For an account of the Bengal movement before 1939, see Ranga and Saraswati, *op. cit.*, pp. 132–38.

Relations between the Kisan Sabha and the new Praja (later Krishak Praja) party were uneven. In Bengal's 1937 elections, the Krishak Praja party, founded by A. K. Fazl-ul-Haq, won 35 seats in a house of 250, while Congress and its supporters won 60 seats, and the Muslim League, 40. Fazl-ul-Haq formed a coalition government of his Praja party, the Muslim League, the Scheduled Caste party, and a number of independents. Because he was unable to forge an alliance with the Congress party, Fazl-ul-Haq's new government increasingly relied upon a consolidated Muslim movement. He himself soon abandoned his own party to join the Muslim League, where he remained until the close of 1941. He continued in office until March, 1944, when his coalition ministry was replaced by a Muslim League government.

While the Kisan Sabha was initially sympathetic to the Praja party, and at one point even advocated merger with it, it soon became a critic of the Fazl-ul-Haq government. The Sabha criticized the government's Bengal Tenancy Amendment Bill (1938) as being inadequate, and was also critical of amendments to the Moneylenders Act and the Debt Conciliation Act. The government thereupon appointed a commission, under the chairmanship of Sir Francis Floud, to examine the system of land revenue in Bengal with particular reference to the Permanent Settlement. The hearings of this commission provide considerable information on the extent to which peasants, landlords, and others with agricultural interests were organized in Bengal before the war, and on the background of agrarian politics during and after the war. Dozens of associations testified,[7] few of which opposed the *zamindari* system. Of special interest is the fact that the Permanent Settlement was supported by a number of middle-class associations as well as by the *zamindar*'s. The commission recommended that the *zamindari* system be abolished, and suggested in its place a system which would transform cultivators into government tenants.[8]

[7] Landholders' associations testified from Bakargang, Bankura, Burdwan, Chittagong, Dinajpur, East Bengal, Faridpur, Hooghly, Howrah, Jessore, Khulna, Malda, Midnapore, Mymensingh, Nadia, Noakhali, and Sundarban. Bar associations from all the districts testified on behalf of the *zamindari* system. The opposition to the Permanent Settlement came from the Bengal Provincial Kisan Sabha, several Muslim tenants' associations, and the Krishak Praja party. The Indian National Congress did not testify.
[8] See *Report of the Land Revenue Commission, Bengal* (Alipore: Bengal Govern-

The Land Revenue System in Bengal

The Permanent Settlement, which Lord Cornwallis had established in the latter part of the eighteenth century, had assured the government a constant and fixed revenue from the land by establishing as permanent landlords Bengal's tax collectors, known as *zamindar's*. While the revenue collected by the government was considerable by eighteenth- and early nineteenth-century standards, an increase in the amount of cultivated land and a subsequent rise in land values and agricultural prices during the nineteenth century eventually resulted in a substantial surplus for the *zamindar* after he had collected his rent from the cultivator and had paid what was due to the government. Land became an increasingly attractive investment, not only because it was profitable, but also because landownership became increasingly devoid of responsibility. The law-enforcement and administrative powers of the *zamindar's* were greatly reduced as the British administration expanded. Earnings from business and commercial activities, government service, and the legal profession went into the purchase of *zamindari's*, *talukdari's*, and other rent-collecting rights; and the late nineteenth and early twentieth centuries witnessed the growth of an intermediary landlord class. Families dreamed of securing a safe income from land upon which they might live without working. A substantial number of individuals succeeded; and it was this landed-gentry class which took so rapidly to Western education in the late nineteenth century and out of which came the leaders of the Bengal renaissance.

Along with the growth of the landed gentry, other intermediaries multiplied: *zamindar's* sold their collecting rights to subsidiary interests; more prosperous peasant cultivators turned part of their lands over to tenants or sharecroppers and entered the *bhadralog* (gentlemen) class. There was an increase in tenancy and sharecropping as indebtedness grew and moneylenders let out their land. The resulting system was extremely complicated, involving many different types of tenure holders: *zamindar's* created by the Permanent Settlement, landowners who let out their holdings to sharecroppers, intermediary rent collectors, supervisory farmers, cultivators with tenancy rights, sharecroppers, and agricultural laborers were among the more common types.[9] The number of intermediaries

ment Press, 1940). The decision to take action, however, was postponed until after the war.

[9] These all have specific terms in Bengali and indicate particular socio-economic classes. Supervisory farmers are often called *dhani chasi* or *dhani grihastha;* cultivators

rose throughout the late nineteenth and early twentieth centuries. Although there are no accurate statistics on the number of intermediaries, estimates made before the Land Revenue Commission in 1939 ranged as high as ten million.

In the mid-twentieth century, the number of intermediaries further multiplied. The 1951 census of West Bengal reported that only 56.5 per cent of the agricultural population cultivated its own land, while another 21 per cent were tenants or sharecroppers, 21.4 per cent were agricultural laborers, and 1.05 per cent were non-cultivating rent receivers.[10] During the time the population was expanding and subinfeudation was rapidly growing, agricultural productivity remained nearly constant. The middle class grew in size, but its profit from land decreased. As a result, the pressure for more education and for more positions in law, medicine, and government service increased. Movement to the cities accelerated so rapidly that by 1951 only one-third of Calcutta's population had been born in the city; 26 per cent were from East Bengal (some of whom were Hindu refugees), 26.6 per cent from other states of India (mostly Bihar and Orissa), and 12.3 per cent from other districts of West Bengal—

---

with tenancy rights are called *chasi grihastha;* sharecroppers are called *adhiar's* or *bargadar's* and agricultural laborers are sometimes called *kisan's* or, more often, *kisan mazdoor's.* Paradoxically, legislation to improve the security of holdings may have contributed to an increase in the number of rent-receiving intermediaries. The Tenancy Act of 1885 conferred on the tenant the right of mortgaging and subletting his land; tenants soon began to create subordinate interests by a process of letting and subletting. S. K. Basu, minister of land and land revenue in West Bengal said: "The bigger *raiyat* (peasant) progressively gave up agriculture and got to the position of intermediary receiving rent for his interest in land. In the meantime, the impact of other powerful economic forces led to expropriation of the smaller tenant. On the one hand, due to steady growth of population and decline of rural industries there was a progressive overcrowding on land and indebtedness and impoverishment of the tenant. On the other hand, the new individualist laws led to increasing foreclosure and sale of holdings. By the turn of the century the small peasant proprietor proceeded to extinction and land concentrated in the hands of bigger raiyats and jotedars. So a very peculiar tenancy system has been evolved. Many of those who are tenants in the eye of law do no longer cultivate land. Very often, the real cultivators in the present set-up are the bargadars and landless laborers, who are in reality expropriated peasant proprietors. Between them and the State there is a wide gulf which very largely frustrates the agricultural policy of Government." Government of West Bengal Home (Publicity) Department, *Estates Acquisition and Land Reforms in West Bengal* (Alipore: West Bengal Government Press, 1955), p. 5.

[10] However, Asoka Mitra, the author of the 1951 West Bengal census, reports that tenants and *bargadar's* (sharecroppers) often claimed proprietorship, while landlords claimed cultivating status. These figures therefore should be viewed as very poor approximations. See *Census of India, 1951,* Vol. VI, Part 1A—*Report,* pp. 345–51. When the Zamindar Abolition Act was passed in 1954, the West Bengal government announced that proclamations had been served to 1,300,000 intermediaries.

Calcutta had become a city of immigrants from the countryside. The politics of Calcutta inevitably reflected these immigrants' origins. It would probably not be too far wrong to say that while the nineteenth-century liberals and twentieth-century moderates—the leaders of the British India Association, the Liberal Federation, and the many civic-philanthropic associations—came largely from families of *zamindar's*, ranking judges, and bureaucrats, the early twentieth-century terrorists, extremists, and later Marxists and Subhasists (followers of Subhas Bose) came for the most part from families of smaller intermediaries and junior officials. While this latter group was active in Calcutta, its influence also radiated into the countryside and district towns. Midnapore and Comilla, for example, were major revolutionary centers throughout the twenties and thirties. Although the revolutionaries failed to win control of the Bengal Congress party organization, the moderates did lose out to the more militant sections led by C. R. Das and Subhas Bose.

Wartime and Postwar Agrarian Politics

During the Second World War, Communists, Socialists, and Marxist-left politicians continued their attempts to build up strength in the countryside. Kisan Sabhas were organized by sons of petty intermediaries who were graduates of the University of Calcutta or at least of the local secondary school. Had it not applied the Marxist doctrine of class struggle, this leadership might well have succeeded in winning peasant support. But at least three factors mitigated any large-scale attempt to organize the peasantry of Bengal around the principle of class struggle. Firstly, there was no clear-cut peasant-landlord dichotomy, since a vast number of rent collectors existed between the cultivator and the *zamindar*. Moreover, caste and kinship ties between some cultivators and their rent collectors diminished the prospects for class struggle. Second, the Krishak Praja party and later the Muslim League won the support of the Muslim peasantry in Bengal; community consciousness, not class consciousness, grew. And third, attempts by peasant political workers to organize the *bargadar's* (sharecroppers) and, to a lesser extent, agricultural laborers alienated some peasant cultivators for whom the *bargadar's* and agricultural laborers worked. In short, even among cultivating peasants, conflicts of interest existed; and any attempt to build a movement on the basis of class tended to alienate one section or another of the peasantry.

   The Indian National Congress almost disappeared in Bengal during the war. A Muslim coalition government controlled the state government.

The Forward Bloc and the followers of Subhas had the support of those who opposed the war effort, and the Communist party had the support of those who favored the war. But fortunately for the Congress party, the Forward Bloc failed to build up any effective organization before Bose's death, and the Communist party's *kisan* organization was not able to tap more than a fraction of the countryside.

At the end of the war, Partition weakened the leftist parties—a substantial number of their workers had come from East Bengal—and the leftists were thus in a good position to organize refugees, but not to organize the West Bengal peasantry. The Communists also made the mistake of organizing an agitation of *bargadar*'s, which alienated many of the peasants for whom *bargadar*'s worked. On the other hand, after 1947 the Congress organization increased its strength in the West Bengal countryside. The more prosperous peasantry and rural gentry—the heads of local school boards, the members of union (local government) boards, petty merchants, shopkeepers, and professionals—joined Congress. The Congress doctrine of rural-village harmony was most attractive to those already in positions of local power; and while the notion of village harmony is as much of a myth as the Communist conception of class struggle, it has been politically more effective. The result is that the Congress party today is well entrenched in the countryside, while the Communists and Marxist-left parties control Calcutta. The leftists can paralyze the city, rally the students, the refugees, and the middle classes of Calcutta, but they are ineffective in the countryside.

Leadership, Tactics, and Targets

The bulk of the leadership of the All-India Kisan Sabha in West Bengal is derived from intermediary families that own but do not till the soil. Of the fifty-one members of the executive council of the Kisan Sabha in 1957, eight had peasant fathers, but thirty-one were members of the rural gentry. Many of these intermediary families from which political workers come have been forced to supplement their meager rural income with other forms of employment. Brothers, and sometimes fathers, of the Kisan Sabha organizers are teachers, local lawyers, clerks, or petty government officials. A few Muslims have become *kisan* workers, but most of the organizers are Hindus. In 1957, only three members of the West Bengal Kisan Sabha executive council were Muslims, while at least seventeen, and possibly more, were Brahmans.

Before Partition the movement was particularly strong in East Bengal, where political activity among the Hindu minority was very high. After Partition, many of these Hindu *kisan* workers migrated to West Bengal, thereby virtually destroying the East Bengal Kisan Sabha,[11] but not necessarily strengthening the West Bengal movement proportionally. The Kisan Sabha had been, for example, particularly strong in Mymensingh district in East Bengal, the most heavily populated district in all of India. The Mymensingh organization virtually fell apart after 1947, but this migration did not strengthen the West Bengal movement, since most of those who came over had to rebuild their homes and find employment, and were not in a position to participate in political work.

The Kisan Sabha in West Bengal had about 150,000 members in 1957, although its membership had been as high as 219,000 in 1955–56 and 185,000 the previous year. The decrease is attributed by the Sabha to the fact that Kisan Sabha workers were busy during the elections working for leftist candidates, and so had little time for *kisan* work. The organization's annual state conference is attended by about four or five hundred delegates.

The head Kisan Sabha office in Calcutta spends Rs. 2,500 or 3,000 per year ($500 to $600), while the budget of each district office is Rs. 1,000–1,500 a year ($200 to $300), plus whatever they can collect for the annual district conferences. Most districts have a full-time worker. The state office has three or four full-time workers and four or five part-time workers. These men receive small sums from the Kisan Sabha, and earn additional money through collections or have private incomes. Kisan Sabha leaders claim that in the past (but no longer) the Communist party helped the organization financially. Ten of the Kisan Sabha leaders are Communist members of the West Bengal Legislative Assembly and thereby support their own work.

Since 1947, the All-India Kisan Sabha in Bengal has been active in a number of agitational movements including *bargadar* protests, movements for the reduction of canal rates, agitations for the abolition of landlordism, and protests against the high prices of certain consumer goods, such as mustard oil. In addition, the leadership of the Kisan Sabha takes some credit for the abolition of the *zamindar* system through the Estates Acquisition Act. In addition to these agitational movements, the Kisan Sabha conducts a certain amount of welfare work. Food and money are collected in urban regions for relief of distressed areas. Sometimes medi-

[11] Of the forty-three members of the executive committee of the West Bengal Kisan Sabha whose birthplaces were known, eleven were from East Bengal and thirty-two from West Bengal.

cal assistance is also provided, such as aid from medical students active in the Communist-controlled student federation. One Kisan Sabha leader, describing the activities of the organization, said:

> There is a lack of drinking water in some areas, so we try to get government or relief organizations to build tubewells. In the Sundarban area, high tides from the bay have created floods, bringing salt water and destroying drinking water. But now the situation is improving with government-built tubewells.

> The Kisan Sabha also fights for opening up primary schools. Sometimes the Sabha has its own evening classes, but usually they approach the local government to open schools. Sometimes if a schoolboy finds his parents cannot afford to send him to school, the Kisan Sabha will raise subscriptions. Sometimes popular lectures are given by Kisan Sabha workers on local government, elections, prices, and how capitalists make exorbitant profits on the jute the peasants sell to them.

This Kisan leader then proceeded to discuss the ways in which the Kisan Sabha approaches government.

> The first step is to send one or two Kisan Sabha workers to see local officials about local grievances. If this fails, they send a mass petition, and this is followed by a mass demonstration. If necessary there is then civil disobedience. One problem they often see local officials about is getting agricultural loans. There is a union board for several villages. The president of the board is empowered to give loans which he often gives to his pets. The board is elected by restricted franchise of taxpayers and the nine members of the board select the president. The government money for loans is distributed through the board president after consultation with officials. This year only Rs. 11,000,000 have been allocated for loans. M.L.A.'s are trying to get more. The M.L.A.'s were successful last year in getting more relief from government during last year's flood.

In the 1957 elections, the Kisan Sabha actively supported the candidates of the Communist-supported United Front. But in contrast to the Congress party, it is so weak that the impact of its activities on the rural vote has been limited.[12] The Sabha's main strength—what little it has— is among some of the tenants and *bargadar's*. Congress, on the other hand, is well entrenched with the influential rural gentry, small shopkeepers, and peasant proprietors. Kisan Sabha leaders argue that Congress is able to win many areas simply because the Kisan Sabha lacks the money to send in its own workers. Furthermore, they claim that Congress has the support of local officials and therefore uses relief distribtuions to win peasant support; and that local merchants support Congress in order to obtain permits from local officials. But whatever the reason, the fact is that the rural vote of the Congress party in West Bengal is built in large part upon the local gentry, members of union boards, the presidents of union boards and of village *panchayat's* (councils), and local merchants, all of whom wield considerable influence among the peasantry.

The Communist party of West Bengal, aware of its weakness in rural areas,[13] has established a new program and new targets for the Kisan Sabha since the 1957 elections. The thesis adopted by the Kisan Sabha conference in 1957 stated that since landlordism had been abolished, the main problem which remained was the reconstruction of agriculture. A sharp decline in the purchasing power of the peasantry, large-scale evictions, unemployment of agricultural laborers, and scarcity of credit were among the most severe problems to be solved; and these required "new slogans." The Kisan Sabha therefore advocated a removal of tax burdens, an inquiry into illegal transfers of over twenty-five acres (the

---

[12] Election results for the West Bengal Legislative Assembly in the 1952 and 1957 elections from rural constituencies were as follows:

	1952		1957	
	Votes	*Per Cent*	*Votes*	*Per Cent*
Congress party	1,618,195	39.2	2,626,521	47.9
Communist party	419,166	10.2	864,090	15.7
Socialists	583,722	14.1	577,288	10.5
Marxist-left parties	207,567	5.0	358,529	6.5
Hindu communal	357,344	8.6	194,003	3.5
Independents	944,035	22.9	871,696	15.9
Total	4,130,029	100.0	5,492,127	100.0
Electorate	9,352,699		11,182,721	

[13] The Communist party doubled its Calcutta vote in the 1957 elections from 12.9 to 24.8 per cent and in the process won a majority of the seats to both Parliament and the legislative assembly from Calcutta. The CPI's main obstacle to winning power in West Bengal (through the ballot) is now the rural vote. While the Communist rural vote increased from 10.2 to 15.7 per cent, Congress increased its rural vote from 39.2 to 47.9 per cent.

Estates Acquisition Act limits individual agricultural holdings to twenty-five acres), the application of the land ceiling to families rather than to individuals, an increase in government credit facilities, the establishment of price parity between agricultural and industrial commodities, the establishment of small irrigation and drainage schemes, a reduction of indirect taxes, and an increase in co-operatives.

Political Organization and Rural India

Although the Kisan Sabha is the oldest and largest national organization which claims to speak for peasants per se, there are, of course, other peasant organizations: the Congress-sponsored Farmers' Forum, N. G. Ranga's various peasant organizations in Andhra, a Socialist-sponsored organization in Andhra, a Socialist-sponsored organization known as the Kisan Panchayat, the Marxist-left legacy of Swami Sahajanand Saraswati, the United Kisan Sabha, and a number of smaller, local peasant groups. Supplementing these groups, there are organizations of peasants organized not as peasants but as members of particular religious, tribal, linguistic, or party movements. Peasants are organized, for example, as Congressmen, or as members of the Sikh Akali Dal (in the Punjab), or as members of the tribal Jharkhand party (in Bihar and Orissa). They are also organized in credit societies, in marketing, seed, and credit co-operatives, and in caste *sabha's*. These organizations, in so far as they make demands upon state and national governments, do so on behalf of either the whole community or parts of the local community. Attempts by tenants to organize against landlords, peasant proprietors against *zamindar's*, and cultivators against moneylenders have occurred, but they have been confined to a few areas, have lasted for limited periods of time, and have rarely resulted in continuous and effective political organization.

At the heart of the controversies between the Kisan Sabha (and other peasant organizations) and the Indian National Congress was a harmonious versus a class-struggle image of the countryside. The controversy obviously involved more than a sociological appraisal of the character of rural India. It involved basic strategies of both organizations. In effect the Kisan Sabha argued that even if class struggle did not exist, it ought to exist, while many Congressmen believed that even if class struggle did exist, it ought not to exist.

To understand fully the efficacy of these two doctrines of rural harmony versus rural class struggle, one must view the ideologies against the realities of Indian rural social structure. We have shown that the history of *kisan* movements in India has not indicated any widespread and continuous class conflict in rural areas. Anthropological studies of India's villages do not, however, reveal a picture of harmonious living.[14] Factional conflicts within villages are common and leadership tends to be factional rather than village-wide. These factions, writes Alan Beals in his study of leadership in a Mysore village,

> need not represent opposed castes, a conflict between progressive and conservatives, or a conflict between economic groups. . . . Brothers, for example, frequently belong to opposed factions because of hatred generated in the course of the division of family property. . . . Underlying the factional structure of social relationships in the village are a series of more stable familial and clique groups. . . . In nearly every case, cliques include relatives, friends, and persons bound together by economic ties, such as employee-employer or borrower-lender relationships.[15]

Local elections do not reveal any pattern of village harmony. In his description of a local election in a north Indian village, Morris Edward Opler writes:

> . . . Thus the election was really a translation into political terms of a struggle between two village stalwarts and the rival factions they headed. The existence of factions of this type has been noted in most of the studies of Indian villages that have been issued recently. Indian social organization emphasizes hierarchy and notions of prestige, and infringements in these areas lead to retaliation, dispute and division. In an atmosphere of friction and tension, an election is simply a means of giving a new turn to an old quarrel.[16]

[14] For village studies which describe internal factional conflicts, see the following: *India's Villages* (Calcutta: West Bengal Government Press, 1955); McKim Marriott (ed.), *Village India* (Chicago: University of Chicago Press, 1955); and *Leadership and Political Institutions in India,* ed. Richard L. Park and Irene Tinker (Berkeley: University of California Press, 1959), especially the papers in the section on leadership and change in the villages.
[15] Park and Tinker, *op. cit.,* p. 433.
[16] *Ibid.,* p. 149.

That the village is, however, capable of acting as a unit is argued by other anthropologists. M. N. Srinivas points to the pattern of ties existing within a village which cuts across both caste and faction.

> When the village is threatened with an epidemic or drought or floods or fire, or when the government passes an order which the villagers regard as unjust, or on certain religious occasions, or in a fight with a neighbouring village, the unity of the village reveals itself in an unmistakable manner.[17]

In fact, this capacity to unite in relation to the outside world is increasingly being tapped by political parties during general elections that cut across villages. In elections for state legislative assemblies and for the national Parliament, virtually all parties, including the Communists, emphasize those issues which appeal to villages as villages. Thus the Congress party stresses the beneficial effect of its community development programs, of local irrigation works, new schools, new roads, and other rural improvements. The opposition parties criticize the government for high taxes, for high food prices, for inefficient programs of grain procurement, for administrative corruption, and for lack of adequate credit facilities, irrigation works, or schools. In West Bengal, as elsewhere, rural demands are increasingly directed at the government and not against groups within the rural community. While leftist attacks on *zamindar's*, *jagirdar's*, and other types of landlords were common in the 1952 elections, the legal abolition of the landlord system in most states between the 1952 and 1957 elections eliminated this important class-struggle issue.

The Kisan Sabha is now attempting to build itself upon the unity of all the peasants, and tries to minimize conflicts of interest through the "principle of village solidarity." Kisan Sabha workers try to negotiate settlements between agricultural laborers, sharecroppers, and small peasant proprietors. This willingness to play a brokerage role in the countryside grows out of the fact that much of the Kisan Sabha support comes from *bargadar's*. Eager to win the support of small peasant proprietors, it wants to minimize conflict between the proprietors and its *bargadar* supporters. Many small owners have twenty or twenty-five *bigha's* of land which, for financial or status reasons, are cultivated by *bargadar's*. These small peasants depend entirely on their land; the

[17] *India's Villages*, p. 7.

bargadar's, in turn, are dependent upon the small peasants for seeds, plows, bullocks, and water.

The fifteenth provincial conference, meeting in 1957, announced that the Kisan Sabha favored compensation for those small intermediaries whose holdings were confiscated by government. It further declared that the organization would launch agitations for agricultural loans, improved irrigation facilities, manure, education, health, and drinking water, and would continue agitation against excessive irrigation taxes and other taxes, including a proposed development tax. The Sabha also announced that it would work within the existing legislative framework, would take the initiative in forming *panchayat's* (local government councils) under the new Panchayat Act, and would support credit co-operatives, marketing societies, handicraft co-operatives, and even the government's Community Development Program and National Extension Service. In short, the Kisan Sabha proposed to minimize agitations and maximize the benefits peasants (and the Kisan Sabha) might receive by working within existing legislation, while at the same time putting pressure on the state government for greater rural expenditures. Rural harmony rather than class conflict was the new theme of the West Bengal Kisan Sabha.[18]

With the growth of political activity in rural areas, direct conflicts have developed within the Congress party organization itself between urban and rural sections. Urban politicians tend to dominate the state administration, while those from rural areas are rapidly gaining control of the party organization and the state legislature.[19] In the West Bengal Legislative Assembly, for example, Congress M.L.A.'s are organized by district for convenience in pressuring the state ministries, especially those responsible for public works, agriculture, and community development. To minimize this conflict the chief minister has sought to balance the state government by distributing positions in the cabinet to members from a variety of districts.

With the disappearance of the landlord-abolition issue as a major ques-

[18] A similar position now guides the national All-India Kisan Sabha. The groups in Kerala, Bihar, Assam, and Tripura all want a moderate *kisan* position. This is all part of the present Communist program of working within the existing framework, which is as much a consequence of Soviet-Indian relations as it is an outcome of Communist experience in India's rural areas. Nonetheless, the new strategy may prove to be more effective for working within the framework of democratic elections. In the 1962 elections, the Communists improved their vote in the rural areas of West Bengal, but at the same time suffered some losses in Calcutta.

[19] For a study of the rise of rural leadership in West Bengal during the past forty years, see Weiner, "Changing Patterns of Political Leadership in West Bengal," in *Pacific Affairs*, XXXII (September, 1959).

tion in Indian political life (although in practice petty landlords still control much of the land), conflicts between urban and rural sectors are likely to grow. The rapid growth of the national extension scheme, the increase in expenditures for rural education, and other rural social welfare programs have in some measure resulted from the pressures of rural politicians. Given India's rural social structure, land tenure systems, and the growing role played by government in economic development, together with a system of universal adult suffrage, pressures from rural areas against the government are likely to increase steadily.

Public Policy and Agrarian Demands

The major outlines of government agrarian policy since Independence have been shaped in New Delhi and subjected to remarkably few influences from outside the government or Congress party. The various proposals for land reform, such as abolition of *zamindar's*, *jagirdar's*, and other intermediaries between the cultivator and the state, ceilings on landholdings, reforms of tenures, and minimum wages for sharecroppers, have come from the national and occasionally from the state Congress and governmental leadership. Communists and Socialists and their respective peasant associations have also pressed for these reforms; but outside of a few local areas (such as parts of Hyderabad), one could not find a ground swell for reform. Likewise, the decision to establish a Community Development Program with its emphasis on the development of many aspects of village life, and the decision in the early 1960's to direct greater resources toward the production of food, were intragovernmental decisions. Similarly, the decision by the Congress party to press for the creation of a nation-wide system of agricultural co-operatives in which, ultimately, labor and produce would be shared was arrived at within the halls of government and the ruling party, virtually uninfluenced by external pressures.

Thus far, the Indian countryside has not produced effective peasant movements capable of exerting a major influence on government policy. The very absence of strong farm lobbies in the states has meant that many state governments, especially those in which landlords have considerable power, have not acted for reform unless pressure has been exerted by the central government or by the Congress party Working Committee in New Delhi. Indeed, although the constitution gives state governments responsibility for agricultural development, India's agricultural policies have come from New Delhi, not the state capitals. The capacity and skills for innovation and, above all, the financial resources are greater in the center than in the states. In agriculture, as in industrial relations policy, the states have generally deferred to the center's guidance.

The absence of strong farmer associations has lent a note of uncertainty to agricultural policy. Policy is debated—often hotly debated—within the Ministries of Community Development and Co-operation, and Food and Agriculture, the Planning Commission, and the Congress party. Other political parties, and intellectuals in general, have heatedly discussed the relative merits and defects of ceilings on landholdings and, most recently, proposals for co-operative farming. But one could write a history of postwar agrarian policy in India, and of the political struggles which have entered into making such policy, with little or no reference to farmer organizations.

One consequence of making policy in such a rarefied atmosphere is that it is exceedingly difficult to implement. Scholars and journalists have referred often to both the Indian penchant for elaborate planning and their lack of skill in implementation. Deficiencies either in Indian administration or in the Indian character are among the most popular explanations. But one must remember that the very ease with which Indians—and foreign experts—find it possible to experiment with new programs is a function of the relative distance separating those decision-makers from the citizenry and from popular political pressures. Also, most notably in agriculture, there is no nation-wide organization made up of and controlled by farmers, which can effectively serve to propose new policies or criticize government proposals. Failures in implementation are not subjected to the scrutiny of vigilant local organizations.[20] Failures by

[20] The difficulties in the implementation of tenancy legislation, for example, have been related to the lack of power—and organization—of tenants. Gulzari Lal Nanda, summarizing from the report of the Tenancy Committee of the Land Reforms Panel of the Planning Commission, reports that "no organized effort was made to make the tenants understand the law and to ensure that they take advantage of it. *Even where the tenants are aware of their rights they are generally in too weak a position—both economically and socially—to insist on their rights.* . . . In some states, there are no village records from which a tenant can establish his possession. Even where his name is entered the *landlord has so much influence in the village that frequently it is very difficult for the tenant to establish his possession.* In some cases the attitude of the Revenue Officers may at times be unconsciously against the tenants. . . . After all, ideas about the evolution of tenants' rights as against the landlord have been of a comparative recent growth. The conception of land as property and the rights and privileges of the owner of property is deeply rooted. The rights and privileges of the actual cultivator of the land are not yet fully comprehended" (Gulzari Lal Nanda, "Progress of Land Reforms in India," *All-India Congress Committee Economic Review*, IX, No. 10 (September 15, 1957), 17). [Italics added.]

government officials to provide seeds, water, fertilizers, and credit at the precise time in which they are needed are not quickly called to the attention of higher authorities. Disillusionment with government policies has often occurred, therefore, when in fact the policies have not been satisfactorily tested.

This is not to say that rural needs and demands are ignored by the government. In at least three major areas, rural interests have been reflected in public policy and administration: land reform legislation, the Community Development Program, and rural taxation.

The impact of certain special rural interests on the formulation, and particularly on the implementation, of land reform legislation has been widely described, although it is not easily documented. The effectiveness of legislation on land ceilings has, for instance, often been impaired by the influence of wealthy peasants on those who control local land records. Indeed, although the central government has pressed for ceilings on landholdings, state governments have been reluctant to adopt such legislation for fear that it might dispel their own sources of power; many states have imposed ceilings on new acquisitions but not on existing holdings. In the few states where legislation places ceilings on current holdings, the limits often apply to individuals, not to families, permitting easily arranged transfers of title. Government efforts to reduce rents through legislative action have also had little effect. Similarly, tenancy legislation has often been ineffective—indeed, has frequently resulted in the large-scale eviction of tenants by landlords who thereby conform to legislative loopholes permitting them to retain title to lands under direct cultivation.

The bias in implementation of agrarian reform legislation is due largely to the distribution of political power in rural areas, but one must also remember that this bias is favored by the existing land-man ratio. The short supply of land in relationship to demand reinforces an economy of high rents and a high rate of tenancy, and encourages an attitude of acquiescence on the part of the landless and the tenant farmers. The temptation is great for the more prosperous peasantry and landlords to evade legislation.

Special rural interests have also been reflected in the progress of the Community Development Program. As originally conceived,[21] the program was to bring together all government agencies engaged in rural de-

[21] Albert Mayer *et al.*, *Pilot Project, India.* (Berkeley: University of California Press, 1958).

velopment activities to pursue a systematic program for changing many aspects of rural life, including agricultural techniques, sanitation, health, and transportation. The program was to be begun in a few areas of rural India and expanded as fast as competent personnel could be trained. However, seven years after the program was launched, some thirty-five hundred development blocks had been created, with approximately seventy thousand village-level workers and fifteen thousand officials. Government reports have admitted that this rapid expansion without adequate numbers of trained personnel meant a marked deterioration in the program. The program has been attacked for, among other things, failing to accelerate the country's food production sufficiently (there has been an average annual increase of 3.3 per cent during the first two five-year plans). It has also been reported that many of the benefits from the program have accrued to wealthier peasants. It is clear, however, that much of the premature expansion of the program during the second five-year plan was the result of efforts by members of Parliament, members of state legislative assemblies, state ministries, and local Congress party organizations to spread the program into their constituencies as quickly as possible.

While hope for political dividends has impelled government officials to take positive action—albeit, as some have argued, premature action—in community development, in the area of rural taxation politicians have felt impelled not to take action for the same reason. Approximately 45 per cent of India's national income is derived from agriculture, but land taxation takes less than 1 per cent of the gross value of agricultural output. In 1959–60, land revenue accounted for only 6.5 per cent of the country's total tax revenues (11 per cent of the state governments' revenues), compared with 16 per cent in 1938–39 (30 per cent of the state governments' revenues in that year).[22] Land reform legislation has provided some increase in revenue, but this has been because peasants now pay their taxes directly to the state rather than through landlords, who had taken a substantial share. Since the peasants are not paying higher taxes, the land reform legislation has only temporarily arrested the long-term trend toward a reduction of total government revenue derived from land taxation. Similarly, rural income taxes have remained low, while income taxes on non-agricultural incomes have increased in the urban areas. Despite the recommendations of many government economists that

[22] Ayodhya Singh, "Land and Agricultural Taxes," *Economic Weekly*, XIII (January 21, 1961), 91.

agricultural taxes be increased,[23] state governments have been reluctant to act. The reason is obvious: state governments derive their political support from rural areas, especially from the more prosperous sections of the countryside, which would be most affected by increased agricultural taxes. Indeed, as urban discontent has risen, the Congress party has felt more and more dependent upon rural support, and less and less inclined toward pursuing taxation policies which might erode that support.

One encounters a marked change in attitudes toward agricultural policy as one leaves the offices of ministers and planners in New Delhi and enters the homes of state legislators. At the top, there is support for more substantial land reform measures, for greater concentration of public resources and skilled personnel in limited areas, and for higher rural taxes; while at the state and local level, the sentiment is against tampering with the prevailing land system, is in favor of greater public investment throughout the rural areas, and is reluctant to see any major increases in taxes. The differences in viewpoint are clearly related to differences in political position; the distance of the national leadership from rural political pressures disposes them toward a program which they justify primarily on economic grounds, while state and local leaders are sensitive to sentiments within their constituencies and are therefore disposed toward policies based on political considerations. On no issue has the conflict between policies based on economic considerations and those which are politically oriented become so clear as in the controversy concerning co-operative farming.

India's first five-year plan proposed that small and middle farmers should be encouraged and assisted to group themselves into co-operative farming societies. In a few states, especially in Bombay, it has been reported that some of the co-operatives were doing well; in general, however, there has been little sustained effort and little success. At a conference of state ministers for co-operation, held at Mussorie in July, 1956, it was agreed that an effort should be made to create at least one co-operative society in every National Extension Block during the second plan period. A delegation under the sponsorship of the Planning Commission visited China in 1957 to study agrarian co-operatives there and to make recommendations for India. They returned with strong recom-

---

[23] See *Report of the Taxation Enquiry Commission, 1953–54* (Delhi: Government of India, Ministry of Finance, Department of Economic Affairs, 1955), III, 529–38 and *passim.*

mendations for an active co-operative program. The delegation took the position that India must

> think in terms of so reorganizing the agrarian economy that a planned use of land, manpower, capital resources, and managerial skill become possible. This calls for the pooling of land, manpower and capital resources by cooperative action so that it may be possible to fully utilize the available resources and also obtain the economies of large scale production. In a cooperative farm, the considerations of outlay and return apply over a much larger area. The pooled area constitutes a single farm. . . . It becomes possible to intensify agriculture over the entire area of the farm and undertake improvements of labour-intensive nature without consideration of cost. Fruit and vegetable growing can be taken up. Dairying can be developed. A part of the surplus labour force can be utilized for the improvement of village communications and housing, for provision of other social amenities including education of children and adults, etc. . . . . The capital resources will be utilized more fully. Costs will be reduced. A portion of the released resources could be made available for the development of cottage and small scale industries. . . . Without the producers' cooperatives, the needs of each one of the 50 million families engaged in agriculture have to be ascertained and provided for. With the producers' cooperatives, the State will have to deal ultimately with less than half a million cooperatives which will become the organ of the State in implementing its welfare programmes. Besides, the producers' cooperatives will provide opportunities of working together for the various groups of people now held apart by social and communal divisions and thus bring about increasingly an emotional integration of the people into a living entity.[24]

Support for the delegation's position grew within the national government and the national leadership of the Congress party. Sentiment was particularly strong in the Ministry of Mines and Oil, the Ministry of Com-

[24] *Report of the Indian Delegation to China on Agrarian Cooperatives* (New Delhi: Government of India Planning Commission, May, 1957), p. 134.

munity Development and Co-operatives, and the Planning Commission. The socialist-minded "ginger" group within the Congress party also lent their support. In January, 1959, the Congress party passed its now-famous Nagpur resolution on "Agrarian Organization Pattern." [25] This resolution took the position that India's future agrarian pattern should be that of co-operative joint farming in which farmers would continue to retain their property rights but would pool their land for joint cultivation and obtain a share from the net produce in proportion to their land. Those who worked on the land, whether they owned the land or not, would receive a share in proportion to their work. Service co-operatives were proposed as a first step prior to the institution of joint farming. To the criticisms that the Nagpur resolution would lead ultimately to collectivization and compulsion, Nehru, in an address to Parliament, declared that he firmly believed "in the rightness of joint cultivation" but that his government would not use coercion to bring the peasantry into such a program. "If they do not agree, I cannot put it in operation." [26] But, he said, a one-acre holding would always keep its owner in semi-starvation, and this called for joint farming since "there are certain improvements in the land which we can profit by if we had larger pieces to plough, to cultivate." [27]

The initial opposition to joint farming came from state politicians concerned with the political consequences of the proposal. Gulzari Lal Nanda, a member of the Planning Commission, reported that

> many State Governments have been lukewarm in promoting this programme. Some of the objections which have been raised to the programme of cooperative farming from time to time are that there is a strong attachment to land among peasants and, therefore, cooperative farming cannot be brought about on any large scale except through coercion or force, which has to be ruled out in any democratic country; the cooperative farming would retard initiative and hamper the growth of farmer's personality; it may even hinder the development of democratic institutions.[28]

[25] The full text was published in *The Hindu* (Madras), January 9, 1959.

[26] From Jawaharlal Nehru's reply to the debate on the president's address in the Lok Sabha on February 19, 1959, reprinted in the *A.I.C.C. Economic Review*, X (March 1, 1959), 5.

[27] *Ibid.*, p. 6.

[28] Gulzari Lal Nanda, *op. cit.*, p. 17.

Outside the Congress party, objection to joint farming was even stronger. The Indian Cooperative Union in New Delhi, a voluntary non-governmental co-operative, expressed its staunch opposition to co-operative farming. N. G. Ranga, one-time leader of the All-India Kisan Sabha, a political leader in Andhra, and now a leading supporter of the Swatantra party, declared that he and the Swatantra party viewed co-operative farming as collectivization in disguise.

Although the primary argument of those who have opposed joint farming has been that it is neither politically feasible nor politically desirable within a democratic system, a few opponents have taken the position that the proposal is not, in fact, likely to solve India's agrarian problem. According to this argument,[29] no reorganization of agriculture can alter the basic man-land ratio. It might be advisable to enlarge the farming units if land and capital were abundant relative to labor and it were therefore feasible to mechanize agriculture on a large scale. Large-scale mechanization is a device for increasing productivity per man, not per acre. But so long as there is much labor and proportionately little land, the basic problem is one of increasing production per acre, not per man. Where the man-land ratio is high, as in Japan, production has been increased through intensive cultivation and by employing new methods. Intensive cultivation requires considerable care on the part of the peasant, and such care is only possible when the peasant owns and cultivates his own land. For "peasants the world over have consistently demonstrated their reluctance to work wholeheartedly under any collective arrangement which deprives them of a sense of secure personal possession of the land they cultivate and the crop they harvest."[30] In India, it is also argued, the Indian peasant is deeply attached to his land and will not voluntarily pool his land no matter how much he is exhorted to do so. "The very fact that at every succession a joint family holding is subdivided among the decendants is enough proof of its truth. What thinking could be more wishful than that which leads one to expect that where the members of a joint family—a natural cooperative—would seldom keep their holdings together for joint cultivation, large numbers of unrelated families would pool them?"[31]

Though in the minds, and occasionally in the words, of supporters of joint farming, co-operatives represent a "higher form" of human organiza-

[29] See Raj Krishna, L. C. Jain, and Gopi Krishan, *Cooperative Farming: Some Critical Reflections* (New Delhi: Indian Cooperative Union, 1956), pp. 6–11.
[30] *Ibid.*, p. 11.
[31] *Ibid.*, p. 12.

tion than do individual farms, their case has been presented almost exclusively on economic grounds; whereas the opponents, in spite of what appears to be a strong economic case, have preferred to stress political considerations. One critic has defined the dispute as involving a choice between two broad visions of the future agrarian society:

> (1) the vision of a village of peasant proprietors or secure tenants with small, consolidated, independent holdings, aided by service cooperatives in respect to supply, credit, and marketing and the use of expensive equipment; and (2) the vision of a village of one or a few big cooperatives or collective farms, managed by bureaucrats, controlled by the state, with collective cultivation and/or collective ownership and with members performing their assigned tasks and receiving wage-payments according to work norms. There are, of course, all kinds of intermediate arrangements between these poles of the owner-cultivated family farm and the state-dominated collective farm, but even in the choice of the intermediate forms, every one starts from a predilection in favor of one or the other of the polar models. . . .[32]

Both of these models, however, are largely in the minds of intellectuals, for no mass peasant movement either for or against joint farming has been launched, not even by the ideologically-oriented, party-controlled *kisan* organizations. As we have already noted, agrarian demands have largely been short-term, limited demands; and this is especially true since *zamindari* abolition has been carried out. Clearly, the more wealthy peasantry is not likely to give up control of land and its produce voluntarily. Given the power held by small landlords and well-to-do peasants, and their close association with local administrators and the local Congress party, it is unlikely that any large-scale agrarian reorganization in the form of co-operatives could take place without substantial coercion.

Paradoxically, the distribution of local power which provides so much strength for the Congress party and ultimately for stable government in the center is a bottleneck for structural changes in rural areas advocated by many national leaders. Tenancy reform has often been slowed, if not invalidated, by the influence of landlords on local record-keepers; state governments are reluctant to place ceilings on landholdings because to

---

[32] Raj Krishna, "Agrarian Reform in India: The Debate on Ceilings," *Economic Development and Cultural Change*, VII, Part I (April, 1959), 315.

do so might disrupt their own sources of power; where ceilings do exist, there are loopholes which prevent their effectiveness; intensive community development programs have been put aside for a more rapid, often hasty, expansion under the pressure of state and local leaders; and central pressures for an increase in land revenue taxes have gone unheeded by state governments. Indeed, one can say that the national government and party leaders have failed to consider the character of their own party organization in proposing and pressing for many of their policies. No amount of exhortation by the center will change the political configurations within which state governments must make and implement agrarian policies. Political movements of the peasantry may have been frustrated by the sociological realities of Indian rural life, but Indian policy-makers have been equally limited by the political realities of rural India.

VII. STUDENTS

In virtually all underdeveloped areas students have played an active role in politics. The prestige which educated men enjoy, the freedom of students from responsibility, their acute political awareness, their idealism and their energy, propel them into the political arena. In India students played an important role in the nationalist movement and today they continue to be politically active. What political activities do they engage in, why, and with what consequences for the development of Indian democracy, are the questions to be explored here.

Historically educational institutions in India have been centers of modernization and Westernization. Missionaries conceived of their schools and colleges as entering wedges for proselytization. Government officials sought through education to provide both the requisite learning and moral standards to prepare Indians for admission into administrative positions. English evangelists and utilitarians, although they differed in many ways, shared a faith in the liberating effects of education.

British educational policy in India underwent numerous changes throughout the nineteenth and twentieth centuries, but certain trends persisted. Indigenous educational institutions were, on the whole, neglected; secular schools, in spite of missionary efforts, multiplied; English displaced vernacular languages at many levels of education; literary studies received precedence over science and technology; and finally, perhaps most important of all, education was given a relatively low priority on government budgets in spite of its recognized importance, with the result that literacy—not to mention higher standards of learning

—increased at a lower rate than in most European countries or in Japan and the Philippines.

At the time of Independence, although nearly one hundred years had passed since the Wood Dispatch outlined the main course of development in Indian education in 1854, the number attending educational institutions was relatively small. In 1946–47, only 241,794 students were attending universities in India, 2,681,981 were in secondary schools, and 10,525,943 were in primary schools. Except in a few localities, there was no compulsory primary education. Wastage—students who fail to complete four years of primary school, the requisite period for permanent literacy—was and still is considerable. Today, perhaps no more than one-fourth of the entering university students obtain degrees.[1] The total number of students who received the benefits of a "modern" education at the time of Independence was small—at best 12.2 per cent of the population, if one uses the literacy figures as indicating the maximum limit. In 1949 only 1 out of 2,206 persons in India was attending a university, compared with 1 out of 837 in Great Britain, 1 out of 225 in the United States, and 1 out of 300 in Russia.[2]

India's politicians have been recruited out of this relatively small store of educated persons. Few Congress leaders, few members of legislative assemblies or Parliament, few leaders of peasant organizations or trade unions, have not had some college education, and fewer still have not completed high school. If one compares the educational level of India's top leadership with that of other major countries, one finds little difference.[3] Education is at least as much, if not more, of a necessity for political leadership in India as it is in educationally and industrially advanced countries. Under the British, knowledge of English was a prerequisite for government and commercial employment. Even communication with government—in the courts, in labor tribunals, and in much of the administrative network—required a knowledge of English. People who were not fluent in English looked up to those who were as being capable of communicating and influencing the makers and administrators of public policy. Those who held university degrees were in fact at the pinnacle

---

[1] In 1951, for example, of the 123,000 students who reached the examination stage at the universities, only 69,000, or 56 per cent, passed. If one includes intermediate examinations, which cover the first two years of college, the percentage who passed was 46.6.

[2] Quoted by Syed Nurullah and J. P. Naik, in *A History of Education in India* (Bombay: Macmillan and Co., Ltd., 1951).

[3] See Donald R. Matthews, *Social Background of Political Decision-Makers* (New York: Doubleday & Co., Inc., 1954).

of the status ladder. They held jobs in administration, journalism, and law; they led the major political organizations; they had the greatest access to government.

Since relatively few reached this level of education, those who had university degrees and even those still in the universities were acutely aware of their own political potential. This awareness was enhanced by the political character of the educational system under colonial rule. Knowledge was not and could not be conceived of as universal, but as parochial, or more precisely, as Western. The medium of instruction was English, a foreign language. The content was heavily literary and consisted primarily of English literature. What religious teaching there was, was in a European religion. Both the uniquely modern content of education (science and technology) and its national aspects (such as Indian history, culture, and religion) were marginal, although it is largely in these two areas that Indian scholars came to distinguish themselves.

In the mid-nineteenth century, Indian reformers welcomed the creation of a Westernized system of education. Leaders of reform, such as Raja Ram Mohun Roy, supported the "Anglicists," who advocated Western learning through English, in the conflict with "Orientalists," who advocated traditional learning through Sanskrit and Persian. The many Hindu reform movements that emerged in the nineteenth century were intricately related to the new system of education. But by the beginning of the twentieth century, when revivalist and nationalist movements were emerging, Indians began to think of the British educational system not as a liberating influence but as a denationalizing one. Indians condemned the universities for ignoring India's national culture and traditions. They attacked the universities as institutions intended to prepare Indians for utilitarian jobs in the British administration.[4] Therefore the student in the twentieth century regarded neither utilitarian motives nor an idealistic search for knowledge as the sole ends of a university education. Entering a university took on the overtones of a political act and implied opposition to nationalist aspirations.[5] Those who left the universities often com-

[4] But as Humayun Kabir, onetime secretary of the Ministry of Education, has observed, if the British had intended the universities solely as institutions for the training of low-level civil servants they would have emphasized commercial law, business administration, secretarial training, etc., rather than literary learning (Humayun Kabir, *Education in New India* [New York: Harper & Bros., 1957], p. 98).

[5] ". . . the educational movement has in a certain sense been political from the outset. That is to say, in the very nature of things, and by reason of the essential constitution of the mind, it was impossible to educate a single native of India without thereby affecting his relation to British rule. Education enables a man to understand better society, government, and his own relation to both. An educated man is able to

mitted themselves to a lifetime of political agitation, and many who remained experienced pangs of guilt. It was in this environment that the first student organizations emerged.

Student Organizations and the Nationalist Movement

The line between early student movements and early nationalist movements is difficult to draw, since the leaders who created nationalist organizations in the 1870's and 1880's were products of the new English universities at Bombay, Madras, and Calcutta.[6] The earliest evidence we have of direct political activity on the part of students records an incident in Calcutta during the first decade of the twentieth century. In 1905 students in Eden Hindu Hostel (a dormitory) burned Lord Curzon in effigy and boycotted college examinations to protest against the government's decision to partition the province of Bengal. During the next few years, Bengali students were among the most active participants in the early revolutionary parties. According to a report of the government's Sedition Committee in 1918, 68 out of 186 arrested in Bengal between 1907 and 1917 for revolutionary crimes were students; another 16 were teachers in schools and colleges. Students in Maharashtra and in the Punjab were also deeply involved in politics. In Maharashtra, Upendra Nath and V. D. Savarkar formed the Young India League in 1906, and in the Punjab a group known as Nai Hava (New Air) was formed to mobilize students and youth groups for revolutionary activities. In Bengal the National Council of Education was inaugurated for the purpose of creating national educational institutions.

For about fifteen years, student activities were directed against British policy in general; but in the early 1920's, student agitation came to be directed against the educational system itself. In September, 1920, the Indian National Congress passed at its annual conference a famous resolution calling for

> . . . gradual withdrawal of boys and girls from Schools and
> Colleges and earnest attempts to establish National Insti-

---

place himself in the universe; to realize better his true relation to what has gone before, and what will come after. If political ideas are in the air, the educated man will make acquaintance with them, and they will alter his mental outlook. So it might have been predicted, and so it was" (H. R. James, *Education and Statesmanship in India, 1797–1910* [London: Longmans, Green & Co., 1911], p. 118).

[6] These three universities were inaugurated in 1857. The University of the Punjab was started in 1882, and Allahabad University was founded in 1887. India's other universities date, in most instances, from the First World War or later.

tutions . . . . By a National Institution it is meant any Educational Institution that does not receive aid from government, is not in any way controlled or inspected by government and is not affiliated to any University established by government.[7]

Agitation for national schools and colleges to replace the government institutions was a major issue in the 1920's. Students at Bangabashi College in Calcutta came out of their classes in January, 1921, to demand that their institution be nationalized. Similar agitation occurred at Ripon and at city colleges in Calcutta. Many students and faculty of these Calcutta colleges resigned and, with the aid of the National Council of Education, created the Bengal National University. At Aligarh University, where Gandhi, Maulana Shaukat Ali, and his brother Maulana Mohomed Ali were urging students to join the nationalist struggle, the students demanded that the university disown all connections with government and revise its curriculums on national lines. Failing to persuade the trustees, the students and nationalist leaders established a new university, the Jamia Millia Islamia (National Muslim University) at Aligarh.

Within a few years after the First World War, a number of Indian-run educational institutions were created. In addition to Jamia Millia Islamia and the Bengal National University (later Jadavpur University of Calcutta), the Bihar Vidyapith, the Kashi Vidyapith at Banaras, the Tilak Maharashtra Vidyapith, and Tagore's Visva-Bharati at Santiniketan in Bengal were founded.

Meanwhile, Gandhi and the Ali brothers toured northern India, urging boys to withdraw from schools and colleges in order to participate in the national non-co-operation movement. In December, 1920, an All-India College Students' Conference was held at Nagpur under the presidency of Lala Lajput Rai, the Congress leader. Rai urged students to participate in the non-co-operation movement; he advised the law students to withdraw from their universities at once, the arts students to watch the situation and withdraw if necessary, and the medical and science students to remain in their classes.[8] Similar national student conferences were held throughout the 1920's, all closely associated with the Indian National Congress.[9]

[7] M. Muni Reddy, *The Student Movement in India* (Lucknow: K. S. R. Acharya, "New Age" [Nayazanana] Office, 1947), p. 78.

[8] *Ibid.*, p. 84.

[9] These were invariably under the presidency of eminent Congress leaders, such as Lala Lajput Rai, Sarojini Naidu, and C. R. Das. Generally several thousand stu-

In 1928 a student organization was formed in the Punjab under the leadership of Lala Lajput Rai. That same year students in Calcutta founded the All-Bengal Students' Association; its first conference was held under the presidency of Pandit Jawaharlal Nehru. In 1929 the ABSA claimed a membership of twenty thousand, published its own journal, was in touch with international student associations, actively demanded that Calcutta University modify the examination system, and was preparing to take part in the *satyagraha* movement led by Gandhi in 1930.

Although the ABSA was officially banned, student militancy in Bengal continued to increase in the early 1930's. Mammoth province-wide conferences including notable Congress leaders were virtually an annual event. Demonstrations of students shouting revolutionary nationalist slogans were popular, and several attempts were made by students to assassinate high government officials.[10] In Mysore and Kashmir as well as in British India, nationalist militancy grew throughout this period.

The first national organization of students was founded in 1936, with the establishment of the All-India Student Federation. Mohammed Ali Jinnah, the Muslim League leader, was its first president, and Pandit Nehru delivered the inaugural address to the first conference in Lucknow in August, 1936. Within two years, the AISF claimed one thousand affiliated student organizations with fifty thousand members. The new organization directed a host of demands to the seven state governments that were then under Congress control: a reduction in fees, the introduction of free and compulsory education, the elimination of antinational ideas from textbooks, the use of vernacular languages as media of instruction, compulsory recognition of student unions by the universities, student representation on the governing bodies of universities, more vocational training, relief for the unemployed, traveling concessions for students on railway and steamship lines, a ban on communal student organizations,

---

dents attended, and resolutions were passed urging students to leave school and college, wear *khadi* (hand-made cloth), and learn to spin and weave.

[10] In January, 1932, a Calcutta girl by the name of Bena Das unsuccessfully shot at the governor of Bengal. In her trial she read the following statement, which vividly illustrates the passion with which students participated in the national struggle: "I fired at the governor, impelled by the love of my country, which is being repressed. I thought that the only way to death was by offering myself at the feet of my Country, and thus make an end to all my suffering. I invite the attention of all, to the situation created by the measures of the government which can unsex even a frail woman like myself, brought up in all the best traditions of Indian womanhood. I can assure all that I have no sort of feelings against Sir Stanley Jackson, the man, who is just as good as my father. But the Governor of Bengal represents a system which has kept enslaved 300 millions of my countrymen" (M. Muni Reddy, *op. cit.*, pp. 124–25).

Students · 164

an end to discrimination, free military education in colleges and schools, compulsory civics, economics and science in secondary education, and the abolishment of degrading punishment such as caning and beating.[11]

Almost immediately after the Student Federation was organized, internal conflicts broke out between Communist and non-Communist students. The Communist section, led by K. M. Ashraf and Hiren Mukerjee (now a Communist M.P. from West Bengal), was critical of the Indian National Congress leadership, and favored more militant measures against the British than Gandhi's limited, non-violent *satyagraha* movement. In December, 1940, at the sixth all-India session of the AISF at Nagpur, the Communists and nationalists parted ways.[12] Thereafter, nationalist students supported the 1942 Quit India movement against the British, while those affiliated to the Communist group supported the war effort. In 1945 the nationalist group, with Congress Socialist support, reorganized themselves into the All-India Student Congress.[13] At the time of Independence, therefore, there were two major national student organizations in India: the Student Federation and the Student Congress.

In addition, several political parties had their own smaller student and youth organizations: the Samajwadi Yawuk Sabha (the Socialist-sponsored Young Socialist League), the Progressive Student Union (Marxist-left parties), and the Hindu Students' Federation and the Rashtriya Swayamsevak Sangh (Hindu communal parties). Non-party student activities centered around college student unions, voluntary student organizations with annually elected officers. Some of these college unions were controlled by politically partisan students, but others remained under non-party student control.

Post-Independence Student and Youth Movements

After Independence, sentiments against the affiliation of student groups with political parties grew. Congress leaders argued that the achievement of independence removed any need for a national student political move-

[11] *Ibid.*, pp. 143–44.

[12] Another split occurred earlier, in 1937, when Muslim students in Bengal seceded from the AISF to create the All-India Muslim Students' Federation. The AIMSF, with the blessings of Jinnah and the Muslim League, was active in Bengal, the Punjab, Bombay, Madras, United Provinces, Central Provinces, Delhi, and Aligarh. It was an enthusiastic supporter of the Pakistan movement.

[13] Humayun Kabir, who later became secretary of the ministry of education, was its first president.

ment. In 1950, in an effort to depoliticize students, the National Congress leadership took the initiative in creating a national, non-political federation of the various student unions. The Student Congress dissolved itself, urged the Student Federation to do likewise, and called for the creation of a National Union of Students. Both Nehru and Jayaprakash Narayan, representing the Congress and Socialist parties respectively, addressed the first NUS conference in September, 1950. But the Communist Student Federation looked upon NUS as an attempt to distract students from the Communist organization. Not until several years later, when the Communist party shifted to a popular front strategy, did the Student Federation lend its support to NUS.

In the same year that the All-India Student Congress was dissolved, an attempt was made by Congress to create a Youth Congress to continue the work of youth associated with the party. Many state Congress leaders were initially unsympathetic to this idea. Factionalism was already so great in many state Congress bodies that Congress leaders feared that a Youth Congress would simply add to their political difficulties. In a few states where young Congressmen had earlier created their own organization, they had run into conflict with the state leadership over the nomination of candidates for legislative assemblies. This new group did indeed become involved in dissensions inside the Congress party. Within a year it was dissolved.

Congress then created a youth department under the direct control of the party organization. In 1955, this department was made into a mass-membership organization, but remained under careful supervision of the parent body. The party organization appointed conveners to start a new Youth Congress in each state; in a few states these appointed conveners have been replaced by elected presidents and secretaries. Neither the national president nor the national council of the Youth Congress is elected by the membership or by the delegates to the national convention. An advisory committee to the Youth Congress is appointed by the president of the Congress party.

In 1957 the Youth Congress claimed two hundred thousand members, with the largest membership in Bihar and Uttar Pradesh. It is organized by district, and claims to be stronger in rural areas than towns. More than half of its members are older than twenty-two, indicating that a majority of its membership is beyond school and college. In many areas, such as Calcutta, the Youth Congress appeal is to established members of the community: young lawyers, businessmen, school teachers, doctors, and small landowners—in short, to the same people who are recruited by the Congress party organization itself.

Partly to avoid factionalism within the party, the activities of the new Youth Congress are carefully circumscribed. Among its major functions are training young people for Congress party work, creating study circles to discuss issues facing the country, organizing social service work to aid in floods and famines, canvassing during elections, and sponsoring sports and cultural activities. The national office of the Youth Congress, which is located in the main office of the Congress party in New Delhi, publishes a monthly magazine for its members. A feature of this magazine is a discussion article by an eminent Congress leader intended for Youth Congress discussion groups. The explicit purpose of these articles and discussion groups is to bring national leaders and young people closer together—that is, to make youth understand the program and principles for which the national Congress party stands. A related part of this program is the organization of study tours for young people to visit dams, community development programs, multipurpose projects, and the like, in order to arouse national pride in the five-year plans. In 1956, for example, four trains carrying two thousand youths toured the country for twenty-five days, traveling some seven or eight thousand miles. Youth camps are also organized to "impart true dignity to manual labor," to repair roads and school buildings, dig wells, reclaim land, and so on. Funds for these camps come from the central Ministry of Education which was allocated 10,000,000 rupees by the Planning Commission for student and youth social service programs. Youth camps have also been organized by the Congress Seva Dal (the Congress social service wing), and the Bharat Sevak Sangh, a non-party social welfare body whose president is the prime minister, which works closely with the government and the Congress party.

Political activity has been strongly discouraged in the Youth Congress. At a Youth Training Camp held in 1955, one state Congress leader told those present:

> There are two types of Congress work—parliamentary and constructive. The AICC has been giving great importance to constructive work. Youth Department is one through which we can carry on work of a constructive nature, and the programme will give lasting results. . . . As regards parliamentary work, Youth Department has got little to do with it.

The same Congressman added:

> Regarding special representation on the Congress Committees, a provision was made for women and backward classes. We never thought that youth should have a demand like this. I think that the Congress should be largely an organization of young people, so that it is an insult to youth and their intelligence that they should need separate representation. They can work in the organization and be elected in due course.[14]

The non-political constructive-work emphasis of the Youth Congress was stressed by another speaker:

> Young people . . . may be given special training in matters like love for the country, respect for the Constitution, obeying the national laws, honour to National Flag, avoiding foul language, removal of casteism, communalism and provincialism, safeguarding public property and helping the Government to check traveling without tickets and other irregularities.[15]

Discussions of controversial political and economic issues are avoided within the Youth Congress. The bulletin of the organization, *Youth Congress*, publishes regular discussion guides, but these are intended to provide information to members about the Congress point of view rather than to elicit discussion. Youth Congress organizational reports have noted that their members are ill-equipped to enter into controversies with students in other political parties; but the absence of seminars, debates, forums, and the like, hardly encourages the development of a well-informed membership. The official attitude seems to be that students and youth must learn about the Congress point of view, not examine it, develop it, or disagree with it. If opposition parties have been successful in winning organized student support at the universities and colleges, Congress has fallen behind by default. Eager to push students out of politics and into development work, Congress lost ground to the opposition parties, who in the meantime were winning student participation for electioneering work against the government and support for various

[14] *Youth and National Building* (New Delhi: All-India Congress Committee, 1955), p. 30.
[15] *Ibid.*, p. 33.

movements against existing authorities. Even now, Congress has no separate student organization, and only in the past few years has it attempted to regain student support and control of student unions.

In contrast to Congress, the Communist-dominated All-India Student Federation has been working continuously with students since 1936. Because it supported the war effort, the Student Federation was the only national student organization that worked freely during the war years. But because of its opposition to the national movement at that time, it lost much of its support. In Bengal it regained some strength by its activities during the great famine in 1943. In 1948 the Student Federation was host for the World Federation of Democratic Youth Conferences in Calcutta, and soon thereafter joined the militant Communist party struggle against the newly independent government. Not until 1951 did the Student Federation, like the Communist party of India, become more moderate in its attitude toward the democratic process and toward the government. The AISF then took increasing interest in organizing and controlling student unions at schools and colleges. In 1955 the AISF claimed a membership of over 100,000, with the largest numbers in Andhra (20,000), West Bengal (16,000), Hyderabad (14,000), Travancore-Cochin (13,000), and Uttar Pradesh (13,000), and a smaller membership in Bihar, Assam, Orissa, the Punjab, and Rajasthan.

But the AISF claims that its influence goes beyond its membership and that it has played an active part in the various student movements that have swept the country. In West Bengal, a center of AISF activity, the Student Federation agitated against fee increments in schools and colleges, and was active in the Bengal-Bihar merger agitation, in the teachers' strike, and in the movement against increased tram fares in 1953 and 1954. On the constructive side, the AISF—with financial support from the university, the Calcutta municipal government, membership donations, and private contributions—built a student Health Home, which has won it considerable support. Though the Health Home is run by the student union, the Student Federation is the most active group within the union. The AISF maintains that in 1955 its membership throughout the country participated in movements ". . . against increment of tuition fees, against difficulties of admission, in support of teachers' demands for better salary, in defence of union rights, for better facilities for education, for recognition of diplomas in technical institutions, against corrupt practices like removing teachers, etc." [16]

[16] *United for Better Education and Service to Motherland.* Reports and Resolutions of the Fourteenth Conference, 59th Session (Lucknow: All-India Student Federation, January, 1955), p. 2.

Two other student movements claim national coverage, the Progressive Student Union, sponsored by the Marxist left, and the Socialist-sponsored Socialist Student Organization. The PSU was started in 1954 and claims thousands of members in Calcutta and tens of thousands nationally. Like members of the Youth Congress and AISF, they are active in attempting to gain control of the various college unions, and have succeeded in a few of the Calcutta colleges. They participated in the 1954 teachers' movement for higher wages, sent volunteers to the Goa *satyagraha* campaign, and agitated against the attempt to merge the states of Bihar and West Bengal. In 1955 the PSU agitated against raising tuition fees, and in 1957 they participated in the protest against high food prices. The PSU is strongest in Calcutta, as are the other student groups in Bengal, and is less active in the rural schools and colleges. Its most active workers, like those of the Marxist-left parties that give it support, have come from East Bengal.

The Socialist-sponsored Socialist Student Organization has some strength in the colleges of Uttar Pradesh and Bihar, but little in West Bengal. The SSO controls a few of the Calcutta college unions, and many of its members are active in other student groups, such as World University Service and the National Union of Students.

Student Indiscipline

A persistent theme of British complaint against the Indians was the extent of "indiscipline" in schools and colleges. Any termination of educational activities, no matter what the cause, was viewed by the British as indiscipline. In the days before Independence, the most common form of indiscipline was the student strike, generally directed against both government and university authorities. The issues and demands around which strikes were organized varied: at Khalsa College in Amritsar a strike started when college authorities attempted to penalize nationalist professors; at Lahore Ayurvedic College students struck when several students were expelled; at Fyzabad (United Provinces) students left their classes when the college fined some students who had gone to hear Sarojini Naidu speak.

As we have seen, the pre-Independence student movement was not united as to its purpose and function: both the demands made and the techniques employed depended upon the orientation of the particular student group. Some students sought to organize on the basis of particular student needs—reduction in fees, changes in the examination system, and so on. These students, many of whom were active in the various student unions, opposed participation in any clearly political program or movement. Other students advocated participation in politics, but opposed the partisan affiliation of students to any particular political organization. Minoo R. Masani, the Congress Socialist leader, summed up this position in an address to the All-India Student Federation Conference in 1938:

> In a conference like this it is unnecessary to affirm that students should and can take active part in politics. One of the objects of the Students' Federation is to prepare students to take their due share in the struggle for complete national freedom. It is very proper objective for the student body, for it is the minimum programme on which almost all students, whether they be socialists, Gandhites or nationalists, can collaborate. While, however, a students' organization should have a political objective, it would not take the place of a political party. It should be political, but non-partisan, and its doors should be opened wide enough to admit students of all shades of progressive thought. I hope you will guard against all attempts by any political party or group whatsoever to dominate and control the Students' Federation.[17]

But as differences developed within the national movement over the ends and means of the independence struggle, it became increasingly difficult for students to draw a line between being political and being partisan. Schisms in the national movement were reflected in schisms in the student movement; as we have noted, the Muslim League created the All-India Muslim Students' Federation, and the Communists gained control of the All-India Student Federation.

University and government authorities sought to prevent all student agitation, but they were particularly incensed by agitations which resulted in violence, including the destruction of school and college property. From the point of view of the student leaders of these organizations, the success of an agitation was not measured solely by whether or not college and university authorities acceded to demands. The student movement was primarily important, they believed, to the extent that it "raised

[17] M. Muni Reddy, *op. cit.,* p. 148.

the students to a higher level of thought and action." [18] Agitation itself, by evoking mass participation and by arousing the social, political, and economic consciousness of students, was useful even if a given strike or agitation did not achieve its stated objective. Action without results was said, in a perversion of the tradition of the Bhagavad-Gita, to be enough. One expression of this philosophy was a tradition of martyrdom which became associated with student agitation. Especially in the Punjab and Bengal, nationalist students criticized Gandhi's commitment to non-violence, and almost everywhere a self-effacing act of violence was greeted as the ultimate in nationalist political action. [19]

Since Independence, student political activities have continued and indiscipline has, if anything, increased. Large-scale disturbances led to the closing of Lucknow University in 1953 and Banaras Hindu University in 1958. In Patna a clash over increased bus fares for students resulted in police firings. Police firings against students also occurred in Gwalior in 1950 and Indore in 1954. In 1959 students at Amritsar were arrested in a pro-Hindi movement; in Calcutta students quit halls in the midst of an examination; in Jaipur students launched a mass movement against an increase in fees; and in 1960 major disturbances occurred in Lucknow and Allahabad.

Many explanations for these outbursts have been offered. The central government's Ministry of Education attributes them to "loss of leadership by teachers, growth of economic difficulties, general loss of idealism, absence of social life, a sense of fear and insecurity and unhappy living conditions." [20]

A detailed study on student indiscipline was prepared by Humayun Kabir, educational advisor to the Government of India. [21] The specific

[18] Prabodh Chandra, *Student Movement in India* (Lahore: All-India Student Federation, 1938), p. 76.

[19] The following incident recorded by Prabodh Chandra illustrates not only an act of martyrdom but the attitude of a student leader toward martyrdom. "On one fateful day sometime in the afternoon, when some students in a group were coming after attending the meeting at Badshahi Mosque, they were stopped by the Police and an Honorary Magistrate and I were assaulted. One of the students, Khushi Ram by name, was fired at seven times but that valiant soldier of the motherland did not move an inch and with the eighth shot dropped down in a pool of blood. But it is significant that not one shot was received by Khushi Ram on his back. The writer himself saw the dead body when it was taken to the cremation ground. The bullets had perforated his chest and it appeared a sort of garland resting on it" (*Ibid.*, p. 61).

[20] Government of India, Ministry of Education, *Education in Universities in India, 1951–52* (Delhi: Government of India Press, 1954), p. 3.

[21] Kabir's memorandum has been reproduced in his *Education in New India* (New York: Harper & Bros., 1955), chap. viii.

proposals contained in Kabir's memorandum were endorsed by the Central Advisory Board of Education in January, 1954. Later in the year a series of letters containing concrete proposals concerning discipline in schools and colleges was sent by Kabir to ministers of education in each of the states.[22] The term "indiscipline" as employed in these official documents, and in non-official writings, is a pejorative, covering a wide variety of student activities. Behind this term lie at least four different kinds of activities:

1. Activities associated with larger political movements in the area surrounding the school, college, or university. In Calcutta students have actively taken part in the Bengal-Bihar merger dispute, the tram fare agitation, the food agitation, and other local movements. In Ahmedabad, some students actively collaborated with sections of the business community in the agitation against separating the city of Bombay from Gujarat. In these and similar movements, student political organizations have been closely associated with non-student organizations: business groups in Ahmedabad, and the many opposition parties in Calcutta.

2. Demands by students upon university authorities. Students have opposed fee increases, demanded an increase in admissions to colleges, and called for the recognition of student unions. Major agitations of this kind have taken place in Lucknow, Banaras, and Jaipur.

3. Student demands upon non-university authorities on issues of special concern. Demands for special student rates on trams are most common. In Kerala, students agitated when special concession rates on the ferries that ply the backwaters of the state were canceled. Likewise, clashes occurred in Patna over bus fares for students.

4. Sporadic, generally unorganized outbursts by students only vaguely associated with concrete demands, such as walkouts on examinations and the subsequent destruction of college property, attempts by students to ride on buses and trains without paying fares, beatings inflicted by students on ticket collectors, and other acts of delinquency. These have increased in frequency.

Although the term "indiscipline" is often used indiscriminately to cover all these activities, it is most properly used to denote the techniques employed by students rather than the demands they make or the targets of their demands. Strikes, destruction of property, attacks upon personnel,

[22] These letters and a letter by Jawaharlal Nehru to state chief ministers have been published by the Ministry of Education in 1956 under the title *Letters on Discipline,* by Humayun Kabir.

and forcible detention of university officials in their homes (such as occurred in Banaras) are common forms of indiscipline.

To understand all the factors involved in the various types of student activities, indisciplinary and otherwise, would require a careful anaylsis of concrete cases. In the remainder of this chapter, we shall take a brief look at two types of indiscipline, one concerned with demands made by students at Banaras on the university authorities and the other involving participation by students in Calcutta in larger city-wide and provincial political movements. From these two types of cases—one within the university framework and the other outside—we may obtain a clearer notion of the political role played by students in India.

BANARAS: AGITATION WITHIN

In October, 1958, student indiscipline at an Indian university reached its high point when Banaras Hindu University was closed by its executive council. Tension at the university had developed over the report of a committee, headed by A. L. Mudaliar, which had been appointed by the President of India to examine the general state of discipline in the university. In view of earlier disturbances, it was also to examine the general workings of the act, statutes, and ordinances of the university.[23]

The committee reported that although the university was under the control of the central government, it had in fact lost its all-India character and had become a "hot-bed of intrigue, nepotism, corruption and even crime." The "real menace to the satisfactory working of the University [lay] in the teacher-politicians and the formation of groups which dominate in all affairs of the University," especially the formation of the dominant "Eastern Uttar Pradesh group." The committee pointed to the unsatisfactory method of selecting teachers, the concentration of power in the hands of principals and its consequent misuse by them, the pressure for admission of large numbers of students, unfair examination practices, and in general the diminution of merit as a standard in university life. Both teachers and students were found to frequent "houses of disrepute." In analyzing lawlessness and indiscipline among students, the committee argued that they were actively guided by teachers.

[23] Government of India, Ministry of Education, *Report of the Banaras Hindu University Enquiry Committee* (Delhi: Government of India Press, 1958). The Committee received about one hundred memoranda and interviewed seventy-four persons.

In order to "root out such group politics" the committee recommended that the President take over the administration of the university, and that an executive council appointed by the President assume responsibility for governing the university until existing legislation could be changed; the President issued an ordinance taking over the university in June. On September 2, 1958, the Lok Sabha (House of the People) passed the "Banaras Hindu University (Amendment) Bill, 1958," which incorporated many of the recommendations of the Mudaliar Committee. A few days earlier students began picketing the residence of the vice-chancellor, who supported reform, and on September 2 they began to picket the residence of the registrar—in both instances preventing the university officials from leaving their homes. On September 6 a crowd of fifteen hundred students collected at the gate of the university to prevent the entry of the vice-chancellor to the university grounds. Later in the month the students similarly prevented the members of the executive council from entering the campus.

Students from the Ayurvedic (traditional medicine) College were particularly active in the attacks against the vice-chancellor. Pamphlets were issued vilifying the university authorities, mass meetings were held almost daily, and the safety of university teachers was threatened if at any stage the authorities were to close the university. On October 7 the executive council decided to close the university. Thousands of students marched to where the vice-chancellor was residing, demonstrated at his gate, and hurled abuses at him. Crowds of students then marched to Bharat Press, which was not supporting the students' agitation, and damaged some property of the press. Orders were issued under Section 144, an ordinance which prohibits gatherings of five or more persons. On October 8 a clash between students and police occurred; stones were pelted and a *lathi* charge (a charge with police sticks) ensued. In all, forty-three students and one ex-student were arrested during the disturbances.[24]

The demand of the students had been two-fold: an open judicial inquiry into the charges leveled against them (particularly those concerning immoral acts) in the Mudaliar Committee's report, and the resignation of the vice-chancellor, Dr. Jha, for subscribing to the report. The agitation and demands of the students were closely backed by sections of the faculty. The correspondent of the *Statesman* reported:

[24] This account is based upon the official statement by the minister of education, K. L. Shrimali, before the Lok Sabha. See *Lok Sabha Debates* (Second Series), XXII, No. 4 (November 20, 1958).

During my two-day stay here I have met leading personalities of the two rival camps. The first comprises members of the University administration who stand for cleaning up the campus of the elements which have brought its dishonour. The other is a group of teachers who have raised an army of students to resist a change. . . .

The teachers of the latter camp startled me with their defence of student behavior. They were a picture of offended innocence. The students have been entirely non-violent, they said. Agents provocateurs had thrown the stones which littered the road after the arrival of the police. The extent to which the teachers went on explaining away student behavior was amazing.

They raise the suspicion that perhaps they are the authors of the agitation in which students have played the role of misguided puppets. The teachers treat the Vice-Chancellor as a legitimate target for criticism, for he leads the new reformist party, supported by the new Executive Council and the Government of India.[25]

The agitation at Banaras Hindu University suggests that close faculty-student relations do not ensure a disciplined and orderly university when factional conflicts divide the faculty or separate the faculty from the university authorities.[26] In Banaras, conflicts existed over the very charac-

[25] *Statesman* (Calcutta), October 15, 1958.

[26] The extent and effects of sectional conflicts were highlighted in a letter by C. P. Ramaswami Aiyar, onetime vice-chancellor of the university, to the President of India: "The background and personnel of the University, due to unchecked and untoward developments during several years are such that I have to devote eight or ten hours a day to routine, petty and often contentious work of a taxing character. Unfortunately, there is no one else who could adequately deal with the almost daily quarrels and intrigues amongst professors and their subordinate lecturers and tutorial and administrative staff. Furthermore, the University is divided into two (in fact three) irreconcilable parties or groups, partly political and partly personal in character, that seek, not only by open and unrestrained disputes among themselves, but also through engineering anonymous and other communications and by other means, to acquire influence in the various academic bodies of the University, e.g., the Executive Council, the Standing Committee and the Academic Council. All but a few of the highest grade of Professors and Readers are engaged in this unceasing and ignoble conflict to the obvious detriment of their legitimate duties towards their students or in the direction of research. Hardly any department in the University but has two groups which are constantly laying their respective complaints against each other. . . ." (*Lok Sabha Debates* [Second Series], XIX, No. 16 [September 1, 1958]).

ter and function of the university. Within the faculty there were those who argued that in effect Banaras should be a provincial university, re-cruiting both faculty and students from the surrounding area, while the university authorities argued that the university should retain its all-India character. Even more fundamental differences existed with respect to the position of the central government's University Grants Commission. This commission held that an expansion in university education should be related to the requirements of the economy; for only by limiting en-rollment could university standards be maintained, discipline enforced, and educated unemployment reduced. Others at the university argued that education is or should be a means of maximizing personal mobility; for only if education at the university level is open to all, is it possible for those lower in the social scale to rise out of their position. This group agreed that an increase in university education meant a growth in edu-cated unemployment, but they felt that those who had an education at least had an opportunity to rise, while those who lacked a university education had no such opportunity. The latter group, with its base in eastern Uttar Pradesh, felt that in the absence of an adequate number of colleges and universities in their area of the state—Lucknow, Allaha-bad, and Agra are to the west—Banaras should expand its number of admissions.

Conflicts also emerged between those who advocated, at least in prac-tice, the application of ascriptive criteria to all aspects of university life (especially to faculty appointments) and those who argued for the appli-cation of merit principles. The former group found support in the prin-ciple of university autonomy (university freedom from central control), devolution of power to principals of colleges, and the adoption of elec-tions in university bodies. While democratic arguments might be used in favor of ascriptive practices,[27] those who advocated the application of merit principles were in effect forced to defend what appeared to be greater authoritarianism. The power of the vice-chancellor was to be increased, that of the college principals reduced; power was to be taken from the elected court of the university and placed in the hands of a smaller, and for the most part appointed, executive council; and an ap-pointed selection committee would be in charge of appointments. In gen-eral, an effort would be made to sever university activities from politics. Elections, which intensify group conflicts, would be minimized; and devices would be instituted for achieving wide representation on all

[27] The Mudaliar Committee listed in an appendix to its report the members of the staff who are stated to be interrelated.

bodies. Those who held important posts in the university would in effect be responsible to the Government of India, i.e., the President, the Ministry of Education, and the cabinet itself. Controversies over educational administration were thus an extension of the arguments concerning the purpose of a university.

CALCUTTA: AGITATION WITHOUT

"I claim to represent the people of Eastern U.P." said one M. P. speaking on the Banaras Hindu University (Admendment) Bill,

> . . . and I can speak from personal experience of many universities, that no university has a greater record of service, none has more patriotic teachers and none was better managed than this university. . . . It was founded by one of the greatest Indians, the late Pandit Madan Mohan Malaviya. In all movements of freedom, in 1921, 1931, and 1942, it played a most glorious part. I remember some of the professors and students of this university worked with me during the "Quit India" movement in 1942 at great risk to their lives. One of its professors, Shri Radhe Shyam, worked in Delhi with Shrimati Aruna Asaf Ali and led an absconding life for three years, exposing his life throughout to the greatest risk. Many other professors did likewise. In fact, the major credit for the glorious part played by East Uttar Pradesh and Bihar in the "Quit India" movement must go to these professors and students of the Hindu University. Today our Education Minister says that they are dangerous persons, and they must be screened by persons who were licking the boots of the British government in India at that time.[28]

Students and professors of universities and colleges throughout India played similar roles in pre-Independence nationalist activities. Before Independence, student movements performed at least two important political functions: students supported the nationalist effort to disrupt British institutions and to destroy the bonds of loyalty between Indians and Britishers; and student organizations served as recruitment centers

[28] Statement by Shri S. L. Saksena, M. P., in *Lok Sabha Debates* (Second Series), XIX, No. 17 (September 2, 1958).

for political parties.[29] Since Independence, political parties in India have sought to build student political movements both as a means of building public opposition to the government and in order to recruit political leadership.

As we have already noted, prior to Independence, Calcutta was a major center of student activity, particularly in support of the various leftist groups within Congress. Since Independence, student organizations, especially those in the opposition, have continued their activities. Students have participated in a number of mass movements, including a tram fare strike, the Bengal-Bihar merger dispute, several agitations over high food prices, and a teachers' strike for higher wages. Student groups have continued to provide a small number of recruits for the various Marxist-left parties and the Communists. During elections, they have actively worked for candidates in Calcutta. But while students have been active participants in these political movements—often providing demonstrators, sign carriers, and slogan shouters—other organizations (political parties, trade unions, and refugee associations) have given the lead and have been the main organizers.

Apart from their direct political activities, Calcutta students are also involved in some "constructive" work, which often has political overtones. A Health Home for students has been sponsored by the Communist All-India Student Federation in Calcutta. Several organizations have small textbook libraries; a few have free coaching classes for school boys. Student relief committees work in flooded areas distributing clothing and medical supplies, often with the financial support of parent political parties.

In the main, students of Calcutta have not played a substantial role in influencing elections in the rural areas of West Bengal. Relatively few Calcutta students come from rural areas. Rural students in West Bengal are likely to attend the district colleges scattered throughout the state rather than those in Calcutta. Students in other cities of India, however, play a more active role in influencing rural elections because of their rural origins. In neighboring Patna, Bihar, for example, and similarly across the border in Dacca, where students come from predominately rural backgrounds, their participation in elections in rural areas has been considerable. Then too, although a large number of Calcutta

[29] Jyoti Basu, Phani Bora, Basava Punniah, Y. D. Sharma, and other Communists were among those who received their early organizational training as student leaders. See Gene D. Overstreet and Marshall Windmiller, *Communism in India* (Berkeley: University of California Press, 1959), p. 398.

students are highly politicized, their influence in political organizations throughout the state, rural or urban, is limited by the prevailing high state of political organization. In environments in which peasants, workers, and the middle class are effectively organized and appropriate channels exist for affecting public policy within an established framework, student organizations are likely to play a restricted role. In the absence of an effective party organization to conduct elections, and more generally to win public support, political parties find it necessary to turn to students for political support. Colleges and universities are centers of modernity; students have a greater awareness of the wider world than do other sections of society; their political awareness, considerable prestige, and relatively high degree of self-assurance in dealing with authority make them attractive recruits for political parties. The rising proportion of students from the rural areas has also increased their attractiveness to political parties as a source for recruitment. Thus the political role played by students from rural areas is related to the character of the recent growth in India's educational institutions.

India's Educational Explosion

In spite of the caution urged by many Indian educators, there has been an enormous expansion in India's educational facilities at the college and university level since Independence. In 1946–47, a total of 241,794 students were attending the universities; nine years later the number had reached 681,179; and in 1958 the University Grants Commission estimated the number at 750,000. By the end of the third five-year plan, it is estimated that it will be about 1,300,000. The number of students on the rolls of universities has thus been increasing by about 50,000 per year and may soon be increasing by 80,000 per year. In the period between 1950 and 1960, high-school enrollment jumped from 1.2 to 2.9 million, middle-school attendance from 3.1 to 6.3 million; and the number of primary-school children nearly doubled from 19 to 34 million. Most impressive was the estimate by the Ministry of Education that between 1947 and 1960 the percentage of children of elemenary-school age who actually attended school increased from 30 per cent to 61 per cent. By the end of the third plan, it is expected that 76 per cent of the children between the ages of six and eleven will be in primary school.

Many Indian educators, including the minister of education, saw a necessary connection between economic growth and a literate population. The inculcation of agricultural skills, they argued, required a literate rural population. Of the Rs. 1,448 million which the central government allocated for education in 1955–56, Rs. 540 million were invested in primary education, Rs. 154 million in middle schools, and Rs. 376 million in high schools. Substantial amounts were also invested in vocational-, technical-, and special-education schools (Rs. 81 million), and professional and technical colleges (Rs. 70 million). Although the minister of education has continually argued with the Planning Commission that a still larger part of the plan should be devoted to education,[30] investment in education has increased at a faster rate than during any other period of modern Indian history.

While educators have on the whole advocated growth in primary, secondary, and technical training, they have cautioned against increases in college and university enrollment. The official position was stated by C. D. Deshmukh, chairman of the University Grants Commission, when he said:

> I have no doubt myself that we shall have to restrict University education by and large to the number of university educated men and women that the country will be needing from time to time and that as regards the rest, the nation will have done its duty by expanding and extending as well as diversifying Secondary education, especially of a technical character.[31]

Considerations other than national economic needs, however, have affected the growth of university education in India. The desire of each state to have its own university in which the regional language, literature, culture, and history could be taught has been a major factor in the increase. Between 1937 and 1947 four new universities were established: Travancore, Utkal (in Orissa), Sauger (Madhya Pradesh), and Rajputana; and shortly after Independence, Baroda, Bihar, Gauhati, Gujarat,

[30] Members of the Planning Commission have opposed further expansion partly on the grounds of giving priority to agricultural- and industrial-development programs and partly on the grounds that the constitution assigns education to the states, not to the central government.

[31] Government of India, Ministry of Education, *Indian University Administration* (Delhi: Government of India Press, 1958), p. 16. This important document contains the proceedings of the vice-chancellor's conference on university administration held from July 30 to August 1, 1957. Perhaps no other single document states so clearly the attitudes of university educators toward the functions and structure of universities in India.

Jammu and Kashmir, Karnatak, Punjab, Poona, and Roorkee universities were created. Existing colleges and universities were also expanded; Banaras, for example, which had 4,872 students in 1946–47, had 8,586 in 1957–58.[32] While it is difficult to ascertain precisely what proportion of the growth represents students from rural areas, the Ministry of Education reports that in 1955–56 241,854 of the 681,179 students attending universities and colleges—or approximately 35 per cent—came from rural areas.

The increase of admissions into colleges and universities is often greatest in those fields in which the costs of education are lowest, and in which, unfortunately, opportunities for employment after earning a degree are at a minimum. Investment per pupil in professional, and especially technical, programs is high, but the expansion of arts and law programs involves a relatively small per capita expense. Many colleges and universities carefully restrict entrance into technical and professional programs, but freely admit all students into arts or law schools. In the Banaras agitation, it was reported that the most active students were those in arts, astrology, and Ayurveda (the traditional system of medicine)—fields which have comparatively low professional standing, low admission requirements, and few employment opportunities; and fields which, as they are taught in India, do not usually inculcate into the student any sense of self-esteem in the pursuit of knowledge.

Student Indiscipline and the Authorities

Intimidation of college and university authorities by students has not been uncommon. Vice-chancellors have been forcibly detained in their homes, and students have denied executive councils the right to enter university property. Many university authorities live in fear not only for their own physical safety but for the well-being of their universities. When city-

[32] The growth of Indian universities is also related to pressure by both students and parents. "The main problem in some of our universities," reports C. P. Ramaswami Aiyar, onetime vice-chancellor of several Indian universities, "of which I have had personal experience are those of autonomy and the intrusion of politics. Thus political and public pressure is brought to bear directly upon the Vice-Chancellor and indirectly upon those university bodies which may have, tangentially or otherwise, something to do with admissions, to admit a number of students especially in the Arts faculty, larger than what the university can adequately supervise and control with regard to educational facilities and opportunities. And what is more, it was argued once in a newspaper that the insistence upon standards is a fetish and that a university is not meant for intelligent students but for the lesser bright ones who cannot help themselves! This was also stated in the Academic Council of the University" (*Ibid.*, p. 25).

wide agitations occur, universities and colleges often close to avoid physical destruction by students. This fear is often accompanied by aloofness. University authorities are reluctant to meet with students to discuss university problems, even those involving students, for to do so, in their eyes, might involve a loss of authority in relation to the students. Furthermore, student demands are often interpreted as instruments of political parties outside, or of faculty factions within the university, which are trying to use students for their own political or personal purposes. They believe that a student's behavior is not an expression of student will, but of the will of others.

Relatively few colleges and universities have established an effective mechanism by which student dissatisfaction can be transmitted to university authorities. Whitley councils, student government, and department clubs have not been developed. Where student unions exist, they are often not welcomed by university authorities. All too often student unions are the main loci of political party activities on campus, and university authorities are doubly reluctant to deal with such bodies. In a few institutions, however, particularly where conflicts within the faculty are minimal, principals and faculty have been able to cope with student demands.[33]

The Ministry of Education in New Delhi, as well as state ministries and vice-chancellors of universities, has been concerned with the problem of student indiscipline. The main line of attack is a twofold one: to eliminate, in so far as it is financially feasible, the main features of college and university life leading to discontent; and second, to provide alternative activities for students so as to distract them from the proddings of political groups.[34] To this end the Ministry of Education sponsors an annual youth festival, and colleges and universities sponsor cultural festivals and sports activities, and encourage constructive work camps.

[33] The *Statesman*, October 10, 1957, reported that college principals in Rohtak successfully discouraged students in their colleges from participating in a Punjab-wide "Save Hindi" agitation against the state government. In one college, it was reported, the vice-principal spent a sleepless night at the college hostel trying to learn his students' views in regard to the strike move.

[34] K. L. Shrimali, minister of education, has said, " . . . Hon. Members have also suggested that we should make a psychological approach to the whole problem. As far as I can see, the only psychological approach that can be made with regard to Indian education at the present moment is that we must inculcate among our students respect for law and authority. If the students do not respect their teachers, and teachers do not respect the university or the college authorities, there would be no stability in society" (*Lok Sabha Debates* [Second Series], XIX, No. 17 [September 2, 1958]).

Discontent among students is likely to remain a chronic ill within Indian universities for many years to come. Efforts to improve physical conditions at the universities, to provide social, cultural, and sports outlets for students' energies, to restructure colleges and universities so as to minimize the factional conflicts, to provide greater employment opportunities for graduates, and to raise the status of teachers, will all help to prevent acts of indiscipline. These major improvements, however, are so closely tied to India's economic level and so limited by finances available to universities that progress is likely to be slow. Furthermore, economic growth is likely to increase the pressure on the universities for larger admissions, especially from rural areas. The desire for mobility invariably precedes mobility itself. Efforts to hold the line on university admissions will be difficult unless status and employment opportunities are made available through secondary-school vocational and technical-training programs, which are invariably costly.

We have noted that, in part, indiscipline is related to the growing ruralization of Indian colleges and universities. The threefold growth in university education in the ten years after Independence partly reflects a growing rural desire for social mobility. The enrollment at the universities at Patna, Jaipur, and Indore—loci of indiscipline—is of heavily rural origin, and even Allahabad, Lucknow, and Banaras have substantial rural populations along with students from small and medium-sized towns. This is not to argue that rural students per se present greater disciplinary problems than do urban students. Both urban and rural students regard the degree rather than education itself as a prerequisite for employment; and to the extent that employment is not forthcoming, they have no commitment to the educational process. The difference lies in the fact that rural students have a larger political arena in which to operate and are, in the long run, politically more dangerous to the Congress government than are urban students.

We have noted that the commitment to the educational process is low partly because in the late nineteenth and early twentieth centuries Indians began to think of the universities as denationalizing institutions, intended only to train Indians as clerks for the British administration and commercial houses. Although in the nineteenth century an Indian intellectual renaissance evoked interest in Western culture and scholarship, in the late nineteenth and early twentieth centuries the growth of religious and cultural revivalism destroyed this earlier inducement to pursue an education. Commitment to the educational process was further decreased when the educational system itself became a target of nationalist leaders.

Once the nationalists had viewed the system as politically partisan, the important questions became what political objectives should education have and how should these objectives be achieved—rather than how could education be made politically neutral.[35] Once they had begun to think of the educational system under the British as little more than an instrument of state policy, it was little wonder that Indians planned their new educational system largely in terms of inculcating nationalist objectives. Since Independence, educators who have wanted to improve the level of education have been frustrated by students, parents, and politicians who have pressed them to increase the number of university admissions. As a result, a status-defined concept of education continues to pervade Indian society.

It is also no accident that India's new technical and agricultural institutes have had no major disciplinary problems. Since Indian students, like students elsewhere, view education as the door to employment, a closer correlation between the employment needs of the economy and the training imparted by educational institutions is likely to result in a greater commitment to those institutions and a decrease in student indiscipline. Students of medicine and other scientific subjects have often remained aloof from agitations at their own colleges and universities. It is primarily the unemployed students in liberal arts, law, and ayurvedic medicine that have constituted the hard core of student agitations.[36]

It is also no accident that a few of the better colleges have had little problem with indiscipline. St. Stephen's in Delhi, Madras Christian College, St. Xavier's in Bombay, and Scottish Church College in Calcutta—all missionary colleges—and the more distinguished government colleges, Elphinstone in Bombay and the Presidency colleges in Calcutta

[35]At the Asian-African Students' Conference at Bandung in June, 1956, an Indian student said: "Friends, the aims and objectives of education can be arranged under the five heads of (1) democracy, (2) justice, (3) liberty, (4) equality, and (5) fraternity." Typically, neither truth nor knowledge was included.

[36] In an accurate witticism, one member of Parliament referred to the educated unemployed as the "educated unemployable." In all fairness to India's state and central governments, however, it should be noted that the cost per student in liberal arts and law is considerably less than in technical subjects. The argument that Indian students (especially Bengalis) are unwilling to study technical subjects or undertake vocational training is belied by the fact that the demand for admissions into technical and vocational schools (even in Calcutta) far exceeds the number of seats available. Among the more encouraging attempts to deal with these problems have been the growth in "basic" education in the primary schools (a Gandhian emphasis on utilitarian manual training), the creation of rural institutes of higher learning, new polytechnic institutes, and new agricultural institutes. These programs share a common emphasis of providing skills for a new mobile generation of Indians.

and Madras, have attracted the best teachers and, more successfully than other colleges, have instilled a love of learning.[37] These colleges have also been major centers of recruitment for the bureaucratic structure; and this, too, has minimized the political inclinations of their students.

We have tried to suggest that indiscipline within the universities or colleges reflects a breakdown in communication between the university or college authority and the students. Discontent does indeed exist, whether or not it is exploited by factions of teachers or by outside political parties; the development of appropriate channels of contact between students, student organizations, teachers, and university authorities may well be crucial to the maintenance of orderliness and discipline, without which universities and colleges can hardly develop as centers of learning. Grievances will undoubtedly persist, particularly as students from non-modern agrarian backgrounds enter modern educational institutions and develop higher expectations than their society is likely to be able to satisfy. The extent of the gap may be augmented by the prodding of political parties and by the unresponsiveness of university and government authorities. The result may be—and thus far has been—not only to widen the breach between students and authorities, but, more seriously, to widen the gap between politics and public policy in students' minds— the former being thought of as a futile but exciting outlet for personal protest, the latter as the edicts and actions issuing from an aloof and irresponsive government or university. The concrete demands by organized student groups against university and non-university authorities, while often irresponsible in their initial appearance, are often potentially negotiable and manageable. If university authorities are able to develop procedures by which students may present their grievances, universities and colleges will do more than eliminate indiscipline. They will educate students to recognize the relationship between politics and public policy, and thereby strengthen the capacity of students to function as adults within a democratic society.

[37] See Edward Shils, "The Culture of the Indian Intellectual," *Sewanee Review*, LXVII, No. 2 (April-June, 1959), 239–61, and No. 3 (July-September, 1959), 401–31.

VIII. POLITICAL GROUPS AND THE STATE

The choice of techniques employed by individuals or groups to influence public policy and administration is determined not only by the structure of the political system but also by the attitudes within and outside the government. In this chapter we shall examine, on the one hand, the attitudes which underlie certain techniques employed by interest groups to influence government and, on the other, the attitudes government officials hold toward these techniques. Our concern here is not with the desirability of one form of behavior vis-à-vis the other, but rather with how one accounts for particular forms of behavior and what the consequences of certain behavior are for the functioning of the system.

To understand the relationship between citizens and their government, we must be able to distinguish between those techniques of influence or coercion which have the sanction of the system and those which do not. Sanctions may be derived from either law or custom. Acts which are illegal may by custom be acceptable—for example, it is illegal to bribe a policeman, but often acceptable to do so. Conversely, for a government official to accept a gift may not be illegal, but may be viewed as unethical. Ethical standards cannot easily be translated into legal procedures, nor can rules be determined solely by legislation. The distinction between the gift and the bribe, for example, is a difficult one to make, for so much depends upon the attitude of the giver as well as the receiver.

Questions of legitimacy with regard to many techniques of influence are still unsettled in India. It is legal for business houses to make contributions to political parties, for example, but the Calcutta and Bombay High Courts have recommended that legislation ban such gifts. It is, of course, illegal to violate any law, but leftist parties in general, and devotees of Gandhiism in particular, look upon the violation of law for some larger political or social good as a legitimate means of attempting to change government policy. In the first instance, legislation is less restrictive than some sentiment; in the second instance, some sections of the public recognize greater freedom than legislation permits.

The popular belief that non-Western organized groups or diffuse mobs often use violence to influence public policy has some measure of truth. That Western political action is not and has not in the past been devoid of violence, that violence in India and elsewhere in Asia and Africa is often exaggerated in the press, and that the bulk of the demands are presented through other than violent means, hardly needs to be stated here. What does need to be stressed, however, is that much of the violence that occurs is neither sporadic nor anomic, but organized and planned.

Theoretically, mass activities—demonstrations as well as mass violence —may occur under at least two different circumstances:

1. They may be organized and used by government as a device for demonstrating a legitimacy based upon mass support. Few governments throughout the world today claim legitimacy on religious grounds, or on the rights of royalty, or on the right of power alone. Even authoritarian governments claim to be based upon the will of the people; and in so far as that will cannot be expressed through free elections, governments may call out street mobs to demonstrate the support of that will. Moreover, popular authoritarian regimes, such as the United Arab Republic, may also organize such mass activities against the nationals of other countries as a means of coercing other states.

Such mass activities are a common feature of state-citizen relations in a number of Near Eastern and Latin American countries. One must remember that in these countries institutional interests are often well organized, while political parties and voluntary groups are often absent, weak, or simply instruments of the state. In the absence of sturdy voluntary associations, an authoritarian regime is doubly dependent on government-organized mass movements to express a popular support on which its legitimacy can rest.

2. In India, where the Congress party reaches into the far sections of the country, and where three free general elections have been held, government does not need movements to demonstrate its popular support. On the contrary, government is so dedicated to development tasks, and so policy-oriented, that it fears the disruptive influence of mass movements.

Here mass movements are the organized instruments of political parties and interest groups which are concerned with shaping government policy or in the most extreme case with overthrowing government.

Both interest groups and government in India are now in the process of setting standards for their mutual relationship. It is the hypothesis of the author that, in general, central and state governments discourage those techniques that restrict the government's freedom of action, and encourage those techniques that provide the government with information. The government is, therefore, unsympathetic to mass deputations, public relations campaigns by business organizations, strikes, *satyagraha*'s, or *hartal's* (closing of shops), but is willing to listen to private deputations or resolutions proposed by particular groups. In fact, the government often attempts to direct its relationship with organized groups in such a way that these groups will not make demands at all, but will instead lend their support to development programs.

How coercion is used against the government, why it is used, and what effects it has can be clarified by looking at several recent instances of mass activities and violence in the city of Calcutta.

Our first account begins in early July, 1953, when the British-owned, government-regulated tram company in Calcutta announced an increase in tram fares. Leftist parties (including the Communists, Socialists, and several small Marxist-left parties) organized a Tram Fare Increase Resistance Committee, which, after failing to persuade authorities not to raise the fares, launched a *hartal* on July 5. Shops, many schools and colleges, and offices closed. In the north and south districts of Calcutta, which are heavily populated with middle-class Bengalis, it was estimated that only 10 per cent of the shops remained open. On July 7, newspapers reported that a boycott of the trams had begun and that demonstrators were pulling people off the trams. In anticipation of violence, the police arrested five hundred persons during the first few days of the *hartal*. The police encountered great difficulty with students. Taking shelter in the colleges situated on the main thoroughfares of Calcutta, they made periodic forays into the streets to erect barricades and pelt tramcars and the police with stones. The students were chased by the police into the college buildings, from which they continued to throw stones; the police refrained from entering the college compounds. This pattern of barricading tram tracks, pelting tramcars with stones, clashes with the police, retreats into college buildings in the face of police *lathi* (long sticks) charges, and renewed attacks occurred in several areas throughout the city. On July 10, crowds of demonstrators marched into Dalhousie Square (the site of the main government buildings), demanding to see the ministers and calling for a restoration of lower second-class tram fares. The police arrested the crowds for violating Section 144 of the criminal code, which prohibits assembling in groups before government buildings. Violence throughout the city increased. The Congress party issued a statement to its workers to resist "acts of goondaism being committed in the name of the Tram Fare Increase Resistance Committee." On July 16, the police commissioner issued orders under that portion of Section 144 which prohibits the assembly of five or more persons anywhere within the town and suburbs of Calcutta. The next day, after there had been numerous police firings at crowds, the West Bengal government requested that the military be sent into the city. By the eighteenth, mobs had taken control of the southern part of the city. On the nineteenth, the West Bengal government announced that it was referring the question of raising second-class tram fares to a tribunal and that the enforcement of the new rates would be suspended. The Calcutta Tramways Company agreed to the suggestion. A few days later the government withdrew Section 144 and released five leftist leaders who had been arrested under the Preventive Detention Act. The Tram Fare Increase Resistance Committee announced that the government's decision to refer the issue to a tribunal and to withdraw its orders under Section 144 were victories of the people. On August 1, the tram workers, who had supported the strike, returned to work, and the city was back to normal. The struggle, which had ended so victoriously for the opposition parties, had effectively prevented the tramways from increasing the fare by one pice—approximately one-quarter of a cent.

Calcutta has witnessed many other attempts by organized groups to coerce government. Hardly had the debris been cleared from the tram fare incident of 1953, when Calcutta was again plunged into violence in early 1954. The All-Bengal Teachers' Association rejected a wage settlement made by the West Bengal government and launched a sit-down strike near the government buildings. An All-Parties Teachers' Struggle Coordination Committee, in support of the teachers' association, launched a mass movement, violated Section 144, and threatened to forcibly prevent legislators from entering the assembly house. Buses and trams were burned, private cars stoned, street lamps and traffic signals smashed, roads barricaded, and shops looted in various parts of the city. As a result of the general hooliganism that broke out, four persons were killed and sixty-five injured. Immediately following these riots, the West Bengal government announced substantial concessions to the secondary-school teachers; and within a few days the strike was officially called off by the All-Bengal Teachers' Association, their demands having been granted.

But certainly not all the violence has resulted from premeditated acts by organized groups. Indeed, Calcutta constantly appears to be on the brink of violence. One day in 1955 four hundred young men, in protest against one "stiff" question in a school final examination that they were taking, marched out of the halls, and attacked examination centers throughout north Calcutta, smashing furniture, tearing examination papers, and assaulting students who did not agree to come out.

Still another incident occurred in April, 1958, when the Calcutta fire brigade advertised for candidates to fill one hundred posts of firemen at a salary of 55 rupees ($11) per month. Some ten to twelve thousand persons appeared for interviews. Unable to cope with the crowd, the authorities announced that there would be no recruitment that day. The crowd burst into fury, and the police reacted with a *lathi* charge and tear gas. Furniture was broken, windows and doors smashed, and one hundred fifty persons were arrested.

No sooner had the police settled with these unemployed than the refugees of Calcutta began a mass campaign to prevent the government from sending Bengali refugees outside the state for resettlement. Clashes between refugees and police took place daily, with hundreds of arrests. Traffic was blocked by demonstrators, buses and trams were held up, and traffic was entirely dislocated. After a month of agitation, the government agreed that no one would be sent outside of West Bengal against his will. The civil disobedience campaign was called off, and the government released from jail some four thousand refugees and refugee leaders, mostly opposition members of the legislative assembly.

Anomy and Mob Violence

Part of India's violence—but only part—can be accounted for by anomy, that is, that condition of lawlessness in which the participants have no explicit ideological rationale for the violation of law. An anomic outburst is unplanned, and is analogous to the temper tantrum of a child whose violence is directed at all objects within reach. In a mob it is an expression of discontent, undefined or unclearly defined—of inarticulate or poorly articulated demands upon public policy; and it occurs when there has been no organization for the expression of demands.

One component of Indian mobs is the *goonda*.[1] *Goonda*, in Bengali and other Indian languages, means ruffian, hooligan, bully, a rough. The *goonda* is found in every Indian city, and has, in the past, played an active part in strikes, Hindu-Muslim communal riots, and mass, especially violent, movements. In Calcutta, the *goonda's* are watched over by the Anti-Rowdy Section of the Calcutta Police. Between July, 1954, and October, 1954, fifty-five hundred persons were arrested by the Anti-Rowdy Section for various crimes. Of these, some 90 per cent were classified as "hardened criminals," i.e., old offenders. The other 10 per cent were first offenders and were mostly unemployed youths, and school and college students who had been arrested for riotous conduct or indecent behavior toward women. The bulk of the arrested rowdies were from West Bengal or from Bihar. Very few were from East Bengal, indicating that, contrary to popular belief, refugees in Calcutta had not been recruited into *goonda* circles. Most of the *goonda's* were under forty, bachelors or members of families for whom they had no financial obligations, urban, and generally Calcutta-born. Since no more than one-third of Calcutta's population was born in Calcutta, the community from which rowdies are recruited is relatively small.

The rowdy is a professional. He thrives on pimping, pickpocketing, and other illicit activities, including smuggling. The police believe that rowdies are organized into small groups, or gangs, but that there is no syndicate comparable to that in large American cities. This may be related to the fact that the police in India's cities are controlled by the state, not by the municipality. It is therefore difficult for permanent ties to develop between local political parties, the local police, and local gangsters—a combination virtually essential to effective syndicate operations in a modern city. It may be, too, that large-scale organized crime demands a higher level of inter-personal trust and skill in organization than one ordinarily finds in Indian life.

Rowdies are not completely unorganized, however. Gangs of rowdies have ties with business houses in Calcutta and have not infrequently been

[1] In spite of its obvious importance in politics, virtually no research into the social composition of the mob has ever been conducted. Part of the difficulty, of course, lies in getting such data from mob members in the midst of activities; and at the end of outbursts, mobs disperse before data can be collected. Some information, however, can be obtained from police records. In July, 1954, the Calcutta police department created what is known as the "Anti-Rowdy Section" to cope with *goonda's* in the city. The records of that Anti-Rowdy Section were, unfortunately, not available to this researcher, but some data have been culled from newspaper accounts and from an interview with a high police official.

used to break strikes. There are frequent rumors that political parties have made use of *goonda*'s, and that *goonda*'s were used, particularly by the Muslim League, in the 1946 communal disturbances; but these claims are difficult to prove. The rowdies are so eager to foment violence for the looting that results that a highly organized relationship between parties and rowdies need not be hypothesized.

Somewhat disconcerting is the fact that professional rowdies are not newcomers to the city, but long-time urban dwellers. Were the criminal elements recruited from recent migrants to the city, who are faced with the usual difficulties of adjusting from rural to urban life, then as migration ceased or diminished, crime would be expected to diminish also. But since the criminal elements are recruited from that one-third of the population born in Calcutta, the problem may very well increase as the city develops a larger settled population without rural roots. Contrary to popular belief, the migrant's ties to the village and to his family, his uncertainty and perhaps even distrust of the big city, lead to a kind of orderliness; it is the settled urban dweller, dependent upon the city for income and security, who turns more easily against authority and joins the underworld.[2] The rural immigrant needs to be acculturated to urban life before he turns to professional crime. The villager must be taught not to fear authority, but to be contemptuous of it, before he or his descendents will become criminals.[3]

The Organization of Violence

Most of the violence in Calcutta has occurred when leftist parties sponsoring an agitation have chosen not to restrain their participants, although deliberate, planned efforts by the authorities to avoid violence may in some cases prevent an outburst. In September, 1957, for example, a long march of demonstrators moved along one of Calcutta's main thoroughfares. The demonstrators were employees of the city government demanding a Puja (a fall holiday) bonus. A mounted police unit crossed

[2] The argument that anomy is associated with a lack of a sense of responsibility is supported by the fact that the rowdies are generally described as bachelors. According to the 1951 census of West Bengal, there are 570 females to 1000 males in Calcutta. Approximately 17 per cent of the adult population has no married life. The census report suggests that the instability of Calcutta civic life may be attributable in part to this disparity between males and females and the absence of family life, which restrains moods of violence.

[3] Even then, some ethnic groups (such as the Santal tribals from Orissa, or Oriyas in general) rarely turn to professional crime.

the intersection through which the demonstrators were marching. On both sides of the intersection were long lines of cars, horse-drawn rickshaws, bicycles, and pedestrians held up by the marchers. As the mounted police crossed the line of demonstrators, the strikers pushed several of the horses against the backs of automobiles. The horses, hemmed in between cars, reared, but the riders held fast. The demonstrators, apparently attempting to provoke the riders to attack, again pushed against the horses, but the policemen, obviously under orders to restrain themselves, held back. The horses were calmed down, and the mounted police proceeded ahead.

Provocation is described as a technique by one Bengali writer:

> Processions have become a routine affair particularly in large cities. The technique is to have convergent processions surrounding the Legislative Assemblies when they are in session. There is dislocation of traffic when it is even normally most congested and there is passionate shouting of slogans and fire-eating speeches. The processionists are inevitably held in check by an elaborate arrangement of the police force. Questions are raised by the sympathizers inside the Legislature and the Government leaders are requested to meet a deputation from the procession. It is inevitably turned down and the signal for increasing the pressure of the procession is given. The police *lathi-charge* or teargasing the mob is welcomed by the leaders of the processionists in a morbid mood. If there is firing and some are wounded, it is considered a great victory for the day, once again demonstrating the callousness and the brutality of the party in power! [4]

Precisely how much organization, if any, goes into the creation of violence is not known. Often the sponsors of mass movements may indicate by their public statements whether or not it is their intention to restrain violence. Leftist threats of "mass action" are generally interpreted in Calcutta as an indication that the leftists will make no efforts to restrain violence. There is evidence, however, that a decision by the sponsors of mass movements to restrain the participants and to avoid violence can in fact result in a non-violent movement. In the many instances in which government has conceded to violent demonstrators, the

[4] K. K. Sinha, *Towards Pluralist Society* (Calcutta: Writers House, 1957), p. 25.

parties concerned have been able to call a halt to the violence, thus suggesting that there is a measure of control. But when passions are high and leftist parties initiate a mass movement, in the form of either mass demonstrations or civil disobedience, to what extent is it possible for them to avoid violence? The Gandhians, armed with a philosophy of non-violence, insist that it can be avoided; but when the leadership is not committed to the philosophy of non-violence, is it possible? If so, then one could argue that when violence does occur, it is organized, or alternatively, that it occurs in the absence of a decision to restrain the participants. Evidence to this effect can be found in the agitation over the West Bengal-Bihar merger proposal.

On January 24, 1956, the chief ministers of West Bengal and the neighboring state of Bihar announced their intention to merge their two states into one large multilingual state. The proposed merger was immediately endorsed by India's Prime Minister Nehru, for the proposal ran counter to the general movement in India to reorganize all of India's states into unilingual units.[5] Eager to stop what was viewed as a fissiparous movement throughout the country, the chief ministers of West Bengal and Bihar, with the support of the prime minister, agreed to try to call a halt and return to the notion of multilingual states. They also thought that a merger would end the dispute over boundaries between the two states. The chief ministers issued a joint statement to this effect with little prior consultation with local people and with no prior public discussion.[6] In Bihar, the proposal was greeted by mixed, but on the whole favorable, feelings (the proposal was endorsed by a vote of 157 to 25 in the Bihar Legislative Assembly). In contrast, it met with strong opposition in West Bengal, where many feared that in a united province they would be outnumbered by the Biharis.

In the weeks following the chief ministers' statement, Bengali political groups maneuvered to win support for and against the move. The pro-

[5] The government States Reorganization Commission, which had issued its report a few months earlier, agreed to reorganize most of the states along linguistic lines. But from the Punjab, Assam, Bombay, and other states, there were strong and hostile reactions to the report—in some instances because the demand for a linguistic (or tribal) state was not granted, in others because the precise definition of boundaries was unsatisfactory. West Bengal and Bihar, for example, quarreled over several border districts. Sentiment in each state, especially in West Bengal, was against the proposal of the government's States Reorganization Commission.

[6] The joint statements of the chief ministers have been reproduced in *Regionalism versus Provincialism: A Study in Problems of Indian National Unity*, by Joan V. Bondurant ("Indian Press Digests Monograph Series," No. 4 [Berkeley: University of California Press, December, 1958]).

posal was immediately endorsed by the president of the West Bengal Congress party. Many Bengali Congressmen were unenthusiastic about the proposal, but the Congress legislative party gave it a conditional endorsement. The Calcutta University senate, on the other hand, adopted a motion that the proposed merger be dropped. When the West Bengal Legislative Assembly met on February 2, the opposition parties boycotted the opening address of the governor. The opposition-sponsored West Bengal Linguistic State Reorganization Committee demanded that the merger proposal be withdrawn before February 20, or they would launch "direct action" such as general strikes and *satyagraha's*. At a meeting of the committee, opposition leaders emphasized that if a mass movement were to be undertaken they were determined not to allow it to degenerate into violence. Were the opposition parties genuinely against violent demonstrations and were they, in the light of the intense feelings on this issue, capable of avoiding violence? The evidence suggests that they were.

Biharis constitute a substantial part of the population of West Bengal and of Calcutta. A large part of the work force in factories comes from Bihar. Were demonstrations to become violent, the resident Biharis might easily become targets of the Bengali demonstrators. In the excitement of communal fury, no one could say what would happen—but everyone, including the leaders of the opposition parties, remembered the bloodshed of Hindu-Muslim riots. The opposition parties had an additional reason for avoiding violence. The Communists, Marxist-leftists, and Socialists were all heavily engaged in trade union activities. All were organizing Bihari factory workers, and all had their eyes on the textile industry, in which many Biharis worked, as a prime target for further trade union expansion. Battles between Bengalis and Biharis would thus conflict with the interests of the opposition parties.

The Linguistic States Reorganization Committee announced that it would call a general strike and *hartal* in Calcutta on February 24, and that it was preparing for a long struggle to resist the proposed merger. The committee also announced that it would send fifty volunteers to march in front of the main government building in violation of Section 144; and that in order to maintain peace, fire services, ambulances, hospitals, medical personnel, telephones, electric and water supply, and news agencies and newspapers would be exempted from the general strike.

Aware of the intentions and efforts of the opposition parties to avoid violence, the government itself took steps to maintain peace. Authorities of the state transport service said that they would not run any of their vehicles on that day. The bus syndicate and taxi associations indicated that private buses and taxis would probably not run on the day of the general strike. It was also announced that the trams would not run. Congress members of the legislative assembly slept in the assembly building overnight because they feared there would be transport difficulties the next day.

Both government and opposition were prepared. Both realized that intentions were not enough. The shadow of violence hung over this volatile city; and if violence were to be avoided, it had indeed to be conquered. The police feared that professional rowdies might precipitate violence. The Anti-Rowdy Section of the Calcutta police moved in. The night prior to the general strike, the police rounded up four hundred fifty persons on their roster as a "precautionary measure" against any incidents. The arrests were made on a variety of pretenses—vagrancy, questioning, and so on—so as to get the rowdies out of the way during the first day of the demonstrations.

On February 25 a complete *hartal* occurred in Calcutta. The city held its collective breath. Commercial establishments, factories, bazaars, shops, and cinemas were closed. Trams and buses were off the streets. Even schools and colleges were closed. Fifty-three persons were arrested for violating Section 144 before the main government building in Dalhousie Square, but no violence was reported.

Linguistic agitation took place elsewhere in the country at this time, and violence did occur, especially in Bombay and the Punjab. Nehru announced that he would not give in to violence. The Linguistic States Reorganization Committee in Calcutta announced that it would continue its demonstrations and its violation of Section 144. By mid-March some six hundred persons were in jail for violating this law. Small batches of demonstrators were arrested daily. Still no violence in Calcutta was reported. B. C. Roy, the chief minister, issued a statement saying that he would not force a merger of the two states, but would leave it to the people to decide. In mid-April, an opportunity was found for the people to choose. As a result of the death of a member of Parliament, a special by-election was scheduled for a northwest constituency of Calcutta. Congress nominated Asok Kumar Sen, a prominent lawyer, and the opposition parties united around Mohit Moitra, the secretary of the West Bengal Linguistic State Reorganization Committee. For three days before the elections the opposition parties suspended their agitation. On May 2 the results were reported: Mohit Moitra had defeated his Congress opponent by a vote of 84,953 to 51,880. On May 4 the chief minister announced that he was withdrawing the merger proposal, "bowing to the opinion of the people as expressed in the Calcutta Parliamentary by-election." The next day the agitation was called off; the opposition parties were elated; the committee called it a great victory for the people of West Bengal; joyous processions marched through the city to celebrate the victory. Moitra, secretary of the committee and now victorious candidate for Parliament, said that the people had really settled the merger problem "on the streets," in spite of Mr. Nehru's threat.

The Bengal-Bihar merger dispute illustrates that both opposition parties and government were aware of the volatile character of the city and of the role played by professional rowdies in precipitating the city into violence. Both sides assumed that violence need not be planned in order to occur, that on the contrary non-violence had to be planned. This raises the difficult question of why Calcutta is so volatile—why it is that large numbers of people can so easily have their emotions set off by rowdies. We may be able to find a partial answer to this question by examining more closely those demonstrators and rioters who join in the fracas along with the professional rowdies.

The Demonstrators

From newspaper accounts and eyewitness reports, we know that demonstrators may be Bengali and non-Bengali workers, and that refugees have taken part in many Calcutta demonstrations. Occasionally, but less commonly, there are demonstrations of villagers who have come into the city, generally from the Sundarban region south of Calcutta, a marginal agricultural area easily affected by poor weather. Above all, the Bengali middle classes—white-collar workers, the educated unemployed, school and college students—are active participants in demonstrations.

Demonstrators, then, come from many social classes, but those demonstrations in which the middle classes form the core are most likely to be violent. The 1943 famine, which impoverished the Bengal countryside and killed hundreds of thousands of villagers, resulted in little violence. Working-class strikes in Calcutta only rarely involve violence and almost never involve the entire city; and the many refugee agitations held in Calcutta have largely remained non-violent. In contrast, the violent agitations in Calcutta have been those involving the middle class: the strike against an increase in tram fares, the strike for an increase in teachers' salaries, and a small but violent agitation in 1954 of orthodox Hindus calling for a government ban on the slaughter of cows. The threatened post and telegraph workers' strike, the bank employee strike, and the West Bengal-Bihar merger agitation—it was these that immediately alerted the police for possible large-scale violence.

It is not easy to discern why the urban middle class of Calcutta is so prone to mass demonstrations and acts of violence. Part of the answer may lie in a high level of political consciousness[7] alleged to prevail among the middle classes, combined with a low level of political organization and action through legally prescribed channels. Voting turnout, for example, does not reflect this purportedly high degree of interest in politics. In 1952 the voting turnout in Calcutta's twenty-six constituencies for the legislative assembly election was 37 per cent. In contrast, a sample of ninety-four totally rural constituencies had a voting turnout of 44.6 per cent.[8] In the 1957 elections the Calcutta vote rose to 46.9 per cent, but the rural vote had risen to 52.2 per cent. This disparity demonstrates that the popularly believed proposition that illiteracy results in a low voting turnout, and literacy in a high turnout, is patently false. A close examination of the urban vote in West Bengal further indicates that those constituencies which have a high working-class population generally have a higher turnout than those which appear to be more heavily middle-class.[9]

Although middle-class participation in civic associations is not common in Calcutta, trade unions have mushroomed among white-collar workers since the war. Employees in banks, mercantile houses, post and telegraph departments, city employees, and insurance workers are now unionized. Many members of the Bengali middle classes are also active in political parties, although the number of actively participating members in these parties is not large. In any event these parties are oriented toward national and state issues, and are rarely concerned with municipal

[7] "Political consciousness" is a phrase widely used in India. In Calcutta and in other urban areas, politicians agree that Calcutta has one of the most politically conscious populations to be found anywhere in India. Unfortunately, survey data on levels of information, interest, opinion, participation, etc., are not available.

[8] Data from Baldev Raj Nayar, "Impact of the Community Development Program on Rural Voting Behavior in India" (Master's thesis, Department of Political Science, University of Chicago, 1959).

[9] The turnout for the working-class constituencies in Hooghly was 49.3 per cent in 1952, 65.4 per cent in 1957. The Howrah vote was 43.1 per cent and 54.9 per cent. In contrast, the heavily middle-class constituencies of Calcutta were far lower. Alipore was 37.1 per cent and 44.2 per cent; the Fort was 32.3 per cent and 38.3 per cent. (Data compiled from *Report on the Second General Elections in India*, II (1957), *Statistical*.)

matters. The few prominent civic activities (e.g., hospitals and some welfare institutions) are largely supported by business and commercial interests in the city.

In so far as the middle classes of Calcutta are organized, they have not been able to satisfy those demands which are of major concern to them. As we have noted, Calcutta residents look upon government, not private industry, as the institution responsible for maximizing employment, increasing wages, improving housing, and providing more food, more clothing, and medical and educational facilities.[10] But efforts to obtain these improvements from the government are likely to remain frustrated, for the demands are vast and basic—more jobs, lower food prices, higher wages, better living conditions—and they cannot readily be met by simple concessions from government. For reasons which are not obvious, the Bengali middle classes in Calcutta have taken no steps to organize their civic lives so as to improve local conditions. Since political parties are concerned with broader ideological questions or with larger issues of public policy, they make no effort to elicit public support for civic activities. Community efforts to clean the streets, provide play and recreational facilities for young people, eliminate begging, and encourage queues before tram and bus stops are almost non-existent.

The absence of civic activities in Calcutta cannot be explained in terms of the citizens' incapacity for corporate enterprise. In Calcutta there are many neighborhood (or, in Bengali, *para*) activities and associations, but these are focused on cultural activities. During the Durga Puja holidays, *para* associations collect money to build images to the goddess Durga, and plan festivities, processions, music, and so on. During Calcutta's winter season, many neighborhood groups organize music conferences—large-scale enterprises that tens of thousands of people often attend. Bengalis have also established hundreds, perhaps thousands, of small one-room libraries throughout Calcutta. But while the middle classes believe that cultural activities can best be organized by people acting in a voluntary capacity, the same middle classes believe that non-cultural civic matters are the affair of municipal, state, or central government.

Although the Bengali middle classes believe that non-cultural civic matters are an affair of the state, they also appear to believe that government is controlled by men who will not take action unless they are forced to do so. This image of government is in part a carry-over from the

[10] See chap. ii above.

colonial era, when government was in fact often unresponsive—*sarkar* (government) was against the people and not subject to its will. Since Independence, the government has sought to change this image, and in many areas it has succeeded; but it has been less successful in West Bengal than elsewhere. Perhaps this is because the economic situation in West Bengal has deteriorated, or because government there seems particularly inefficient and unresponsive; perhaps it is because leading Bengalis were alienated from the Congress movement in the late 1930's, with the result that some of the most respected Bengalis, who might have helped the middle class make an adjustment to the new government, were themselves in opposition to the Congress party. Whatever the reason, the fact remains that the Bengali middle-class image of government appears to have changed little since Independence.

As we have suggested, the use of mass pressure against the government (that is, the encouragement of large numbers of people to violate a law or declare their opposition to government policy through such public acts as demonstrations, strikes, and the closing of shops) is more than a legacy of the past. Since Independence, more sober attempts to influence public policy have often failed, whereas the chief minister of West Bengal, many of his ministers, and his administrative personnel have frequently proved more responsive to mass pressure. The reasons for their aloofness toward the more moderate demands of many organized groups are diverse. Under some circumstances, of course, they are confronted with conflicting interests, or may themselves favor inaction. The sympathies of an official toward landlords or businessmen may, for example, impede action on a petition. Demands made by mass organizations under the influence of opposition parties are naturally less likely to be considered than those pressures which come from within the Congress party. Unresponsiveness may also result from the lethargy which characterizes a substantial portion of the lower echelons of Indian administration, a lethargy that is reinforced by inflexible adherence to the formal rules of administration. Still another factor, although an intangible one, is the reluctance of government officials to respond to demands coming from a hostile source. Style of presentation is an important factor in the success of a petition. A militant attitude, a tactless entrance into a government office, or the failure of a petitioner to present his case through a "respectable" intermediary may cause the government official—whether elected or appointed—to be unsympathetic and unresponsive. And finally, government officials believe that their decisions with respect to some policies must be made solely in terms of some abstract consideration of the public good.[11]

Because of these considerations, teachers' demands for higher wages, or the demands of refugees for more assistance, or the desire of refugees not to be moved out of the state involuntarily, have often been initially rejected by the government without regard for the intensity of the feelings of those making the demand. Only when public order is endangered by a mass movement is the government willing to make a concession, not because they consider the demand legitimate, but because they then recognize the strength of the group making the demand and its capacity for destructiveness. Thus, the government often alternates between unresponsiveness to the demands of large but peaceful groups and total concession to groups that press their demands violently. Indeed, since 1947, some of the major concessions made by the government have been to mass movements, violent or non-violent.

It would be an oversimplification, however, to view mass demonstrations and violence solely as devices for influencing public policy. Parties and interest groups also look upon mass movements as a means of augmenting their organizations and winning mass support. Many groups in Bengal have not been effective in building themselves up as organizations. Membership is often indeterminate—except for a few hard-core militants—dues-paying is irregular, finances are uncertain, records are badly kept, regular meetings are rarely held, and there is no continuous organizational work. In the absence of a well-knit organization, their cohesion often comes from the general appeal of ideologies and broad slogans, the dynamism of the organization's leadership, and the mass movements in which the organization participates.[12]

[11] The chief minister's attitude is expressed in this statement: "If I hate anything in public life it is the creation of political sectors or groups for the sake of controlling political opinion. I am convinced that this universally practiced political manoeuvring cannot lead to the greatest good of the greatest number, and abuses, nepotism and dishonesty follow." Quoted in K. P. Thomas, *Dr. B. C. Roy* (Calcutta: West Bengal Pradesh Congress Committee, 1955), p. 189.

[12] The following story was told to me by a leading Praja Socialist party organizer in Calcutta. He had been asked to assist a local party organization in north Bengal. When he met with the local leaders he was told that they were in the process of building their organization, and that to do so they needed a popular issue on which to agitate and on which their party workers could get a reputation for self-sacrifice for the cause of the peasantry. There were many issues on which they could agitate —for lower irrigation taxes, lower food prices, and so on; but the party workers wanted to violate a law which would result in their arrest. By going to jail they would clearly demonstrate to the peasantry the extent of their devotion to the *kisan*

In contrast, the Congress party, with all its weaknesses, has a local organization with a regular membership and many activities. Only the Communists and the Hindu youth group, the Rashtriya Swayamsevak Sangh, have as effective an organization, and they do not cover the wide territory reached by the Congress party. In any event, the Congress party is in power, and therefore does not have to mobilize people to demonstrate its strength.

The use of mass movements by parties to strengthen their own organization is not without dangers, for the organization may be weakened if their mass movements do not in fact affect government policy. Political groups have learned that some of the most successful movements have been those to prevent the government from taking action—such as the movement to prevent an increase in tramway fares, or the agitations against a West Bengal-Bihar merger or a tuition increase at the University of Calcutta.

Political groups have tried with less success to coerce the government to take action. Within those groups launching such agitations, there have often been long discussions over the tactical advantages and disadvantages of particular movements. One such debate occurred before the September, 1957, food demonstrations in Calcutta. An All-Party Committee on Food was organized by the opposition parties in West Bengal to pressure the government into taking steps to bring down the price of food. The leftist parties demanded that government confiscate rice stocks from dealers, stop bank advances, which they believed encouraged hoarding, and store large government rice surpluses to maintain a constant supply, thereby reducing prices. Most of the parties in the committee felt that a general strike would hasten government action, and several of them also felt that the public was restive over high food prices and that an agitation at this time would strengthen leftist parties. The All-Party Committee met shortly before the Puja holidays and agreed to launch a four-day *satyagraha,* the high point of which would be a mass violation of Section 144 before the main government building. Every effort would be made to fill the jails.

One member of the All-Party Committee, the representative of the Revolutionary Socialist party, argued that a movement before the Puja

---

(peasant) movement. But what law could they violate? Section 144 was not in effect anywhere in the area. They could attack a government building or even the police headquarters with a few stones, but the Socialists were committed to non-violence. With the official from Calcutta, the local party leaders tried to find a law which they could violate non-violently, but to no avail! The local organization finally decided to launch a few demonstrations, but no civil disobedience movement.

holidays would be unsuccessful. Without the likelihood of a continuous movement, he argued, one that would persist for weeks as had the Bengal-Bihar merger agitation, the government would not give in. And, if peasants were to come into the city and march into the jails, as the All-Party Committee was advocating, they would want to see some results. The other parties on the committee overruled the RSP representative, however, and the agitation began. For four days, peasants, workers, middle-class supporters, and a few students violated Section 144 and flocked into the jails, but the movement ended with no change in government policy. Despite its objections, the RSP took part in this agitation because they did not dare oppose the decision made by the other leftist parties for fear that the RSP would thereby be isolated and accused of lagging behind the masses. After the campaign, an RSP representative in jail reported to his party that the peasants in his cell were quite restive since the government had not informed them whether they would be released from jail before the holidays began. Many were eager to return home for the festivities. Furthermore, many of the peasants wanted to know what results had come from their going to jail. The political workers, of course, could not answer. By taking part in the agitation, the RSP lessened the efficacy of mass movements; but if they had not taken part, they would have been in danger of being isolated from other leftist parties.

Legitimation and Violence

No Indian party or group publicly advocates violence. Some of the smaller splinter-left parties, such as the Revolutionary Communist party of India, do believe that nothing short of a violent revolution will overthrow the bourgeois order. But for the present, at least, even these groups believe that strikes, demonstrations, and *hartal*'s need not be violent. But these parties often welcome violence, look upon police attacks as a vindication of their argument that the state is an oppressive instrument of the ruling classes, and interpret the counterattacks by demonstrators as an indication of a growing revolutionary surge. But there are times, such as in the West Bengal-Bihar merger dispute, when the opposition parties have shown their capacity to avoid violence in spite of the passionate feelings aroused by the issue over which they were agitating.

There are groups, on the other hand, which look upon any act of violence as illegitimate. The Gandhians, and many in the Praja Socialist party who have been influenced by them, not only reject violence, but will take steps to prevent it as part of the preparation for civil disobedience. The Gandhian justification for the non-violent violation of the law grows out of an elaborate philosophical position.[13] Basically, those party leaders who claim to follow Gandhi's precepts argue that unjust laws ("unjust" as they define them) should be broken. For example, Suresh Chandra Banerjee, the Socialist refugee leader, attempted to justify a refugee *satyagraha* in 1950 in these terms:

> As regards to laws, I would like to mention with all humility that under the leadership of the father of the nation we have been taught how to break lawless laws, and if need be we will break laws again. Therefore the question of legal forms and other shibboleths are too late in the day. To us, life is more precious than legal forms. The refugees are trying to get shelter wherever they can and the question of legality or illegality is simply begging the question.[14]

Since Independence, the Congress leadership has argued that civil disobedience no longer has a place in India. So long as the government was run by aliens and laws were created undemocratically, Indians were justified in violating the law, they say. But now that laws are made by democratically elected Indian legislatures, laws should be obeyed; and those who oppose them should use their vote to change the representation in the assembly. While this argument has much support within Congress, the non-Congress Gandhians argue that the government is not adequately responsive to the people, that elected Congressmen are forced to vote as the party whip instructs, and that in any event, so long as the Congress party has such a strong hold on the legislatures, minorities suffering from injustices have no other alternative than to violate the law.

As Dr. Banerjee forcefully stated:

> Mainly we organize a demonstration because if a particular bill we oppose is not changed there will be a fight. If we are going to defy a law later, we must prepare the refugees for a fight, if necessary. This is also a way of expressing support. We may be tear-gassed and there may be *lathi* charge,

---

[13] For a systematic analysis of this philosophical position as it relates to *satyagraha*, see Joan V. Bondurant, *Conquest of Violence: The Gandhian Philosophy of Conflict* (Princeton, N.J.: Princeton University Press, 1959).

[14] West Bengal Legislative Assembly, *Debates*, April 11, 1950.

but it is a legitimate action to commit *satyagraha*. In a demonstration the people must have the right to violate the law. Peacefully, of course. If there is violence, it is because the government acts violently, not the people. Gandhi taught them this. *Satyagraha* and demonstrations are very effective on legislation. If speeches in the Assembly are backed by demonstrations outside, the speakers will be more effective than by merely arguing. Three of the four demands the opposition M.L.A.'s [members of the legislative assembly] made on the government this past July were granted. The government was not moved by persuasion, but by the force of public opinion. I have taken part in many mass movements. The tram strike that we led to force a cut in fares wouldn't have been successful otherwise. Or the Bengal-Bihar merger movement! Or the teachers strike! [15]

Again, the justification for the violation of law was the government's unresponsiveness. Were the government willing to consider the repeal of laws which certain groups considered unjust, were the government willing to take action to satisfy the demands of groups, and were the government willing to act as a result of a peaceful petition or group deputation—then, say the advocates of mass demonstrations and civil disobedience, such techniques for influencing public policy would be unnecessary.

A fundamental incongruence lies behind the relationship between organized political groups and the state—an incongruence between both their respective notions of the principles that should guide public policymakers and the appropriate methods for influencing the formulation of public policy. We have seen these differences dramatically at work in Calcutta, but it remains to be shown that these differences are at work in other parts of India. Clearly, these differences are not universal, but they do affect the relationship between organized groups and government frequently enough to disturb—often in dramatic and alarming ways—the maintainence of public order.

A conflict in 1956 between the central government and the state government of Assam (supported by many organized groups in Assam) provides a good illustration of the points which have already been made in respect to Calcutta. In the fall of that year the Indian government appointed a technical-economic committee of experts to investigate various

[15] From an interview.

sites in India for the construction of a refinery to process oil discovered in Assam in 1953 and 1954. The refinery was to be built by the government of India in conjunction with Burmah Shell. The commission investigated sites in Assam, West Bengal, and Bihar; and on the basis of the merits and demerits described by the commission in each of the sites, the Indian government decided to locate the refinery in Bihar at a point accessible to railway lines, far from the unsettled borders of Pakistan and away from the labor problems endemic to the Calcutta area. Almost immediately after the decision was announced, the opposition parties in Assam launched a mass campaign against the central government; and even the governing Congress party in Assam, though more restrained, joined in the opposition to the central government's decision. Pressure was so great that the central government announced that its initial decision was a tentative one and that it was prepared to reconsider if the Assam government could offer additional arguments of a technical-economic nature. The Congress party in Assam hired a foreign oil expert and sent members of the Assam state cabinet to Europe and the United States to marshal evidence on their behalf. Meanwhile, the opposition parties organized the All-Assam Oil Refinery Action Committee, which then proceeded to launch a series of *hartal*'s and *satyagraha*'s. Hundreds were arrested for acts of civil disobedience. Finally, in December, 1957, the Government of India announced that it had revised its decision and that the refinery would be built in Assam, but that a second refinery would be erected in Bihar. The central government declared that technical considerations, rather than Assamese agitation, had motivated their change of policy, but gave no evidence to support its reversal.[16] The central government cabinet had clearly decided that in this incident political considerations deserved priority—or at least that national economic considerations were not of first priority. Assam's proximity to Pakistan, Tibet, China, and Burma, the uneasy relations between hill and plains people in the state, and the danger of having a politically unstable state along such a strategic border, may have been decisive in the minds of members of the cabinet. Assam's appeal on the grounds that it is a particularly underdeveloped state and therefore deserves special consideration may also have been a factor in the final decision. Although the center wished

[16] James A. Steintrager, in "The Politics of Planning in an Underdeveloped Area: The Case of the Assam Oil Refinery Controversy" (Master's thesis, Department of Political Science, University of Chicago, 1960), produces evidence that in the judgment of at least one technical adviser to the Government of India, the technical arguments were clearly in favor of the sites in either Bihar or Calcutta, and not Assam. The description of the case provided here is taken from Steintrager's study.

to make the decision as to the location of the plant on the economic principle of achieving the maximum return for the lowest investment, Assamese political groups were primarily concerned with improving Assam's own economic position. The eruption of civil disobedience in the state led to a rethinking of the issue by the central government and, ultimately, to a reversal of its decision. It is particularly important to note that whatever considerations did in fact lead to a reversal of the decision, the reversal was interpreted in Assam and in the rest of the country as further evidence that the central government would succumb to pressures exercised through civil disobedience.

In so far as civil disobedience has been a successful instrument for influencing government policy and administration, one can understand why this device is increasingly becoming part of India's political culture, almost assuming the regularity of lobbying in the United States. Unfortunately, no statistics are available on the magnitude of civil disobedience in India, but some data has been put together in a recent study by David H. Bayley.[17] Bayley reports that in six alternate months of 1955, the *Times of India* reported thirty-seven separate riots in India in which 63 individuals were killed, 252 were injured, and 2,973 were arrested; police firings occurred seven times. In six alternate months of 1958 the *Times of India* reported forty-four riots, 17 persons killed, 480 injured, 7,283 arrested, and ten police firings.[18] An examination of the violence reported in the month of March, 1958, shows a wide variety of incidents: dock workers marched in a procession to the office of the Union minister for shipping in Bombay; townspeople agitated against the government's decision to shift the district headquarters to another town; students rioted for cinema price concessions; central government employees in Bombay demonstrated for changes in the rules of employment; in a village near Ahmedabad, farmers began a hunger strike to protest the removal of their names from the land revenue registry.[19]

From 1953 through 1957, agitations over the issue of states reorganization were prevalent in many parts of India, with those in the Telugu, Maharashtrian, Gujarati, Punjabi, and Naga areas the most serious. One of the more novel forms of public protest occurred in Ahmedabad in August, 1956. The Gujarati opponents of the bilingual state of Bombay, which was supported by the central government, formed a People's Curfew Committee to exhort or shame people into staying indoors after a

[17] Bayley, "Violent Agitation and the Democratic Process in India" (Ph.D. Thesis, Department of Politics, Princeton University, 1960).

[18] *Ibid.*, p. 15.

[19] *Ibid.*, pp. 17–19.

certain hour. Curfew passes were issued for persons engaged in essential services and thousands of volunteers patrolled the streets to enforce the curfew. The government and the police, eager to avoid violence, stood idly by.[20] Violence was not completely avoided, however. Late in the month, students organized a public meeting attended by some seventy-five thousand persons to oppose the pressure exerted by the Gujarat Pradesh Congress Committee to retain a bilingual Bombay. Thereafter, Congress-sponsored rallies were violently attacked; and in at least one rally—addressed by Morarji Desai, then chief minister of the state of Bombay—two hundred persons were injured. In the city of Ahmedabad, buses and cars were burned, vandalism broke out, and police firings took place.[21]

In contrast with many of the agitations in Calcutta whose primary concern was the vetoing of government action, the states-reorganization agitations were directed toward forcing the government to take positive action. And as we have indicated earlier,[22] in almost every instance of agitation for a major reorganization, the central government has conceded. The Telugus won their Andhra state; Bombay was bifurcated into Gujarati and Maharashtrian states; the Nagas were granted a separate state, carved out of Assam. In the Punjab, where government has thus far refused to take action, agitation continues. The merits and demerits of state reorganization have been much argued both within and outside of India, and it is not our purpose to reopen the issue here.[23] In so far as the dispute throws light on the relationship between organized groups and the state, however, conclusions may be suggested. First, the central government was apparently unaware of the popularity of the demands, or was unwilling to take action to reorganize the states on the basis of these demands. Second, as usual, organized groups concluded that civil disobedience or some other form of coercion was necessary to force the government to take action. Third, when government finally agreed to reorganize some of the states, it did so on an *ad hoc* basis rather than by formulating some general principles which could be used for accepting or rejecting demands.[24] Fourth, in the absence of the application of

[20] *Ibid.*, p. 30.
[21] *Ibid.*, pp. 35–36.
[22] See chap. iii above.
[23] Some of the most important relevant documents can be found in *Introduction to the Civilization of India: Developing India*, I, *Readings Selected by Myron Weiner* (Chicago: Syllabus Division, University of Chicago Press, 1961).
[24] Some had argued that the central government should concede the principle of establishing states along linguistic lines for those languages listed in the constitution as the country's official languages, and that each state should consist of those contigu-

consistent principles by the central government, those communities which felt that their demands were unsatisfied—particularly in Bombay, the Punjab, and Assam—concluded that through continued civil disobedience government would finally concede. And fifth, government action with respect to states reorganization has largely been shaped by the extent of local agitations.

Civil disobedience is thus more than a legacy of the Gandhian era. The regular channels of communication between voluntary associations and the various governments have often proved to be inadequate; or, alternatively, government has very frequently refused to act—initially, at least—merely on the basis of information available to it, and as a result organized groups throughout the country have turned to various forms of civil disobedience. The very frequency with which mass action has succeeded in vetoing government action, or in positively modifying public policy, has strengthened the public belief that such measures are both desirable and effective.

Petitions and Deputations

Lest one imagine that the mass movement is the sole means by which groups attempt to influence government, it should be pointed out that direct contacts between the government and common citizens are still common in India. Formerly, the *durbar*—that regal display of royal wealth and power—served as a means for the citizen, either directly or through his village headman, tribal chief, or smaller raja, to place his needs before the state. The royal *durbar* is gone. But in its place are the tours through the villages of district magistrates, government ministers, and party leaders, who hear the petitions of individuals or groups. Poor and low-caste villagers sometimes present their case directly to the visiting authorities; or more often, it will be pleaded for them by someone of local standing. This pattern of dealing with authority through an intermediary is quite common in the villages and is often carried over into dealings with state and national, as well as local and district, officials.

Precisely how such petitions are presented to the state can be seen in the ways East Bengal refugees in West Bengal present their grievances

_____

ous units (which might be villages, or *tahsil's*, or districts) which shared the same language. In effect, however, the States Reorganization Commission recommended that the reorganization take into account economic viability and a host of considerations peculiar to each region. The central government therefore found it difficult to justify the decision to maintain a bilingual Bombay on the grounds of any principle, with the result that it was exceedingly vulnerable to organized popular pressures.

to the state government. Refugees in camps in and around Calcutta, or squatters in public places in the city, usually go directly to camp administrators or officials of the Refugee and Rehabilitation Ministry with their complaints. If they are unable to obtain results directly from these authorities, refugees then turn to local refugee leaders. These leaders are often non-refugee political party officials, and their files are full of petitions from individuals or groups of refugees asking them to present complaints to the appropriate officials. A group of refugees may, for example, ask help in getting their names recorded in land settlement operations; or a school teacher may seek aid in rehabilitating himself and his five dependents; another refugee may ask for a house loan; still another may request that his old father be placed in one of the permanent camps for the old and infirm. The refugee leader turns over the petition, with his supporting recommendation, to the appropriate officers. Since administrative officials—including district magistrates, divisional officers, and block development officials—have small sums of funds for distress and relief work, they may provide assistance in individual cases. The chief minister and the minister of relief and rehabilitation also have funds that they may allocate at their discretion to those in need. In many instances where the refugee has been ignored, a refugee leader, particularly one with effective government contacts, may obtain results. Local administrators, otherwise callous to the numerous soulful petitions presented to them, will heed the advice of a distinguished refugee-party leader.

The role of the intermediary in the petitioning process is well illustrated in the relationship between Suresh Banerjee and B. C. Roy, the chief minister of West Bengal. Banerjee's files are filled with carbon copies of the petitions he has forwarded to his friend, the chief minister, with covering letters endorsing the petitioners' demands. In these exchanges with the chief minister, Banerjee has justified his own role as an intermediary. When Roy wrote to Banerjee:

> . . . I agree with you that the Government should always attempt to appreciate the depth of feeling of sufferers, but the feeling in such cases is greatly modulated by political opposition, as you yourself admitted in one of your letters to me. This makes it difficult for the Government to gauge the depth of suffering. If the refugees were left alone, we would have got a better view of the nature of their trouble. But perhaps you will not agree with me.

Banerjee replied heatedly to the chief minister:

> . . . I should be much obliged if you will please let me
> know the letter in which I stated that the feeling of sufferers
> is modulated by political opposition. I cannot speak about
> other political workers but regarding myself I can categori-
> cally state that the intensity of my feeling is always less
> than that of sufferers. Hence instead of their feelings being
> modulated by me, my feeling is modulated by them. As far
> as the Charbatia refugees now living at Sealdah [a train
> station in Calcutta] are concerned they contacted me only
> a few days back. Before that, I am told they did not ap-
> proach any other political leader but did make written
> appeals to . . . the Relief Minister . . . and to other rele-
> vant Government authorities but with no effect. . . .

Petitions may also be combined with a mass movement, in which case
the petition becomes not an instrument for eliciting sympathy from government, but part of the movement to force the government to take
action. The following exchange of correspondence shows how a petition
may be used by the organizers of a mass movement to permit their followers to articulate their demands even when the government has
already been informed. S. C. Banerjee wrote to the chief minister, B. C.
Roy:

> My dear Dr. Roy:
> I shall be glad if this note be considered confidential.
> I am forwarding to you a copy of the petition which I, as
> president of the Bastuhara Sammelan (Refugee Associa-
> tion), desire to present to you on 13th September next.
> The presentation procedure will be this: There will be a
> rally of the refugees at the Wellington Square at 3 P.M. on
> Monday (13th September) next. Myself, Dr. P. C. Ghosh
> and Srijukta Leela Roy may address the gathering. Then
> the refugees will march in a peaceful procession along
> Dharamtalla Street towards the Assembly House. They
> have no intention of violating 144. They will therefore stop
> wherever the Police obstructs them. Then they will ask the
> Police Officers in Charge to take to you a copy of the

Petition. In the petition appeal has been made for an interview with you at a time and place convenient to you. The time should of course be as soon as possible. During the interview the representatives will press you for a time limit within which the Government intends to complete regularization of Squatters Colonies, Industrialization of Colonies and regularization of Exchanged property. The Government have already expressed their intention of doing these three things. The refugees now only want to know within what time these things will be completed. . . .

The chief minister's reply was prompt and succinct:

Dear Suresh:
Your letter. You know very well what we are attempting to do. My Rehabilitation Minister and myself can see you next Monday, 20th September at 12 noon in my office room.

Banerjee's argument for such a demonstration was that it might force the government to act more quickly. To what extent it was also his intention to strengthen the unity of the refugee association can only be surmised. In any event, it is interesting to note the way in which the interest-group leader, by informing the government of his group's course of action, seeks to restrain his own membership.

The most successful link between government and local groups, whether a formally organized association or a collection of individuals who temporarily share a common interest, is the local Congress party organization. In rural areas especially, the leaders of the district and *taluka* Congress committees are very active in coping with a wide range of local demands. The creation of *panchayat samiti*'s in some areas, with substantial budgets for rural development, has improved the capacity of local Congress leaders to cope with specific local demands, for they often control not only the *samiti* but the district co-operative bank and local co-operative and educational institutions as well. Indeed, since the same people who staff the local party organizations are now being called on to operate the many semigovernmental co-operatives and credit institutions being created at the local level, the line between the party and parts of the local administration is sometimes blurred. The district administration, too, tends to be sympathetic to problems brought by Congress party leaders. As a result, small landowners and shopkeepers needing assistance or permits from the local administration may seek the aid of local Congress leaders. And when local demands can be satisfied only by action at the ministerial level, the local Congress leaders and Congress M.L.A.'s will lobby for their constituents in the state capital. Thus, where the Congress party is strong, local administrative officials and the state government generally tend to be sensitive and responsive to local pressures. It is in areas where the Congress party is weak that the channels of communication between the public and government are not well developed. Occupational or ethnic groups which have no working connection with the local Congress party are the ones most likely to resort to militant efforts to influence government and administration.[25]

Conditions for Violence

To summarize, violence is not the only means by which groups attempt to influence public policy. Business and trade unions take part in various consultative bodies; group lobbying is not uncommon, especially in the state legislature; petitions and deputations are frequently made by refugees, students, and other mass organizations. Also, violence itself is only one form of the technique of coercion; others include mass demonstrations, *hartal*'s and civil disobedience.

Violence is not used by groups solely for the purpose of influencing public policy. Mass movements, with or without violence, may be attempted by organized groups to win popular support or to build greater cohesion within their own organizations. And for the professional rowdies, violent movements provide an opportunity for pilfering goods from store windows and shops and for committing destructive acts.

But neither the rowdies, with their propensity for violence, nor the political leaders, with their liking for any mass movement that will mobilize support, could foment mass movements or violence were the population not willing to participate in such movements.

We have suggested that many Calcutta citizens, particularly members of the middle classes, turn to coercive and sometimes violent methods in their attempts to reach the government in the belief that only through such coercion is it possible to obtain government help or to prevent the government from making an unpopular decision. There are many reasons for this great distrust of authority, not the least important being that

[25] In a forthcoming study I shall explore the functioning of the local Congress party organizations in five districts.

government officials are in fact unresponsive to many of the demands made by the urban middle classes. The government official may respond to a case of individual distress (particularly when it is brought to his attention by some eminent and reliable figure), and he may give in to mass pressure, but he is less able or willing to respond to the varieties of demands between these two extremes. The quiet demand of a group of petitioners, the requests made by those who have no outside leadership, and the deputations without mass backing are little noticed by the government official. The requests of university students that tuitions not be raised, or of teachers that cost-of-living allowances be provided, or of many groups that the West Bengal-Bihar merger be rejected, are ignored. But when such requests become demands, develop into mass movements, and threaten to disturb law and order in the city, the government concedes. To interpret mass movements or violence as resulting only from the lawless activities of rowdies, or as caused by the political calculations of opposition party leaders, is to ignore the basic sentiments of the many who participate in such movements and who give them their mass character.

In short, we would say that the following beliefs of Calcutta's Bengali middle classes may explain their behavior as we have described it.

1. In so far as non-cultural functions are concerned, civic affairs are the responsibility of government (state or municipal). While a few wealthy citizens may contribute part of their fortune to building hospitals, schools, and other civic institutions, the average citizen can do nothing.

2. Although the government ought to provide more services for its citizens, including more and better food, wages, employment, clothing, education, housing, and medicine, government officials are too concerned with enriching their own pockets or enlarging their power to tend to such matters. With rare exceptions, virtually all men in positions of authority are corruptible.

3. Activities to change government personnel are not nearly so important as activities which will coerce the government into taking—or not taking—action. Since most men, irrespective of party, ideology, or social class, are corruptible when in power, it is more important to coerce those in authority than to take action to remove them.

4. Rational efforts to persuade government officials rarely succeed. But men in authority do respond to mass demonstrations, civil disobedience movements, and violent action. It is important that citizens participate in these activities, for they are the most effective instruments for changing government policy.

Together these beliefs of middle-class Bengalis may help us understand their low voting turnout and low participation in civic activities, despite their high political interest and a tendency toward mass activities and violence.

Our examination of the techniques by which organized groups seek to influence government has led us to explore the attitudes of group leaders, their followers, and government officials. We have suggested that individuals generally present their demands, for themselves or their groups, either directly to a government official or, more often, through an intermediary. Where the local Congress party organization is strong, its leaders often serve as a link between the public and the government and administration. But we have also suggested that a wide range of demands are not being satisfactorily handled by the government or administration on the local, state, or national levels. The demands of many ethnic groups are overlooked on ideological grounds. Movements led by opposition parties often find that their demands are rejected because their motives are suspected by state officials. And local administrators often ignore the demands made by people whose position in the local power structure is weak, and respond more favorably to those who have greater wealth and status. The advent of representative government has encouraged the political organization of certain communities which formerly hesitated to organize in the face of a formidable administrative hierarchy. Nonetheless, the aloofness of many local, state, and national leaders, both administrative and representative, has encouraged opposition politicians to move politics from the conference room to the streets.

IX. POLITICAL DEMANDS AND MODERNIZATION

The establishment of universal adult suffrage, the extension of political rights and privileges to all the people, and more generally, the expansion of governmental activities in social and economic life have been accompanied by a rapid rise of organized interests in Indian political life. In the course of our study we have tried to indicate the main patterns of this development.

First, political parties have sought to organize interests and gain control of them. Trade unions, student organizations, peasant organizations, and many cultural groups, welfare associations, and refugee organizations are dominated by political parties. Business associations are the only major type of association—apart from ethnic groups—which is free from party control.

Second, ethnic identifications play an increasingly important part in the development of organized interests. Although some of the ethnic associations demand political independence or the creation of new states within the Indian union, most of these associations are primarily concerned with the economic and social welfare of their membership. We have suggested that in the immediate future the developing economy may foster an increase rather than a decrease in the number of groups organized along the lines of caste, religion, and tribe.

Third, though organized interests do have an impact on the formation of public policy in India, to a large entent this influence has been a negative one—that is, it has been directed toward preventing government from pursuing some course of action. At the state level, for example, agrarian interests within the Congress party have prevented an

216

increase in agricultural income taxes or land taxes. Attempts by state governments to increase tuition fees at colleges and universities, introduce higher levies in areas which have profited from developmental activities, or move refugees from one area to another, have often been delayed or halted by organized interests.

Fourth, organized groups largely influence the administration rather than the formulation of policy. Since the ideological framework of Indian politics does not support many of the goals of the business community or of local but often powerful agrarian interests, these groups find it difficult to affect the main outlines of public policy. And since their influence is felt in the state governments to a greater extent than at the center, and by administrators more than by policymakers, it is at the administrative level in the states that these interests are most effectively exercised.

Fifth, government officials at the state and national levels respond easily to some kinds of pressure but have often been unresponsive to other types. Petitions presented by the opposition through mass movements are often not acted upon, and government has responded more readily to demands made from within the Congress party than from without. More generally, administrative officials and state politicians react sharply when demands are made which attack their authority, often without considering the merits of the demands. In some areas, especially but not exclusively where local government and administration are in the hands of an ethnic group which differs from the majority of the local citizenry, a breakdown in communication and a rise in civil disobedience or even violence are not uncommon. Indians are far from agreed on the appropriate methods for citizens to influence the formation and implementation of policy; nor is there agreement within government and administration as to the appropriate attitude for dealing with organized demands.

Sixth, the growth of organized interests at the state level is an important factor in the development of conflicts between the state governments and the center and between several state governments. The expansion of colleges and universities within the states at a faster rate than the University Grants Commission and other central government authorities have approved is a result of pressures within the states for admitting more students into higher education. The increasing requests by state governments for greater investments by the center in the states' public sectors, and their pressures on the center to grant more private businessmen permission to open new factories, are clearly related to the growing political pressures within each state. In the conflicts between states over the allocation of water resources, no chief minister would ignore local interests and suggest that the decision be made on the basis of maximizing the country's total productivity—unless, of course, such a criterion would be in his favor.

The growth of organized interests in a developing area raises two fundamental questions. *To what extent does the growth of organized interests imply a reduction in systematic governmental planning or a slowing down of the developmental process? And how do emerging groups affect the development of a political community in which those who govern and those who are governed share a similar outlook with respect to political matters?*

There are many Indians who view the growth of organized pressure groups with alarm for the country's modernization efforts. They believe that ideas as distinct from interests should guide policy formulation, and that once government succumbs to the pressures of organized groups no rational government is possible.

It is further assumed that worker, peasant, tribal and religious groups, and other organized elements are being exploited by self-seeking, ambitious politicians. These politicians, according to this view, are concerned solely with their own success, or with the enhancement of the particular group which they lead, and have no regard for the broader public interest. It is necessary, therefore, that the Indian government seek to minimize the destructive effects of such politicians—always, of course, within the limits imposed by the democratic framework. To accomplish this, the Congress party has tried to establish and control mass organizations of workers, peasants, women, and students so as to harness such groups for developmental activities and, perhaps even more important, to prevent them from being exploited by opposition politicians. To this end, also, the system of compulsory arbitration has been created to cope with labor-management disputes which threaten to result in work stoppages. Many demands of organized groups, in spite of the apparent popularity of the demands, have initially been rejected by the state and national leaders, who have viewed such demands as threats to national unity (such as the demand for states reorganization) or to economic development (such as Assam's demand for an oil refinery). Finally, coercive measures have been employed against those groups and individuals who have threatened, or who have actually resorted to, the use of force or civil disobedience.

Throughout this study we have tried to suggest that government efforts to control, restrain, ignore, and repress organized demands have resulted in a myriad of difficulties. The production-oriented, responsible-minded Congress unions have often lost out to those unions emphasizing conflict and the redistribution of wealth. There is no evidence that the system of compulsory arbitration has in fact substantially diminished the number of work stoppages. The national government's opposition to "provincialism, casteism and communalism" has not resulted in the disappearance or weakening of community organizations; on the contrary, government policy has often been a factor in the development of such groups, and government opposition to many of their demands has set in motion a number of local outbursts. Finally, government intransigence in the face of organized groups has been interpreted by many of these groups as a further justification for mass movements, civil disobedience, and even violence.

The assumption upon which much of the strategy rests—the selfish qualities of political leaders of organized groups—holds some measure of truth. Implied is a comparison with politicians in the West, or more specifically Great Britain, where it is assumed that politicians are concerned with the public interest, the general good, and above all with ideas. If, however, American and British politicians today seem more moral or generally less corruptible than their counterparts of a half century ago, it is not because of a change in heart resulting from religious or educational activities, but because the character of the American and British politicial systems has so changed that certain kinds of moral behavior— or at least the appearance of moral behavior—are essential to achieve and maintain power. The politician concerned with his own advancement and with the advancement of his own special interest has learned that this can best be achieved by couching his demands in terms of the public interest; and those politicians who strive for higher office find their altruistic motives reinforced and not threatened by the political necessity of reconciling diverse viewpoints. As in an economic market, the politician will assess his market and produce those commodities (appeals) that yield the maximum return. Some may miscalculate the market and be unsuccessful, but others will find the combination of products (or appeals) that will find a market. The national leadership may decry the organization of tribal, religious, and caste bodies as catering to the parochial sentiments of the Indian people; but politicians seeking to win power in India find it opportune to appeal to such sentiments, just as other Indian politicians find it opportune to appeal to workers, refugees, or students. No amount of exhortation is likely to change the kind of appeals made by local politicians seeking office so long as consumers consider the demands worthy and the methods for making demands acceptable.

But the fact is, as many Indians argue, that organized interests have often hampered the passage of legislation at the state level and the administration of state and national legislation. Local groups concerned with preserving the existing local social, economic, and political power structures may impede policies with respect to land ceilings, land redistribution, and taxation. And mass organizations may force investment in social welfare activities at a time when the country's greatest economic need is an increase in savings, capital investment, and general productivity.

How, then, is the state to cope with the enormous range of demands now being made and those which are yet to come? How can the state satisfy demands without making economic planning an impossible farce and without denying the demands of organized groups to so great an extent that political democracy is destroyed?

To find a simple resolution for the problem posed here is beyond the range of any scholar. Indeed, to a large extent the countless decisions and acts made each day by government leaders will set the tone of any government. Nonetheless, there are basic policies which the state can pursue to deal with the problems posed here, policies which can set the tone within which day to day decisions will be made. It is not our intention to prescribe any such set of policies; it is, rather, to suggest several alternative methods that the state can pursue to cope with the great number of demands made upon a government that is concerned with economic planning, national unity, and public order within the framework of free institutions. We shall deal with these methods under two categories: (1) methods for reducing demands on the state, and (2) methods for dealing with these demands.

Methods for Reducing Demands

There would appear to be at least five methods for reducing the pressure of political demands on government planners. One method would reduce the role played by government in settling certain types of political and economic controversies; a second would attempt to improve the channels of communication between government and organized groups; a third would increase the power of local institutions; a fourth would permit administrators to make decisions in a field now within the domain of politics; and a fifth would aim to develop a public philosophy within organized groups.

First, and perhaps fundamental among structural reforms, the government can avoid involving itself in conflicts which do not immediately threaten the broad public interest. To pursue our earlier analogy to the economic market, one might note that the political market, like its economic counterpart, has some self-regulating mechanisms. Some group demands do not automatically involve government, but only competing and conflicting elements within the society. Management and labor make demands upon one another; as do landless laborers and peasant proprietors, tenants and landlords, students and university administrators. For purposes of equity or ideological commitments, the state may choose to support one side against another; or the state may pursue some special notion of the general good (such as maximizing production) and thus inquire into the merits of a dispute. But, alternatively, the state may choose to intervene only in the event that the public order is disturbed; or to put it another way, the state may define the rules within which the free market may operate. One important consequence of such a policy of minimal interference by the state in the political market is that all group demands are not focused on the government; many are dissipated in conflicts within the society. Labor and management, for instance, would tend to look to each other and not to the state for a resolution of their conflicts. Such an attitude involves greater self-confidence in the stability of government and the responsibility of citizens, perhaps, than has characterized the present leadership. Certainly, the maintenance of public order is essential, lest civil disobedience, violent or otherwise, result in the collapse of government, the paralysis of economic life, or a general erosion of the legal system and of popular respect for existing institutions and procedures. On the other hand, one must recognize that a certain amount of violence is built in to the process of modernization. Tensions between social groups, tension associated with the shift of individuals from rural to urban environments, the displacement of individuals from occupations and from places of residence as new industries and new dams are built, and changing economic relationships in the countryside as barter systems are replaced by cash transactions— all contribute to a readiness to act in a violent fashion. Clearly many of these tensions result from the very success of modernization; they are the price paid for any substantial social change. While the public sector may take steps to mitigate some of the tensions, inevitably many individuals will feel a sense of deprivation and will experience a loosening of those bonds which have previously imposed restraint on their behavior. Demonstrations, strikes, civil disobedience, and even violence are simultaneously expressions of and outlets for social tension. What India—and many other Asian and African states—experience today has been experienced by Western nations in the nineteenth and twentieth centuries.

Although the breakdown of public order may endanger development activities and lessen respect for legal practices in the locality in which it occurs, in a federal system such as that of India, the effects on overall governmental stability are often minimal. A breakdown of public order in Kerala toppled the government in that state, but the central government remained relatively unaffected. In fact, only a handful of state governments have toppled since 1947 as a result of violence and civil disobedience. West Bengal has had much violence—especially in Calcutta—but the strength of the government in the countryside has increased, a single chief minister has held office for over ten years, factionalism within the government and the party has been less pronounced than in other states, and by any index the government has been relatively stable. The effects of a breakdown in public order on economic development may also not be as great as one might expect. In spite of intermittent struggles between the Sikh Akali Dal and other political groups in the Punjab, in spite of widespread demonstrations, civil disobedience, and even violence, the Punjab has sustained one of the highest rates of growth of any of the Indian states.

Though the state can and must take steps to minimize violence, clearly the system can tolerate a considerable amount of disorder without seriously endangering either the stability of the government or the growth of the economy.

A second device for minimizing the gap between organized demands and government capacity is already in use. Consultative bodies, which provide opportunities for organized groups to consult with government agencies, have been in existence for many years. There are few ministries in the central government that do not have one or more consultative bodies representing a wide variety of organized groups. But the need for consultative bodies on the state level, where organized groups are now multiplying, is obviously great. Many exist; but they have not grown with the expansion of state activities, nor are they always representative of all important interests. Such bodies are important not only because they facilitate contact between the government and organized interests, but also because they provide an opportunity for organized interests to negotiate and bargain among themselves and thereby be-

come aware of alternative demands upon the limited government resources.

Unfortunately, there has been a tendency for both the state and central
governments to create consultative bodies that are mere forums for ministerial policies. The ministries generally attempt to place the organizations that they consider to be the most responsible on the consultative
bodies. They also tend to select the individuals who will represent the
interest groups rather than allowing the groups themselves to make the
selection, another procedure which decreases the representativeness of
consultative bodies. In the absence of institutionalized methods of communication, organized groups often resort to mass demonstrations and
civil disobedience as a means of impressing government with the serious-
ness of their demands; and governments often issue pronouncements
without first having discussed the proposals with those groups most
likely to be affected. Consultative bodies, and in general an improvement in communication between government and organized groups,
might in time reduce the use of violence and civil disobedience, and
might also serve to make the demands of organized groups less extreme.

The strengthening of local-government institutions may constitute a
third strategy for limiting demands upon the state and central governments. The merits of a federal system—and within that system a wide
dispersal of authority to local units—are often overlooked by contemporary critics, especially when they concentrate on the need for rapid
centrally directed planning and development. But in an ethnically diversified society, a federal structure is particularly helpful in minimizing
conflicts by dispersing conflict among many levels of government.

In India the Constituent Assembly granted wide powers to the states,
including the sole right to tax lands, control education, pass land reform
legislation, and regulate health and welfare. But while resolutions of
the Congress party speak of the need for decentralization of power, much
of the government's legislation produces the opposite effect. Though states
share with the center the power to regulate industrial relations, develop
education, and pass legislation in the field of local government, in practice state legislation is almost non-existent (as in the field of industrial
relations, where central legislation is followed by most states), or is a
mirror of the recommendations of the center (as in local-government legislation). While local-government legislation is in theory intended to be
the cornerstone of a program of decentralization and the strengthening
of popular government, in practice local government has often been an
arm of the central government's development program, and its success

or failure has been measured in terms of its contribution to development.[1]

It is not easy to decentralize power so that local units may have, for example, greater taxing powers and the authority to build and maintain schools, local roads, irrigation works, and sewerage systems. Where skills are not easily available, and where factional conflicts often make effective government almost impossible, it is difficult to increase responsibility.[2] State officials, especially members of the state bureaucracy (in particular, those involved in the revenue services), have hesitated to take the risks of reduced efficiency, perhaps even corruption, which might accompany any strengthening of local-government institutions. But in spite of the obvious difficulties, the need for strengthening local government in India is strongly supported by many Indians. Apart from the strong moral argument that self-government is preferable to efficient government (an issue, after all, on which Indians took a strong stand in their struggle for independence), there is a further argument for increasing the powers and finances of local governments. If local governments were required to match funds provided by the state or central governments for the development of schools, roads, irrigation schemes, and the like, local groups would in effect be encouraged to divert their demands toward local, rather than state or national, institutions. Moreover, the encouragement of local demands upon local-government institutions might also force local authorities to make more effective use of tax sources which are made available to them by state governments but which thus far have not been fully utilized.[3] (In view of the perennial

[1] See Margaret H. Case, "Panchayats and State Administrations," *Economic Weekly,* August 6, 1960. Recently there have been new efforts in several states, particularly Rajasthan and Andhra, to strengthen local-government institutions by providing village *panchayat*'s with greater revenue powers and control over the community development program. The new program is popularly referred to as "panchayati raj," and plans are to extend it throughout India. It is still too early to see what effects the new program will have on the local distribution of power. For a preliminary report, see Ralph H. Retzlaff, "Panchayati Raj in Rajasthan," *Indian Journal of Public Administration,* VI, No. 2, 141–58.

[2] Nonetheless, many Indian critics have pointed out that financial support for local-government institutions has been short of desirable. See P. P. Agarwal, *The System of Grants-in-Aid in India* (published under the auspices of the Indian Institute of Public Administration [Bombay: Asia Publishing House, 1959]). Agarwal writes: "Though grants to local bodies have increased in recent years, the existing scale of assistance towards education, medical relief, public health, communication, etc., is inadequate. In contrast to the heavy dependence of the States on the resources of the Centre, the local bodies do not receive sufficient assistance which would enable them to carry out many responsibilities under the purview of their activities" (p. 74). One difficulty, it might be added, is that the Indian government makes no direct grant to local bodies, but only to state governments.

[3] *Ibid.,* p. 77.

reluctance of local bodies to increase taxes, it has been suggested that state bodies take on the responsibility of setting the rates for local taxes.) Finally, the strengthening of local-government institutions will serve to further strengthen, not weaken, state and central governments. In a modernizing state, power is not a fixed quantity to be rationed but an ever expanding element. The ability of one level of government to carry out its tasks makes it that much easier for another level of government to perform its responsibilities.

These three strategies—to minimize government involvement in social conflicts, to increase group representation on consultative bodies as a means of strengthening the channels of communication between government and organized groups, and to strengthen local governments—are alternative ways of relieving the state and central governments of some of the demands made upon them. An even more direct device for decreasing demands upon government would be to give to the administration sole responsibility for certain economic decisions. The question here is: To what extent can certain types of economic decisions be withdrawn from the realm of public demands and public controversies?

Investment-location decisions obviously affect the entire nation, if only because an inappropriate decision results in increased costs or a lower return. While there are clearly political questions associated with the decision as to whether the nation should build an oil refinery at all, once the decision is made it should be possible to determine the site of the refinery on the basis of strictly economic considerations. Here, then, the government could legitimately attempt to remove from political consideration questions that can be decided on a technical basis without infringing the public's welfare. In India, however, questions concerning the location of investments are decided at the ministerial and cabinet level, i.e., at a political level. Invariably, then, location decisions have been subjected to considerable political pressures; and in fact, no institutions now exist to remove these decisions from the public arena.[4] Moreover,

---

[4] All decisions concerning the formation of new public enterprises by the government must be approved by the Lok Sabha. In fact, even reinvestment of "surplus" or profit by public corporations must be sanctioned by government. Capital expenditures cannot be incurred above a fixed limit by state enterprises without the approval of the government. For the Indian Airlines Corporation and Air India International, capital expenditures exceeding $300,000 must be approved. For Sindri Fertilizers, Nangal Fertilizers, Bharat Electronics, and several others, the limit is approximately $400,000. In many cases, salary appointments of more than Rs. 2,000 ($400) per month require the government's approval. Contracts exceeding $5,000 often have to be referred by the public corporation to the Ministry of Finance for prior approval. Parliamentary budget grants to public corporations are generally on an annual basis. It is obvious that the Indian government leans in the direction of rigid government

policymakers have themselves been unclear as to whether investment decisions should be made exclusively on the basis of economic considerations (where can one get the maximum return at the lowest cost?) or should take into account social justice, which would require that backward areas receive priority. If the question of locating new public sector enterprises is to be removed from political controversy, than at least three means of doing so might be explored. First, the present uncertainty as to the criteria for locating new investments should be clarified. So long as non-economic considerations remain an important though unavowed factor, political pressures from chief ministers and other state leaders will continue. Second, the economic rationale for a location decision must be explicit and precise. This requires greater research into economics and location theory than has thus far been conducted in India. Chief ministers must not only be persuaded, but they must be given data which they can use to protect themselves against criticism within their state. Third, in a society as poor and as politicized as India, it would be difficult to persuade political groups to refrain from exerting pressure and even coercion on government for the location of government-built factories, as long as the decisions concerning location are made at a political level. When it is evident to all that politicians are making the decision, no declaration by the prime minister or a cabinet member that the decision is technical, not political, is likely to influence opposition parties, local pressure groups, or even the state Congress party and state government. One possible solution would be to create a public investment body, the broad policies of which might be shaped by the planning commission, but which would have responsibilty for determining specific public investments, including their location.[5]

However, there is a strong case for the alternative strategy of using

control of public corporations. See C. P. Bhambhri, *Parliamentary Control over State Enterprise in India* (Delhi: Metropolitan Book Co., 1960), esp. chap. vi, "Financial Control over State Enterprise," pp. 68–74.

[5] This is not the appropriate place to discuss the technical problems of creating public investment corporations that achieve some measure of balance between autonomy and accountability, since our major concern has been to call attention to the political difficulties that arise as a result of the present preference of the Indian government for having direct control over public investments. Some economists may argue that the difficulty could be resolved by having few public investments and by leaving all investments (except for schools, roads, communication, and other "pre-investment" or social-overhead projects) to the private sector. This solution, of course, raises other political problems. I have tried to suggest here, however, that even within the present Indian government's preference for public investments, there can be devices for minimizing negative political consequences, which have not thus far been sufficienlty explored.

public investments as a means of strengthening national unity and even of strengthening the political position of the governing party. Government could choose to invest most heavily in potential "trouble spots." Such a strategy would, of course, reduce the economic returns on investments. Furthermore, areas which wanted a project but did not obtain it would be more likely to defect from the government if government decisions were clearly made on the basis of political considerations. And finally, the area which got the project would not necessarily be won over by the government, for there are often socially disturbing consequences of a development project, which turn sections of the local populace against the government.[6] But until and unless there is more precise information on the political consequences of public investments, it would probably be wiser to remove investment decisions from the political arena. This does not preclude giving special attention to the more backward areas, but would simply mean that those areas would be encouraged to develop the industries which from the point of view of comparative economic advantage they are capable of developing.

Underlying any strategy for reducing demands on government must be the goal of changing the attitudes of organized groups. Indeed, perhaps the most critical question with regard to the relationship between organized demands and government is, How can one develop within organized interest groups and political parties a concept of the public interest or, in the words of Walter Lippmann, a public philosophy? Organized groups must learn to limit their demands by an awareness of what is possible; they must learn to consider the effects of their demands upon others; and they must make demands within the rules of a democratic system. The development of such a sense of responsibility obviously depends upon the kinds of relations that develop among groups and, most important, between groups and the government. The extent to which the government indicates that it is prepared to negotiate with organized groups can be a critical factor in the development of a sense of responsibility concerning organized demands. But building a relationship in which negotiation, rather than group violence or government coercion, is the normal method of contact is by no means easy. Institutional devices, such as consultative committees and public hearings, on

---

[6] A study of the effects of community development programs on voting behavior in rural districts in West Bengal in the 1952 and 1957 elections (Baldev Raj Nayar, "Impact of the Community Development Programs on Rural Voting Behavior in India" [Master's thesis, Department of Political Science, University of Chicago, 1959]) showed that the vote for the Congress party increased more in areas which had no community development projects than in those which did.

both the central and state levels are one way; increased personal contact and conversations between government officials and the leaders and rank and file of organized groups are another. But when such groups have no responsibility for the implementation of government policy and little opportunity for participating in its formulation, their initial behavior is often of an irresponsible and parochial variety. In the long run, however, as groups seek to influence government and as they discover the conditions under which government is responsive, they are likely to learn to couch their demands within a public-interest framework and employ reason rather than violence to attain their ends.

Those who wield authority can play an important role in developing a greater understanding within interest groups of the problems of development. The decision-maker can often set the framework for a public discussion of a policy issue. One example might help to illuminate this view. A state university confronted with increased costs, and insufficient government aid to meet these costs, naturally considers raising student tuitions. If the issue is seen narrowly from an economic point of view, the vice-chancellor might well decide to increase tuitions. But if the issue is seen from a political viewpoint, the decision itself is less important than the way in which it is made. The vice-chancellor could choose to treat the issue as an important opportunity to raise the level of public discussion of India's educational goals. He could choose to raise the question before his university senate and before the city's educated community: "Given our shortage of funds, do we raise tuitions, thereby denying opportunities to our poorer students but maintaining our existing standards; or do we keep our tuitions as they are but add to our revenue by admitting more students, enlarging our classes and thereby depressing our educational standards; or are there other alternatives for us?" By raising the issue one might improve the state of public discussion, temper public feelings, and hopefully diminish the likelihood that a decision would be followed by violent outbursts on the part of the student body. In any event, public understanding of whatever decision is made is more likely if the decision follows public discussion than if it is made within the confines of the vice-chancellor's office.

Although we have spoken primarily of approaches that the Indian government might pursue in order to reduce the pressures of demands upon it, we have said nothing about how the attitudes of the voluntary associations themselves might limit individual demands upon the state. Throughout this work we have tended to treat all voluntary associations as sources of demands upon the state, a bias inherent in the theme of this study. We would be remiss, however, if we did not call attention to a strong tradition in India which emphasizes the limitation of wants. This tradition of "renunciation" was harnessed and modified by Gandhi and his disciples to a view which emphasized not renunciation, but limitation and, above all, self-help;[7] this view has facilitated the development of what is referred to in India as "constructive work." (Essentially, "constructive work" refers to voluntary activities for local improvements.) Reinforcing the Gandhian attitude is a strong tradition of charitable activities, which is associated with the religious values attached to accruing merit.

An enormous number of social welfare associations exist in India. The Central Social Welfare Board under the Government of India reported that between 1953 (when the Board was created) and 1957 grants were distributed to four thousand institutions in the fields of child welfare, welfare of the handicapped, and general welfare.[8] Caste *sabha's* have been particularly active in building hostels in urban centers to assist members of their castes while they are attending local schools and colleges; and scholarship aid has also been forthcoming from caste associations. In addition, political parties, especially Congress, have been active in providing relief during famines and floods. These activities, although at times sparked by motives unattractive to many of India's intellectuals, have served to draw forth private funds for public activities and have thereby lessened the drain upon the limited public treasury.

The case for voluntary associations is as old as it is obvious. By facilitating individual participation in public life, voluntary associations may contribute to the consensus necessary to maintain orderly government. Though policy may not be, and probably can never entirely become, the creature of public opinion, close ties between voluntary associations and government facilitate the development of a sense of participation— and above all, a sense of justice—on the part of the public. And from the viewpoint of the policy-makers, voluntary associations may serve as a link between the state and society by providing government with information concerning public opinion. They may alert government to felt needs within the society, and of great importance, they may forewarn government of the consequences of its policies.

While the case for voluntary associations in a free society is obvious,

[7] For a discussion of the traditions of "renunciation" and "materialism" in modern India, see Milton Singer, "Cultural Values in India's Economic Development," *Annals of the American Academy of Political and Social Sciences,* CCCV (May, 1956), 81–91.

[8] Agarwal, *op. cit.,* p. 46.

it is perhaps less obvious that voluntary associations may take different forms in different societies and still be able to serve these purposes. We have suggested here that many Indians have chosen, thus far at least, to identify themselves with their caste, religious, or linguistic group or tribe, and have organized accordingly. Even the modern business sector has built its political organization upon the network of community associations. We have also tried to suggest that such associations do not represent the threat to public order, national unity, or modernization that so many fear. These associations are no less concerned with the material well-being of their communities than are occupational associations, and are perhaps even more concerned since they tend to be less ideologically oriented. Then, too, apart from making demands upon the state, community associations have often devoted part of the resources of the community to either serving the less fortunate within the community or providing assistance to those who are mobile—caste associations, not trade unions, have been providing scholarships for their youth. Community associations have also been freer from outside political control than have trade unions or peasant and refugee organizations.

Whether the state can create voluntary associations which are in fact voluntary is dubious; but there can be no doubt that state policy can seriously retard the growth of voluntarism or can turn voluntary associations into enemies of the state. We have suggested that the industrial-relations policy of the government may be a deterrence to the development of strong trade unions. The hostility of some university authorities to student organizations has not impeded the multiplication of such associations, but has often alienated students from the university. Unsympathetic and unresponsive state ministers, district magistrates, and other administrative officials have not prevented refugees or agriculturalists from organizing, but have often provided incentives for political extremism and agitational politics. And finally, the hostility of government to linguistic, tribal, and religious organizations has not resulted in their demise, but has likewise been an incentive to agitation. The government's methods of dealing with existing demands may, therefore, be of paramount importance in its attempts to modernize the society and economy peacefully.

Methods for Dealing with Demands

In reading through this work one might mistakenly gain the impression that the concern of the present Indian national and state governments

for eliminating conflict and achieving their own defined goals has resulted in the creation of a strong, increasingly authoritarian state. In
fact, the dangers to democracy in India, as in many other new states, have
more often been in the breakdown of authority than in its concentration;
attempts to impose central control have often, ironically, had the opposite effect of discrediting authority. For example, pressures for the
reorganization of the states along linguistic lines were opposed by the Indian government—and by outsiders as well—as serious threats to the
unity of India. Although many of India's states were already unilingual,
the Indian government feared that concessions to linguistic demands
would strengthen particularistic, subnational loyalties. As a result of the
central government's unresponsiveness, unexpected large-scale agitation
erupted throughout the country; and anti-Congress parties mushroomed
in Telugu-, Marathi-, and Malayalam-speaking areas. National leaders
treated regional loyalties as antithetical rather than complementary to
national loyalties. The weakening of the Congress party, the growth of
violence, and the intensification of regional and even antinational sentiments represented a self-fulfilling prophecy.

Some state governments have also tended to be uninformed, because
of their unresponsiveness, as to the probable consequences of various
policies, and have often been surprised and dismayed by the responses
to their proposals. An example which comes to mind is the unexpected
reaction to the proposal of a West Bengal-Bihar merger.

The problem of governmental responsiveness as opposed to governmental authoritarianism leads us appropriately to an exploration of the
actual threats to the political system that are posed by community associations. Intense identification with one's community to the exclusion
of a sense of national identification and a concern for the national interest
could be an inhibiting factor in India's modernization. The adoption of
the regional language through the school system and the colleges could
decrease mobility of both individuals and ideas. Pressures for the employment of members of particular castes or linguistic groups, or for the exclusion of those who come from other states, could decrease efficiency
in administration, in the colleges, and in private employment.[9] And the
pressure of a number of ethnic minorities for the creation of separate
states could, and does, continue to inject conflict, violence, and political
instability into a number of states.[10]

[9] Selig Harrison, in *India—the Dangerous Decades* (Princeton, N.J.: Princeton
University Press, 1960), spells out in detail some of the threats that linguistic and
caste associations present to a modernizing India.
[10] In late 1960, after the demand of the Nagas for a separate state had been granted,

On the economic side, as we have seen, the demands of caste and tribal associations, as well as of peasant organizations and trade unions, present problems for economic planning. In India, as elsewhere in the world, political groups are characteristically more concerned with consumption than with production. Trade unionists want higher wages; peasants want more government assistance; caste and tribal associations demand greater government aid, or more jobs, or the creation of more schools. All groups are inclined to oppose new taxation measures unless they involve the taxation of others. The business sector in India has not been able to prevent increased taxes, but politicians have been reluctant to raise taxes in the agricultural sector. Unresponsiveness to these demands has its dangers, as we have seen. On the other hand, in so far as government accedes to these various demands, economic modernization may be impeded in a number of ways. Demands for patronage on an ascriptive basis may destroy merit considerations in the appointment of personnel, thereby not only decreasing efficiency, but bringing about widespread feelings of injustice. Demands for higher wages and more consumer goods could result in a lower rate of capital investment or in inflationary pressures. The failure to increase agricultural taxes diminishes the revenue available to the state for capital investment in both the agricultural and non-agricultural sectors. Pressure for the location of capital investments made by government may result in the erection of plants, irrigation works, or development programs in sites that are not most productive. And finally, there may be a growth in dependence on the state for goods and services which need not come from the public treasury, but which individuals, local institutions, and communities should, and in many instances could, provide.

However, one must also remember some mitigating elements in the demands of these groups. In the political sphere, as we have noted earlier (see chap. iii), the very multiplication of caste, tribal, religious, and other ethnic associations within a particular state increases the possibility that politicians are less likely to build their careers by seeking to satisfy only one group. Equity becomes politically feasible in a society of many associations. And if an increase in occupational diversification takes place within ethnic communities, primordial loyalties to one's own caste or tribe are likely to be overlaid with other loyalties, with the very likely consequence that the intensity of political demands will be reduced.

One should also not assume that all economic demands impede the de-

a number of tribal groups throughout the hill areas of northern India began to increase their agitation for the creation of new tribal states.

velopment process. In fact, a strong case could be presented for the view that accession to some demands might hasten development in India. The demands for more government investment in rural areas—for credit programs, seed programs, rural educational institutes, irrigation works, and improved transportation—would find strong support among agricultural economists. Local pressures for more schools and for institutions of higher learning, though often reflecting the desire of individuals to succeed by obtaining government appointments, can be satisfied by increased expenditures in much-needed agricultural and technological institutes. Here again, there are many economists who feel that India has not invested sufficiently in human resources—the basic skills that underlie development activities. Again, if urban unrest were to result in greater government attention to town and urban planning, there would be a material as well as a political payoff. Finally, if the pressures of the landless for land could be directed into labor for reclamation projects, a political demand could be converted into an economic asset.

The argument that a more responsive government would be less able to block programs that were against the public interest is hardly tenable since all governments have invariably found it necessary to accede to demands made through force and violence, with the result that respect for constitutional processes has decreased. A more responsive government is, moreover, capable of effectively restraining lawbreaking movements. No government can possibly accede to all demands; and there are times when government must hold the line against the pressure of what is, in its judgment, counter to the public interest. But firmness by those in authority, if it is to be effective in winning public support, must be used infrequently. Unless interest groups are given opportunities to affect policies and their implementation, the danger exists that politics will become—or remain—merely an act of rioting or demonstrating in the streets and of exciting election campaigns without ever becoming oriented toward problem-solving and policy-making.

Responsiveness to demands need not result in a diminution either of effective planning or of the development of national unity. Greater responsiveness—or at least the appearance of responsiveness—on the part of the government helps, in fact, to inculcate a greater measure of consent and loyalty within the society. For the past half century or more, there has been a considerable increase in public participation in politics, but this has yet to be reflected in a greater sense of participation among organized groups in the making of public decisions.

In every democratic society, there is a place for political allocations as well as for developmental allocations; and indeed there are times when one must necessarily detract from the other. In a democracy, skilled political leadership often lies in the capacity to make political allocations that will not detract from developmental allocations, or in knowing how to use symbolic gestures to satisfy political demands. In this respect, a number of individuals in the Indian government have already demonstrated considerable skill.

If one can make any generalizations about a society as diverse and as complex as India, one could say that Indians as a people are acutely status conscious. Awareness of status has not markedly decreased in modern times, although the symbols of status have undergone enormous changes—from turbans to Gandhi caps, from the sacred thread to the western suit or the *achkan,* from chaste Persian or Urdu to English or "high" forms of the vernaculars, from the *pankah* to the air conditioner. India is also a society in which group solidarity has played a powerful social and political role. Status is thus defined in both individual and group terms. The success of a single individual redounds to the status and pride of the community to which he belongs. A college scholarship awarded to a member of a low caste may bring a greater psychic reward to the community than would a general rise in income. A national or international award received by an individual is heralded at home as a recognition of his community as a whole. In 1957, for example, when Satyajit Roy, a leading film producer who received international awards for his *Aparajito,* returned to Calcutta, he was greeted at the airport by the mayor and a host of distinguished Bengalis who presented the hero with an award, not for his film, but for having brought international fame to Bengal and India.

The establishment of a system of national literary awards given by the Sahitya (Literary) Academy, the awards in art and music by other government academies, and the creation of annual Presidential Awards for distinction in various fields are of considerable political importance. However, symbolic status-bearing gestures can be more directly applied in response to political demands. Nehru's visit to Master Tara Singh, the popular leader of the Sikh Akali Dal, and Nehru's words of praise for Tara Singh and his community, did a great deal to bring about a temporary *rapprochement* between the government and the Akali Dal at a time when threats of violence were increasing. The overuse of symbolic devices can, of course, debase the coinage. But in a society in which the solidarity of communities often appears threatened, and whole communities are conscious of their need for social and economic mobility, the use of status-symbols by government is an important political tool.

We have noted earlier that political groups not only try to coerce the state through civil disobedience to achieve their objectives, but very often seek to erode the policies of the state by affecting the administration of decisions. Government and Congress leaders in New Delhi frequently complain that decisions made at the center are lost in the administrative net. Clearly those decisions involving land reform are the most striking examples of recommendations made by the center and passed into law in many of the state capitals which have lost their potency in implementation. Many Indian intellectuals have lost respect for a government which in their eyes has not been able to cope with increasing nepotism and widespread corruption at the local administrative level. These are serious problems; and although in the main they involve individual businessmen rather than the business chambers, individual caste leaders rather than caste associations, and individual landlords rather than landlord associations, they nonetheless threaten some aspects of the government's development policy.

On the other hand, we have tried to suggest in our study that efforts to influence local administration, even through widespread corruption, are not wholly detrimental to political, and perhaps even to economic, development. For reasons beyond the scope of this study, India's administrative structure—like that of many other agrarian societies—is a rigid one.[11] Junior administrators hesitate to take the responsibility of making decisions. A citizen's request to a local administrator may be processed through time-consuming channels before a decision is made; and individual administrators are reluctant to side-step the formal procedures for the sake of speedy action. By injecting a new element of personal motivation, the illegal fees paid by businessmen to local administrators often provide the necessary incentive to speed decisions. Many economic activities would be paralyzed were it not for the flexibility which *bakshish* contributes to the complex, rigid administrative system.

Furthermore, the role played by local Congress party "bosses" in finding jobs, and bringing credit, improved roads, and irrigation facilities to constituents is one played by effective party organizations elsewhere in the world. Tammany-type machine politics may enrich the pockets of

[11] See Fred Riggs, "Agraria and Industria," *Toward the Comparative Study of Public Administration,* ed. William J. Siffin (Bloomington, Ind.: Indiana University Press, 1959).

a few individuals, but it also serves to strengthen the local party organization, which in turn contributes to the maintenance of an effective government at the state and central levels. The paradox of selfish politicians at the local level contributing to the strength of a progressive national organization is, after all, also an appropriate description of many parts of the Democratic party in the United States.

We have suggested in an earlier chapter[12] that from a political point of view, equal opportunity to corrupt is often more important than the amount of corruption, and therefore that an increase in *bakshish* is in the long run less serious than an increase in corruption by ascriptive criteria. So long as the businessman and the peasant can obtain what they want from local administrators through the payment of money, there is less likely to be popular discontent than if those who can and wish to make payments discover that caste and family connections are more decisive. For in that case, those of lower status backgrounds but rising economic success will find themselves blocked, and political disaffection is likely to increase.

There is no doubt, however, that whatever devices flourish unofficially or are pursued by the government to establish a working relationship with the organized citizenry, the gap between organized demands and government resources is likely to continue to exist. Moreover, it is probable that the gap will remain a large one for some time to come, and that many groups will continue to make "irresponsible" demands—demands for non-merit considerations in various types of appointments, including jobs and seats in colleges and universities, or for legislation restricting employment to people from a given locality or region—and will in an irresponsible fashion employ civil disobedience and other forms of coercion to attain their ends. There will be objections and demands which clearly conflict with government development efforts—such as refusals to pay higher taxes, including taxes on agricultural development, or pressures for local projects when funds are simply not available—and these too will often have to be resisted. No simple formula exists that can guide a government in rejecting the demands of organized interests while minimizing political losses. Consistency and firmness are difficult but important attitudes in any government, and concessions to violence and civil disobedience are obviously invitations to more violence and civil disobedience. Given the proclivity of many organized groups in India to such agitation, the government must be confident when it rejects a

[12] See chap. v.

demand that it is prepared to sustain its rejection even in the face of coercion.

In the final analysis, the government must be prepared to use its own coercive authority. Governments may fail for being unresponsive and repressive, but governments have also failed because they neglected to use their authority in matters of clear public interest. For example, the failure of Pakistani authorities to deal with the riots of orthodox elements against the heterodox Ahmediyas at Lahore has been widely interpreted as a factor in the subsequent inability of the Pakistan government to command respect and authority. The West Bengal government, which has so frequently succumbed to coercion, has as a result lost a great deal of support among intellectuals and the middle classes of Calcutta. Whenever authority on the top has been weak—in the vice-chancellors' offices of many north Indian universities, in the offices of a number of ministers, chief ministers, and Congress party presidents in some states, and in the offices of the district magistrates in some districts—corruption has multiplied, merit standards have been cast aside, coercion and intimidation have increased, politics in the invidious sense has grown, *élan* within the organization has dwindled, and popular respect has been dissipated.

In a society in which popular respect for law is not widely developed, forceful measures by government are often necessary to inculcate an acceptance of law. As paradoxical as it may seem, some repressive legislation in the legal code, firm use of the police against rioters, and the widespread arrest of those who practice civil disobedience may be essential to the development of democratic traditions in Asian states. The danger in repression lies not so much in using it to enforce the law, as in using it as a substitute for the day-to-day task of building consent within the society.

Conclusion: Bridging the Gap

Many Indian intellectuals and government officials hope for the day when trade unions and peasant organizations will not be controlled by outside leadership, when caste, tribal, linguistic, and religious organizations will disappear, when all political groups will cease to agitate and will direct their energies toward developmental activities, when a sense of responsibility and rationality will pervade all political controversy. The danger of these expectations—and of other forms of political utopia—is that they often tend to direct energies away from making the present political sys-

tem work. A sympathetic understanding of existing forms of political organization and the attitudes that underlie them is essential if the existing
gap between government and politics is to be bridged.

Clearly, a high level of aspirations and a growing level of political organization present special problems in an underdeveloped country where
resources are scarce. Can this gap be narrowed by economic growth?
First it must be recognized that economic growth, including not only increased productivity but also growth in education and mass communication, generally results in an increase in voluntary political organization,
which in turn causes a widening of the gap between aspirations—or at
least, organized aspirations—and reality. While, on the one hand, economic growth provides government with increased resources for satisfying
organized demands, it is accompanied, on the other hand, by a growing
mobilization of groups exerting pressure on government.

In the short run, economic growth can therefore be politically unstabilizing. Economic growth itself is likely to be somewhat unbalanced. Industrialization, barring some sudden growth in small-scale industries, is
not likely to provide sufficient job opportunities for the growing Indian
population; and given the rapid expansion of universities since 1947, the
numbers of educated unemployed may very well multiply. Population
growth in rural India will increase agricultural density, with a resultant
rise in the number of landless agricultural laborers. Moreover, under the
best of circumstances, some groups and some regions are likely to improve
more slowly than others. Tensions between hills people and plains people,
tribals and Hindus, Kammas and Reddis, Sikhs and Hindus, agricultural
laborers and peasant proprietors, may be intensified as one community or
class perceives that its improvement is not as rapid as that of another. And
perceived differences of this sort are as important as real differences in
personal income.

Economic progress is thus likely to be accompanied by a rise in organized demands. Within a few decades, there may very well be substantial
increases in unionization. Existing caste, tribal, and other community and
regional groups may be better organized. With a rise in educated unemployment, student militancy may increase, and urban areas may become
even greater centers of discontent than they are today. Peasant agitations,
especially of the landless, may be expected; and peasant proprietors may
demand greater government expenditures. As the economic supply grows,
"consumer" political demands may increase even faster. Thus, economic
growth is not likely to diminish the political repercussions of scarcity.
The argument that economic growth provides government with greater

revenue, thus enabling it to satisfy more of the demands made on it, assumes a constancy in demand for which there is neither historical precedent nor theoretical justification. Economic stagnation—even if one could tolerate such a condition—offers no solution either, for demands have already reached such a level that no government and perhaps no political system could survive stagnation for long. Our argument, therefore, is not that stagnation is desirable, but that growth by itself is not only not stabilizing but often politically unstabilizing, and that one must look beyond the sphere of economics to find ways to progress and survive in a polity of scarcity.[13]

The central problem of planning is increasingly that of implementation, and the problems of implementation are essentially those of politics, social organization, and cultural values. Although in recent years increasing attention has been paid to the human factors in development, that is, those factors involving social organization and cultural values, little attention is paid to the facts of local and state political power which affect the implementation of policy. This may be related to the great faith of India's political and intellectual leaders in the efficacy of law. Legislation by the central Parliament abolishing the dowry system, for example, or laws passed by state governments imposing a ceiling on land holdings, have been enacted without regard to the existence of local forces which impede the implementation of such legislation. The result is often a great hiatus between law and reality, between what is willed by the national leadership and what is done at the local level, between the high ideals in New Delhi and the cynicism in the *mofussil* towns. No bridge can be built across this gap unless one constantly asks with respect to any public policy recommendation by the state or central government, What local forces are at work which can be utilized to implement a proposed course of action?

If one views India's primary task as that of achieving maximum economic growth in the shortest period of time, then the developments suggested in this study might be viewed with deep alarm. The freedom of Indian planners to pursue their economic objectives without reference to the demands of organized groups has been steadily diminishing. But there are many planners—and intellectuals outside of government—who look wistfully across the Himalayas where, or so it seems, decisions are made

[13] This argument is developed at greater length in an article I have written jointly with Bert Hoselitz, "Economic Development and Political Stability in India," *Dissent*, VIII (Spring, 1961).

with ease and, above all, are implemented as planned. In the main, however, India's leaders have opted for both democracy and economic growth. Indeed, in spite of India's enormous poverty, her leadership has resorted neither to mass coercion nor to widespread suppression of political groups. Indians are, on balance, willing to pay an economic price for their freedom if need be. Thus, when the goals of economic development and political development do not mesh, Indians increasingly stress their political ideals, not with any sense of guilt, but with a sense of pride. Perhaps the time will come when Nehru's vision becomes the vision—and the reality—of all India, a vision expressed eloquently and yet simply when Nehru said: "My legacy to India? Hopefully, it is 400,000,000 people capable of governing themselves." [14]

[14] From an interview with Norman Cousins published in the *Saturday Review,* XLIV, May 27, 1961.

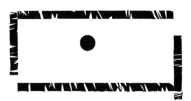

INDEX